I0084644

A History of Rutherford County

Carlton C. Sims, *Editor*

SOUTHERN HISTORICAL PRESS INC

Book Publishers

This volume was reproduced from
An 1947 edition located in the
Publisher's private library,
Greenville, South Carolina

All rights reserved. No part of this publication may be
reproduced, stored in a retrieval system, transmitted in any
form, posted on to the web in any form or by any means
without the prior written permission of the publisher.

Please direct all correspondence and orders to:

www.southernhistoricalpress.com
or
SOUTHERN HISTORICAL PRESS, Inc.
PO BOX 1267
375 West Broad Street
Greenville, SC   29601
southernhistoricalpress@gmail.com

Originally published: Tennessee 1947
ISBN #0-89308-700-9
All rights Reserved.
Printed in the United States of America

TO THE PIONEERS WHO SETTLED
RUTHERFORD COUNTY
TO WHOM WE OWE SO MUCH
ABOUT WHOM WE KNOW SO LITTLE

Preface

This book is one in a series of county histories written at the suggestion of and with the aid of the Tennessee Historical Commission as a part of the sesquicentennial celebration of the State of Tennessee. The authors are, Frank E. Bass, formerly Director of the Middle Tennessee State College Training School and now with the Tennessee Education Association; Doctor J. B. Black, formerly Director of the Rutherford County Health Department; Baxter E. Hobgood, Superintendent of the Murfreesboro city schools; Mary B. Hughes, formerly of the Murfreesboro *News-Journal* staff; Clayton L. James, Professor of Social Science, Middle Tennessee State College; Carlton C. Sims, Head of the Social Science Department, Middle Tennessee State College; Perry Williamson and Ethel M. Womack, teachers at the Murfreesboro Central High School.

No attempt was made to get uniformity in style and method of organization for the various chapters. The reader should soon discover that "War Between the States" and "Civil War" refer to the same event.

An attempt was made to make the work both interesting and accurate. Footnotes for the most part have been eliminated and references incorporated in the body of the text.

When writing a local history, established facts for early periods are indeed few. Rumor frequently enters the picture. To confine one's narrative to facts alone would give a most incomplete picture. It must be remembered that the existence of a rumor is within itself a fact, one that must be considered in getting a true insight into a period. The authors therefore have not confined themselves to well established facts, but have, in some cases, reported mere rumor. Every attempt was made, however, to enable the reader to distinguish between fact, probability and hearsay.

The authors are indebted to many citizens of Tennessee and Rutherford County for numerous and valuable suggestions. Only a few, however, can be mentioned. Those who read parts of the manuscript and made numerous corrections and criticisms include, Mr. Philip Mankin of Vanderbilt University, Professor Clarence Bruner of Tennessee Technological Institute, and Professors Robert Abernathy, Emily Calcott and Richard C. Peck of Middle Tennessee State College. Most of all, the committee is indebted to Judge Samuel C. Williams for his untiring efforts in furnishing much valuable data and many helpful suggestions.

Murfreesboro, Tennessee
August 15, 1947

Carlton C. Sims.

Contents

A History of Rutherford County

CHAPTER I

The Early History of Rutherford County

INTRODUCING THE COUNTY

Rutherford County was the twenty-fourth to be established in Tennessee. Its pioneer history is therefore not as rich as some of the earlier counties. Its economic and cultural development, combined with its Civil War history, and with the fact that Murfreesboro was the capital of the state from 1819 to 1826, however, cause it to rank near the top of the counties of the state in historical importance.

In 1940 the county had an area of 614 square miles and a population of 33,604. During the same year the population of Murfreesboro was 9,495. The geographical center of the state is said to be the flat rock on the Hughes place near the Lascassas highway about two miles northeast of the courthouse.

Geologically the county belongs to the lower Silurian period. Under the soil are limestones and shales. The limestone crops out in various places making the land unsuitable for tillage. This type of land grows blue grass and makes excellent pasturage. Even the most rocky land will grow a variety of timber, especially cedar for which Rutherford is world famous. The county is one of the most level in the middle Tennessee basin. It is surrounded by ridges and hills, some of which cut through the central portion. The elevation ranges from 420 feet to 1,120 (Pilot Knob near Readyville). The average is from 500 to 600 feet, that of the courthouse at Murfreesboro being 617 feet. No minerals of any importance have yet been discovered within the area.

Rutherford County is well watered by Stone's River and its numerous tributaries. Many caves underlie the surface. Some of these have streams flowing through them which make large springs where they reach the surface.

The climate is moderate and the rainfall is near fifty inches a year. Much of the soil of the county attains considerable depth and is very fertile. Such land will grow most of the crops found in the central section of the country.

In transportation facilities, the county is equalled by few in the state with a railroad and twelve paved highways. Although Murfreesboro is rapidly becoming a commercial and manufacturing center, the city is still best known as a center of culture because of its writers, schools, and colleges. The Veterans' Facility, recently located near Murfreesboro, has added materially to the culture of the county.

At present Smyrna is the only incorporated place in the county besides Murfreesboro. There are, however, many prosperous communities worthy of mention. Located on the railroad northwest of Murfreesboro are La Vergne and Florence, while to the south on the same line one finds Rucker, Christiana and Fosterville. The last two were formerly incorporated. South of Murfreesboro and to the west of the railroad is Barfield, while to the southwest are Salem, Rockvale and Eagleville. Eagleville also was formerly incorporated. To the west are located Blackman and Almaville; to the north, Walter Hill, Jefferson and Sulphur Springs; to the northeast, Lascassas and Milton; to the east, Hall's Hill, Kittrell and Readyville, and to the southeast, Gum, Buchanan and Hoover's Gap.

Since Rutherford County is a part of middle Tennessee, as well as of Tennessee and the United States, its history will, wherever possible, be woven into that of the region, the state, and the nation

THE INDIANS AND MIDDLE TENNESSEE

The vast area bounded by the Tennessee and Ohio Rivers and the Cumberland Mountains was long an Indian hunting ground. It was used extensively by the Cherokees who lived to the southeast and the Chickasaws of northern Mississippi, as well as by the Creeks of north Alabama, the Choctaws of central Mississippi, the Shawnees, and other lesser tribes. Even the Iriquois of New York claimed rights in the area and occasionally hunted there.

Antedating the Indians, the mysterious mound builders had villages and even cities in the area later to become Tennessee, but this race disappeared long before the coming of the white man. They appear to have had few, if any villages in the Rutherford County area. Neither did the Indians make settlement here, though the abundance of fish and game and the large springs in the region made it a favorite hunting ground as is evidenced by the large number of arrow heads found on or near the surface.

The Shawnees were probably the only Indians to make permanent homes during the colonial period in what is now middle Tennessee. It appears that part of this tribe which originally lived in the Savannah River area, settled on the Cumberland about the year 1670, near the time of the settlement of the Carolinas. Marquette, in his journal in 1673, refers to many Shawnee villages on the lower Cumberland. Their largest settlement had about five hundred people. They are known at one time to have had a town at the sight of Nashville, though there is no evidence that they ever settled in what is now Rutherford County. The Cherokees and the Chickasaws, however, expelled the Shawnees about 1714. The majority of them appear to have settled north of the Ohio near the Wabash.

When, therefore, the first white settlers came into the middle Tennessee region, the land was unoccupied. Haywood in his history of Tennessee states that there were no signs of villages or of cleared land in the area. Some writers even go so far as to state that the land, as a result of hostilities which had broken out between the Cherokees and Chickasaws, was seldom visited by Indian hunters during the middle of the 18th century. It should be borne in mind that if the Indians to the south would not allow the Shawnees to establish permanent settlements on their hunting ground, and even fought among themselves for hunting rights, they would object more vigorously to the white settler who destroyed their forests and game. There is little wonder, then, that the early settlers were subjected to frequent Indian attacks.

EXPLORATION AND SETTLEMENT OF TENNESSEE

The first white man to view what is now Tennessee was, of course, De Soto who discovered the Mississippi River in 1541. Many years passed without a white man again setting foot on the region. The people next to explore the area were the French who had settled in Canada and were becoming interested in the Mississippi Valley. Marquette and Joliet, in 1673, went down the Mississippi River as far as the mouth of the Arkansas River. In 1682 La Salle reached the delta of the Mississippi, while ten years later Chartier, one of La Salle's men, after staying with the Shawnees on the lower Cumberland for a time, made a trip from French Lick, where Nashville now stands, up the Cumberland and over the mountains to Virginia.

In the following years the French built up a lucrative trade with the Indians in the Mississippi Valley and gradually encroached upon the claims of the English colonies. By 1710 a French trader had opened a "store" at French Lick on the Cumberland. Other French traders came in from time to time, although it is not known how much of middle Tennessee they covered. They might have become familiar with the Stone's River area. In 1682 La Salle built Fort Prudhomme on the Mississippi in West Tennessee, and in 1739 the French built another where Memphis now stands.

The English colonies to the east were continuing their westward expansion and long before 1750 were becoming interested in the fertile lands across the mountains. In 1673 while Marquett and Joliet were on the Mississippi, Needham and Arthur were exploring parts of east Tennessee. In 1700 Jean Couture, a Frenchman, led an English expedition from Charleston to the Cherokee Country and down the Tennessee, Ohio and Mississippi Rivers to the mouth of the Arkansas. By 1711 Eleazer Wiggan had extablished trade with the Cherokees of East Tennessee while in 1730 the English negotiated the first treaty with the Cherokees. Thereafter, contacts with this tribe were frequent.

Prior to 1750 most of the contacts with the Indians of Tennessee were made by traders from Charleston. After that time land speculators and hunters, first from Virginia and later from North Carolina, dominated the scene. In 1748 Doctor Thomas Walker, a Virginia land speculator, explored a part of upper east Tennessee. Two years later he and a party of explorers crossed the mountains, passed through a beautiful gap and discovered a river. They gave the name Cumberland to both the gap and the river, probably in honor of the Duke of Cumberland. The French and Indian War, for a time, checked hunting and exploring parties.

When the war broke out the Cherokees were friendly to the English. They insisted that the English build a fort in east Tennessee to protect them from the French who were allied to the Indians of the north. The English, after much delay which annoyed the Cherokees, finally built two forts in the area. A small one was started by Virginia, while a more important one, Fort Loudon, was built by South Carolina. The Cherokees, however, partly because of French influence and partly because of further agression by the whites on their lands, made war on the English and destroyed Fort Loudon.

In 1761 the English made peace with the Indians and in 1763 the French and Indian War came to an end. The only obstacle to settlement across the mountains was the Indian claim to the land and many were determined not to let that stand in their way. From 1760 to the establishment of the first permanent settlement in Tennessee hunters and explorers for land companies were crossing the mountains in ever increasing numbers. Boone appears to have been in east Tennessee by 1760 when he carved the famous inscription on a tree in what later became Washington County. Several years later he, Scaggins and others were exploring for Judge Richard Henderson, the most famous land speculator of the period. Scaggins probably came as far as French Lick.

Large parties of hunters were also crossing the mountains. They would hunt and trap on the Cumberland and other rivers and float skins and tallow down the Mississippi to Natchez and other ports. One of these parties, that of Colonel James Smith, is of especial interest to residents of Rutherford County.

The following quotation is from Smith's account, given some years later, of his trip:

"We also explored the Cumberland and Tennessee Rivers from Stone's River down to the Ohio." He further states: "Stone's River is a south branch of the Cumberland, and empties into it above Nashville. We first gave it this name in our Journal in May, 1767, after one of our fellow travellers, Mr. Uriah Stone, and I am told that it retains the same name unto this day. This party had passed by the mouth of Stone's River in 1766."

The following quotation from Haywood is also interesting:

"Uriah Stone, one of this company, had come to the Cumberland River in 1767. In that year he and a Frenchman were trapping on the River now called Stone's River, and had nearly loaded their boat with furs. In his absence the Frenchman stole off with the boat and landing. Stone then returned to the settlement, and came out a second time with Mansco and his associates. From this man Stone's River took its name."

The King of England, desirous of keeping peace with the Indians, in 1763 ordered that his subjects go no farther westward than the crest of the mountains. The pioneers apparently paid little attention to this order which they considered unfair. The region was reported to be very fertile and was unoccupied. They could see no reason why they should be prohibited from entering it. However, the king, in 1768, made a treaty with the confederacy of the Iriquois at Fort Stanwix, New York, by which these Indians surrendered their claims to the land bounded by the Cumberland Mountains and the Tennessee and Ohio Rivers. This cession included most of middle Tennessee. During the same year a treaty was made with the Cherokees at Hard Labor, South Carolina. The Cherokees, who had the better claim to the area, however, did not extend to the colonists the right to settle west of the present eastern boundary of Tennessee.

A word should be written about the difficulties of making treaties with the Indians. For a contract to be effective, the parties must have power to make the agreement. Furthermore, the terms of the agreement must be clear. Seldom did a treaty with the Indians conform to these specifications.

On the side of the colonists there was a multiplicity of governments, often causing confusion. Sometimes the representative of the king made treaties with the Indians. Various colonies with conflicting claims often acted independently. In 1776 the colonies became sovereign states. Then the central government, first under the Articles, and, after 1789, under the Constitution, entered the picture. In addition to these governments, private citizens, like Henderson, and even pioneer settlements, sometimes made agreements with the Indians.

The situation was still more confusing on the Indian side. They were divided into tribes which often had subdivisions. The agency in the tribe vested with treaty making power was sometimes none too clear. The ownership of hunting lands was usually obscured by numerous claimants. Consequently, groups within a tribe often felt that they were not bound by a treaty. It was sometimes difficult for the tribe to hold in check its adventurous young members just as the colonial and state governments found it hard to keep white pioneers from settling on Indian lands.

Furthermore, foreign powers were continually stirring up the Indians to make war on the pioneers. The English made alliances with the red men during the Revolutionary War. After the war the English in the northwest and the Spanish in the south were responsible for many of the attacks on the western settlements, though this was apparently the work of individuals without instructions from their governments. Often French traders who lived with the Indians, especially outlaw tribes, were responsible for massacres.

Finally, the treaties were interpreted in different ways by the contracting parties. Often the land was not surveyed, and usually was described by natural boundaries, such as mountains and rivers. The natural boundaries sometimes had two or more names and further confusion followed.

The result was that treaties were frequently made and regularly broken by both sides, the colonists settling on land to which they had no claim and the Indians massacreing whites even on land which the latter rightfully owned.

While the treaties of Hard Labor and Fort Stanwix were being negotiated, and perhaps a year or two earlier, the pioneers were entering east Tennessee for the purpose of making permanent settlements. Some, no doubt, justified their entry on the grounds that the treaty with the Iriquois opened the land to white settlement. Others were determined to come, treaty or no treaty.

The exact date of the first permanent settlement in Tennessee is not known. Many think that the North Holston settlement in the present county of Sullivan between the Holston River and the Virginia line was first, and that it might have been established as early as 1766. It was settled by Virginians coming down the Holston valley. For over a decade it was mistakenly considered as being in Virginia. The Watauga settlement which is usually considered the beginning of Tennessee was started by William Bean in 1769. By 1772, there were two other settlements in this region, the Carter's valley settlement west of the North Holston, and the Nollichucky settlement southwest of Watauga. All of these were west of the line of white settlement as accepted by the British government. John Stewart, in 1770, by the Treaty of Lochaber had the original treaty with the Cherokees modified so as to include the North Holston settlement in the area to be occupied by the colonists. The others were left out. The Watauga settlers, not wanting to move from their newly acquired lands, proceded to negotiate leases with the Indians. In 1772, the Watauga settlers framed the famous compact of government.

With the outbreak of the Revolutionary War the Cherokees again made war on the white settlers. In the early stages of the war the Indians murdered many pioneers. Finally an expedition under Griffith Rutherford into the Indian country destroyed so many Indian towns that they soon sued for peace. In 1777, at Long Island, near where Kingsport now stands, a treaty was made with the Cherokees whereby the settlers in east Tennessee acquired title to the lands upon which they had settled. The line ran to the west of the Nolichucky settlement. Certain of the younger Indian chiefs, however, refused to accept the treaty and massacres continued.

THE SETTLEMENT OF MIDDLE TENNESSEE

In 1770, a party of hunters including Casper Mansker, Abraham Bledsoe, and Uriah Stone came down the Cumberland, stopped at French Lick, and went on to Natchez. In 1775, De Mumbrune built a cabin at a point later called Eaton Station near Nashville. In 1777 he made a trip to New Orleans.

About 1778, Spencer and others came from Kentucky to the Cumberland area. Although the rest of the group deserted him, Spencer planted a crop of corn and spent the winter in a hollow tree. Others visited the region during the 1770's but no permanent settlement was made up till 1779 when James Robertson led a group of settlers from east Tennessee.

In 1775, Richard Henderson's Transylvania Company made a treaty with the Cherokees, who ceded to it all the land between the Cumberland and Kentucky Rivers. Although it is reported that he gave the Indians $50,000 worth of blankets, rifles, ammunition and other commodities, the deed itself recites "two thousand pounds." Actually there were six wagon loads of goods. Though the British and Colonial authorities repudiated this treaty as far as Henderson was concerned, it in a way, marked the beginning of the permanent settlement of middle Tennessee as well as of Kentucky. It appears that Henderson was instrumental in persuading James Robertson to lead the colony to the lower Cumberland.

Robertson and a small group of men, including one Negro, left Watauga in the spring of 1779. They took the land route over the Cumberland Mountains, through Kentucky, north of the Cumberland River, and entering Tennessee in what is now Sumner County, pitched camp at the site of Nashville. They were soon joined by another group led by Mansker. After planting corn, all save three, who were left to keep the buffalo out of the crop, returned to Watauga for their families. Robertson, with over two hundred emigrants, set out late in 1779 for the Nashville area, again taking the land route over the mountains. It was not until January, 1780 that they reached French Lick. The Cumberland was frozen so solidly that they crossed on the ice. This was one of the most severe winters on record.

Soon after Robertson and his followers left Watauga, a number of emigrants under John Donelson, left by water to join Robertson. They went down the Tennessee and up the Ohio and Cumberland Rivers, reaching French Lick on April 24, 1780 after a hazardous trip. Thus, the first permanent settlement in middle Tennessee was established.

It should be remembered that while the Nashville area was being settled, the American Revolution was reaching a climax. In 1780 the battle of Kings' Mountain, in which many east Tennesseans including John Sevier fought, took place. North Carolina, therefore, had little time for providing a government for the new area. The lower Cumberland settlers, therefore, in true American tradition, signed a compact of government for the community. Had not the Pilgrims on the Mayflower taken similar action? Had not many of these same pioneers at Nashville helped to form a government at Watauga before the state of North Carolina, in 1777, established a government for Washington County? It is well that the colonists took such action not only to suppress lawlessness, but, what was even more important, to protect themselves from the Indians who continually attacked them for the first few years. Most of these attacks were made by the Creeks and Cherokees, though the Shawnees and others participated at times. Had it not been for the perseverance of Robertson, the colony would, in all probability, have returned to east Tennessee.

In 1783, the same year that the Revolutionary War came to a close, Davidson County was created by the legislature of North Carolina. It included roughly what is now the upper half of middle Tennessee. The territory of Rutherford County was, therefore, at this time a part of Davidson County.

Prior to the close of the Revolution, certain states had ceded to the Central Government their lands north of the Ohio River. In 1784, North Carolina ceded to the central Government its territory beyond the mountains, on condition that the offer be accepted within one year. The colonists, fearing that Congress would take no action, naturally became panicky. The Indians were attacking them. The Spaniards were apparently secretly encouraging the Indians, and at the same time, trying to win the allegiance of the southwest to Spain. The Mississippi had been closed and Congress had been unable to negotiate a treaty opening the river. There is little wonder then, that the colonists were becoming desperate. They felt that they were being deserted, not only by North Carolina, but by Congress as well. Accordingly, they considered a number of alternatives. One was to secede from the United States and join Spain. Certain leading colonists, including James Robertson, opened negotiations with the Spanish authorities in New Orleans, but the exact nature of their discussions is not known. The settlers in east Tennessee took matters into their own hands and created the "state" of Franklin. Davidson County, however, did not become a part of this "state".

Soon North Carolina attempted to re-establish its authority. For a time, there were two sets of officers in the area, those responsible to North Carolina, and those responsible to the "state" of Franklin. After many clashes, the "state" of Franklin finally collapsed in 1788. In 1790 the territory was again ceded to the United States Government which accepted the offer, and in 1796, Tennessee was admitted as a state. At this time, the state consisted of 12 counties. Rutherford did not yet exist.

THE SETTLEMENT OF THE RUTHERFORD COUNTY AREA

Although some writers claim that permanent settlements in the area soon to become Rutherford County were established by 1790, a more careful examination of the facts indicates that such settlements were not made till 1796 or perhaps the fall of 1795. Attempts to settle no doubt were made before 1790 but none was successful because of the hostility of the Indians.

Before discussing these first permanent settlements, a short space will be devoted to the exploration of the Stone's River area, the activity in real estate, and the Indian troubles which retarded settlement of the region for more than a decade.

As has already been indicated, the French traders might have explored the region in question before 1750. From 1767, when Uriah Stone explored the river bearing his name, to the permanent settlements in the Nashville area in 1779-80, other whites no doubt, explored the region. Often the Nashville settlers, in search of food, went on hunting trips and probably covered Elk and the Duck River valleys, as well as those of Stone's and Harpeth. When reports of the rich lands in middle Tennessee reached North Carolina, much dealing in land followed.

As early as 1780 North Carolina, ignoring Indian claims, promised land west of the mountains to soldiers who would enlist for three years. In 1782 definite steps were taken for surveying and distributing this land. Preemption rights to six hundred and forty acres were given to each head of a family who had settled on the Cumberland before June 1, 1780. Isaac Shelby, Anthony Bledsoe and Absolom Tatum were appointed commissioners to survey the land set aside as a military reservation. The area at first included approximately the northern half of what is now middle Tennessee.

The commissioners, accompanied by a numerous guard, started their work in 1783. The surveying apparently required several years for completion. In 1786 North Carolina made many grants in the Stone's River area to her soldiers. Among the grants for that year, in what was soon to become Rutherford County, one finds the names of Reading Blount, Samuel Hayes, Archibald Lytle, Hardy Murfree, Samuel Wilson, Clement Hall, John Mulherrin, William Blackamore, and Robert Shotswood.

When North Carolina ceded the territory west of the mountains to the United States in 1790, she protected the claims of her soldiers and continued to give title to land in Tennessee until well after 1800. This resulted in many disputes not only between the two states, but between citizens holding conflicting claims. As late as 1818, an act of the Tennessee legislature gave relief to the heirs of Griffith Rutherford for land taken from them as a result of the decision of the United States Supreme Court in favor of the heirs of Nathanial Greene.

There was considerable real estate activity in the Stone's River area after 1786, the original owners often selling their land without seeing it. Real estate dealers also enter the picture buying and selling large tracts of land. Records in the Rutherford County Register's office show that North Carolina made many grants of land in middle Tennessee in the years 1786, 1788, 1793 and 1794.

Many were also made in 1797 after Tennessee became a state. Much of the land in these grants was located on Duck and Elk, as well as on Stone's River.

From 1780 till the close of the Revolution, the fate of the Cumberland settlement hung in the balances. In 1783 the war came to an end. It was thought by many that the Davidson County settlement would rapidly spread until it included most of middle Tennessee. Several factors, however, prevented this hoped-for rapid expansion. The neglect of North Carolina which caused the establishment of the "state" of Franklin has already been referred to, as has the weakness of the government of the Confederation, along with Spanish and English policies. The inauguration of the new government for the United States in 1789 and the establishment of Tennessee into a new territory in 1790 raised the hopes of many for a rapid settlement of middle Tennessee. Again, there was disappointment. Spanish and British intrigue continued and the Indian attacks, instead of subsiding became more fierce. The Spanish were encouraging the Creeks and Cherokees to the south, while the English were egging on the Shawnees, Delawares, and others north of the Ohio. President Washington was anxious to avoid angering these foreign powers. The Cumberland settlement, however, was holding the Spaniards responsible for the Indian massacres and wanted to wage war openly on the Creeks and Cherokees. The Chickasaws had become friends of the Cumberland settlement.

The pioneers of middle Tennessee had a most difficult task in combating the Indian attacks. When the whites and Indians met in open battle, the former were decidedly superior. The Indians, therefore, resorted to a different type of fighting. They would encamp some miles from a white settlement and would swoop down upon an unguarded station, or would break up into small bands and attack those working in the fields. The Stone's River area was a favorite base for such operations by the Indians.

A station was a miniature fort for the protection of a small number of families. The most southern of these stations in Davidson County were Buchanan's and Castleman's near the forks of Mill Creek; Mayfield's, a few miles to the west; and Dunham's, still farther west near the Harpeth river. None of these stations was as far south as the present Davidson-Rutherford boundary line. No stations south of these are referred to in the early history of Davidson County. During 1788 and 1789 these stations were so frequently attacked by the Indians that several of them were abandoned. The Cumberland settlement was therefore contracting on the south instead of expanding into what was to be Rutherford County, as some writers contend.

In order to combat this type of warfare, Robertson and his aides resorted to several procedures. One was to send out scouting parties to locate Indians encamped to the south. The following quotation from Haywood describes such a scouting party sent out in 1792, and also indicates that no white settlers were in the Rutherford area at that time.

"Abraham Castleman, one of the militia soldiers, had withdrawn himself from the army for some days, and at length returned and stated, that he had been as far as the Black Fox's Camp, where he had seen the signs of a numerous army of Indians, and that they might shortly be expected in the neighborhood of Nashville. The General sent off Captain Rains to ascertain the reality of the facts detailed by Castleman; Rains took with him a young man, Abraham Kennedy, and went to the place where Murfreesborough now stands, and halted in the woods, and remaining on the ground all night, he next day made a circuit around the spring where the Black Fox's Camp was. The Black Fox was an Indian chief, who formerly hunted and encamped at the spring not far from the spot where now is the sight of Murfreesborough. In this circuit, he examined all the paths which led to the camp from the direction of the Cherokee country; finding no traces of Indians, he ventured to the spring; he then returned home by way of Buchanan's Station, and informed the people that the traces of an Indian army were nowhere to be seen. Soon after the return of Captain Rains, the troops were marched back to Nashville.

"Two other men, however, were sent off to reconnoitre the country through which the Indians were necessarily to pass in coming to Nashville. These were Jonothan Gee and Seward Clayton, who went on the Indian trace leading through the place where Murfreesborough now stands, to Nashville, eight or ten miles from Buchanan's Station; as they traveled along the path talking loudly, they saw meeting them the advance of the Indian Army, who called to them in English to know who they were, to which question, without disguise, they answered. Upon being asked in return, who they were, they said that they were spies from General Robertson's Station, and were returning home; both parties advanced till they came within a few steps of each other, when the Indians fired and killed Gee dead in the road. They broke the arm of the other, who ran into the woods, but being persued by a great number of them, they overtook and killed him also. Thence they marched rank and file, in three lines abreast, and with quick step arrived at Buchanan's Station, where the people were wholly unapprised of their coming and did not expect it."

The Indians, however, were unsuccessful in their attack.

A more effective means of combating the Indians was that used by Sevier and Rutherford of destroying the Indian villages from which the attacks originated. Robertson therefore, in 1787, at the head of about one hundred and thirty men destroyed the Indian villages near Muscle Shoals. But there were other villages, especially Nickajack and Running Water on the Tennessee River in northeastern Alabama which had to be dealt with. For several years they made attacks on the Cumberland settlement. In 1793 and 1794 they became very offensive. It was rumored that Indians north of the Ohio who had recently ambushed and had annihilated most of the forces of General Saint Clair were attempting to form an alliance with the Creeks and Cherokees for the purpose of exterminating the Kentucky and Cumberland settlements. The Federal Government refused to take seriously the requests of the Cumberland settlement for protection. President Washington, as stated above, was more interested at the moment in negotiating treaties with foreign powers. Some, including the Secretary of War, thought that the pioneers were to blame for this trouble, while most people, on the coast and far removed from the scene, did not understand the Indian problem as is indicated by the following quotation by Putnam from a letter of Pickering, Secretary of War, to Governor Blount.

"Six Indians, Chickasaws and Choctaws, have strolled to Philadelphia without interpreter or guide. We cannot tell the object of their journey except that they might expect to be clothed, and to receive presents. They have been clothed, and each furnished with a rifle-gun and accoutrements, and sent home with a guide. Do keep them at home!"

If Philadelphia was "pestered" by a visit from six friendly Indians, imagine the attitude of the Cumberland settlers who lost to the Indians at least fifty of their number in 1793 and an even greater number the following year.

Finally, the settlers demanded that Robertson take matters into his hands and destroy Nickajack and Running Water. In 1794, an expedition was sent out by Robertson under General Ore (Orr). The expedition "marched to the Black Fox's Camp, and there remained that night; they then crossed the Barren Fork of Duck River, near the Stone Fort where Irwin's Store stood in 1823; thence to Fennison's Spring; thence crossing Elk at Caldwell's Bridge and the Cumberland Mountain, they reached the Tennessee about three miles below the mouth of the Sequachee."

The Indian villages were surprised and destroyed.

This expedition was without the authorization of either the Federal authorities at Philadelphia or of Governor Blount, though

Blount was accused of duplicity in the matter. Apparently, he was in sympathy with the attack, yet did not want to offend the Federal government.

While this expedition broke the back of the Indian attack, some murders continued till 1795 when a series of incidents cleared the way for the rapid settlement of Rutherford County and middle Tennessee.

In 1795, the United States signed the long awaited treaty with Spain, opening the Mississippi. Thereafter, the Spaniards gave up the idea of annexing the southwest and gave little encouragement to further Indian attacks. During the same year, the Chickasaws, who were frinedly to Robertson, with the aid of a few white people decisively defeated a band of one thousand Creek warriors who had come to destroy them. The Creeks soon made peace.

In 1795, the United States negotiated a treaty with England whereby the latter agreed to remove her troops from the northwest forts by 1796. The decisive defeat of the Indians of the northwest by General Wayne, followed by the Treaty of Greenville, with the northern Indians, destroyed the hopes of an alliance between the Indians of that section with those of the south. At last peace with the Indians was a reality for the Cumberland settlement.

The best description of the Cumberland settlement before 1795 is given by Putnam quoting one of Governor Blount's letters to the Secretary of War in 1792:

"I will give you a description of the Mero District. The settlements extend up and down the Cumberland River, from east to west, about eighty-five miles, and the extreme width from north to south does not exceed twenty-five miles, and its general width does not exceed half that distance; and not only this country surrounding the extreme fronties, but the interior part, (which is to be found only by comparison with the more exposed part) is covered generally with thick and high cane, and a heavy growth of large timber, and where there happens to be no cane, with thick underwood, which affords the Indians an opportunity of lying days and weeks in any and every part of the district in wait near the houses, and of doing injuries to the inhabitants . . ."

The happenings of 1795 were soon to change Governor Blount's description of much of middle Tennessee. To quote again from Putnam, "The mischievous Spanish influence being diverted from the Cumberland settlements, large parties of emigrants arrived, especially in the fall of the year 1795, and farms were being opened in all directions from Nashville." During this same year the Walton road from Kingston to Nashville across the Cumberland plateau was opened.

The effect of the Indian attacks upon the settlement of middle Tennessee is well illustrated by a census taken by Governor Blount in 1795. Of a total state population of 77,262 only 11,924 were living in the three middle Tennessee counties of Davidson, Tennessee, and Sumner. By 1800 the seven counties in middle Tennessee, namely Davidson, Sumner, Montgomery, Robertson, Smith, Wilson and Williamson boasted a population in excess of thirty-two thousand. Since the population of the state in 1800 was 105,602, most of the increase during this five year period therefore took place in middle Tennessee.

The exact date and location of the first permanent settlement in Rutherford County is not known. The following quotation from Putnam indicates that settlers were on upper Stone's River in 1797:

"The Indians were very desirous to have permission to hunt on the waters of the Cumberland and to trade with the whites. Some of the Cherokees applied to General Robertson for his sanction, which he gave. In the fall, (1797) Chilcoe and Gentleman Tom, with their hunting parties, commenced their hunt on the headwaters of Stone's and Duck Rivers. The party of Gentleman Tom had their camp on the southwest side of Stone's River, about a mile from white settlers, with whom they were on very friendly terms. But in the neighborhood, a mile above, on the north side of a creek which has two licks on it, there lived some bad white people, who could not restrain their hellish spirit of revenge; and, regardless of the treaty, and danger of renewing the bloody scenes of war, killed two of these peaceable Cherokees, about the 5th of November "

Various communities said to be "first" in the county include Stewart's Creek, Black Fox's Spring, the northwestern part of Cannon County which for years was a part of Rutherford and perhaps others. The most important stream of immigrants into the county came up Stone's River from Davidson County. Some of these turned up the east fork while probably the greater part followed the west fork and its tributaries, Stewart's Creek, Overall Creek, Lytle's Creek and others. Many from Virginia, North Carolina and other seaboard states appear to have left the Walton Road and turned south before reaching Davidson County. These helped to settle the northeastern part of Rutherford and the northwestern section of what is now Cannon County. Another group of early settlers appear to have gone up the Harpeth River from Davidson County into an area soon to be in Williamson and later a part of Rutherford County.

The following description of these early settlements is far from complete and much of it is based upon rumor. An attempt has been made to separate fact from rumor.

Owen Edwards, Thomas Nelson, Thomas Howell, William Atkinson and John Etta are usually listed as among the first settlers on Stewart's Creek. One of Edward's descendents states that he came to the county in 1797. The Atkinson descendents think that Atkinson did not come till after 1800. An early settlement was near the forks of Stone's River but little is known of this community before Jefferson became the county seat. Another early settlement was on the west fork of Stone's River near where the National Cemetery now stands. Samuel Wilson and Nimrod Menifee were probably the first to settle here. Wilson's land was conveyed to him by North Carolina in 1786. In 1789 he is reported to have planted a corn crop near the forks of Stone's River, but did not remain there permanently. He is also said to have killed near the Murfreesboro spring the last elk seen in the county. He probably became a permanent settler before 1800. Nimrod Menifee, at whose home several early meetings of the Rutherford County court were held, acquired his land by a deed dated 1797 which stated that his land joined that of Samuel Wilson.

An early settlement which is especially interesting today was that of the Ruckers on land where the Veterans' Facility now stands. Thomas Rucker was listed in a deed dated 1797 and recorded in Davidson County as being a citizen of Virginia. The land conveyed to him in this deed was on Stone's River and adjoined the land of Isaac Shelby. In 1801 Rucker and others purchased the Isaac Shelby tract of 5,000 acres on the east fork of Stone's River which the State of North Carolina had given to Shelby for his services as a land commissioner. This deed recites that Rucker was a citizen of Wilson County. Since the east fork of the river was at that time in Wilson County, Rucker must have moved into the region between 1797 and 1801. The statement by some writers that Rucker built the first grist mill in the county in 1799 could easily be true.

Another early settlement was that which later became Murfreesboro. Archibald Lytle, Hardy Murfree and others received grants to land in this area in 1786. Lytle, however, never occupied his grant but a relative, Captain William Lytle, came to the county at an early date, probably before 1800. There are several deeds in the register's office in Rutherford County conveying land on the west fork of Stone's River to William Lytle in 1799. These deeds state that Lytle was a citizen of Davidson County. Another early family which appears to have come about the time the county was established was the Bairds who occupied the land where the State College now stands.

The Murfrees did not come to the county till after the death of Colonel Hardy Murfree which occurred in 1809. Some claim that the first house in the county was near the Black Fox Spring. An Indian trading post was in this area at an early date. It was also the first voting place for the Lytle's Creek area. It must have been an early settlement.

Charles Ready after whom Readyville was named is credited with being one of the first settlers in that area. He is supposed to have arrived "about 1800." The records show that in 1802 he purchased land on the east fork of Stone's River from Griffith Rutherford, for whom the county was named. Rutherford, about the same time, sold a nearby tract to George Brandon whose descendents are living on the land today.

The settlement between Lascassas and Milton was also an early one. Nathaniel Overall and William Doran appear to have been there by 1800. The Alexanders and McKnights came in a year or two later. Across the line in Cannon County in territory that was a part of Rutherford County till 1836 is another "first" house but conclusive evidence to sustain the claim is not available.

Absolem Scales appears to have settled near Eagleville before 1800. Other early families, partly from records and partly from hearsay with a reasonable basis for truth, include the Crosthwaits and Millers at Florence, the Searcys at Walter Hill, the Jacksons at Versailles, the Kings, Bradys, Beesleys, Snells, Masons, Bateys and Blackmans west of Murfreesboro, the Butlers, Ransoms, Jenkins and Lillards in the Salem community, the Sheltons and Joneses near Almaville, and the Campbells near Murfreesboro. Other family names that one meets in the early records of the county include, Hunt, Hayes, Woods, Chadwick, Vaughn, Henderson, Waller, Spence, Hall, Sanders, Floyd, Brashears, Wright, Goodloe, Tucker, Herndon, Bedford, Weakley, Nash, Jetton, Cummings and Windrow, the latter giving the name to the famous Methodist camp ground in the western part of the county.

THE ESTABLISHMENT OF RUTHERFORD COUNTY

Since Davidson County as set up in 1783 included most of the northern half of middle Tennessee and therefore embraced the territory that makes up Rutherford County today, and since a large part of the territory now comprising Rutherford County was taken from Davidson in 1803, many writers assume that all of Rutherford County was a part of Davidson continuously from 1783 until 1803. This is far from true.

In 1786 the legislature established out of the territory of Davidson County the new counties of Sumner and Tennessee. Sumner, at that time, included most of the eastern part of Rutherford County. In 1796 Tennessee County was divided into Robertson and Montgomery Counties so that the State might use the name "Tennessee." Evidently there was some misunderstanding about the boundary of Davidson and Sumner County, for in 1798, an act of the legislature made "the main west fork of Stone's River" the boundary line between the two counties.

Wilson County was carved out of Sumner County in 1799. The eastern part of Rutherford County therefore became a part of Wilson County. This is clear from certain deeds registered in 1804 in Book "B" in the register's office of Rutherford County. The first deed recorded in this office was executed by the sheriff of Wilson County. The land conveyed by the deed was formerly owned by John Reed and was located in Wilson County on the east fork of Stone's River about 4 miles from its mouth. This would make the land in question near the village of Walter Hill. The land was sold for taxes at the court house of Wilson County in 1802.

It is of interest to note that this deed was proven before and ordered registered by Andrew Jackson, one of the judges of the Superior Court of law and equity for the state.

Another deed executed in 1801 and registered in 1804)No. 33, Book "B") describes a tract of land "on the waters of the west fork of Stone's River . . . known by the name of Black Fox Camp" as being in Wilson County. This land is about three miles southeast of Murfreesboro.

In 1801 the Legislature passed an act fixing the southern boundary of Wilson County at a line near the present boundary between Wilson and Rutherford Counties. This act returned to Davidson County the eastern part of Rutherford. This is further evidenced by a deed executed in 1803 and registered in Rutherford County (No. 32, Book "B") in 1804 which describes the land at the Black Fox Camp as being in Davidson County.

When Rutherford County was authorized by the legislature on October 25, 1803, it included territory from Williamson County as well as from Davidson. Section three of the act states that "nothing therein contained shall be construed as to prevent the sheriffs or collectors of taxes of Davidson or Williamson County from collecting same within the limits of said county of Rutherford which are due at this time." Various parts of Rutherford County had therefore, before 1803, been at different times under the jurisdiction of Davidson, Sumner, Wilson, and Williamson Counties.

The southern boundary of Rutherford County originally extended to the Alabama territory. When Bedford County was created in

1807, the southern boundary of Rutherford was set at about its present location.

Prior to 1836, the year in which Cannon County was established, the eastern boundary of Rutherford extended to a point about two miles west of Woodbury. When Cannon County was set up, the eastern boundary of Rutherford was fixed at its present location. Since 1836 the boundaries of Rutherford County have experienced many minor but no important changes with one exception. Before the Civil War certain citizens of Eagleville, under the leadership of Chesley Williams tried to interest Franklin and perhaps Shelbyville in a turnpike. Receiving no encouragement, they turned to Murfreesboro and eventually the road was constructed. This pike tended to turn the Eagleville trade to Murfreesboro and agitation for annexation to Rutherford County followed. This was accomplished by acts of the legislature in 1867 and 1871.

GENERAL GRIFFITH RUTHERFORD

The county was named in honor of General Griffith Rutherford. This Revolutionary hero, the son of John R. Rutherford, was born in Ireland in 1731. The Rutherfords were one of the oldest and best known families of Scotland. Although it is claimed by some that their lineage can be traced as far back as the year 800, it is probably safer to start with Hugo de Rodiforde who was living at the time of the signing of the Magna Charta. The family was long identified with Jedburg Abbey, one of the most beautiful in Scotland, the remains of which are still standing. Many of the Rutherfords are buried in its choir.

Sir Walter Scott, whose mother was a Rutherford, makes references to the qualities of this ancient family in his writing. Notwithstanding the prominence and religious bent of the family, it contained many who were classified as radicals in both politics and religion and conflicts with the authorities as well as family schisms were not infrequent.

After the Puritan Revolution many Scots and Englishmen migrated to Ireland, especially to the northern province of Ulster. Some Time after 1700, Griffith's father, John, an uncle Samuel, and perhaps other members of the family joined the procession and moved to Ireland. The motive behind this move is none too clear. Some attribute it to economic causes while others hint that certain of the Rutherfords had lost favor with the government and church because of liberal views and acts. It is interesting to note that this vein of liberalism showed itself early in the life of young Griffith.

Conditions in Ireland apparently were no more promising than those in Scotland and after a brief stay during which John Rutherford married a Miss Griffith and became the father of a son, Griffith, the family set sail for America. Unfortunately, both parents died at sea. Friends took young Griffith to a family in New Jersey. This unfortunate accident probably explains why Griffith Rutherford, though descended from a family of scholars, received such limited formal education. Some writers state that he was all but illiterate. This is an overstatement, however. Official documents show that he wrote a fair hand and that he expressed himself with force. It must be admitted, however, that his spelling was poor and his vocabulary limited.

Practically nothing is known of the early life of Rutherford. It is not known just when he moved to North Carolina. His name appears as early as 1753 on the records of Rowan County where he was the king's surveyor. In 1754 he married Elizabeth Graham, whose father, James Graham had come to North Carolina from Ireland. The records show that Rutherford, like many other adventurous pioneers, bought and sold much land.

His rise in North Carolina was rapid. During the next ten years he fought the Indians in the French and Indian War, was a member of the North Carolina Assembly, sheriff of Rowan County, a member of the court of public claims, a justice of the peace, and a colonel in the military organization of the colony. While a member of the assembly, he was instrumental in the passage of laws creating a militia, establishing a college in Charolotte, and preventing "card playing and other deceitful games."

When the conflict with England began to take form, though a colonial official, he was in sympathy with the revolutionists. At first he counseled moderation but finally broke with the governor and was classed as a radical not only in politics but, like certain of his ancestors, in religion. He left the Episcopal Church because of certain undemocratic practices. He objected especially to the monopoly and high fees charged by the Episcopal clergy for performing the rite of matrimony, and succeeded in getting an act passed permitting ministers of all denominations to officiate at marriage ceremonies. He represented Rowan County as a senator in the Provincial Congress in 1775. The following year he helped to frame the first constitution for the state of North Carolina.

In 1775 he was appointed a member of the district committee of safety for Salisbury and before the end of the year was a member of a similar committee for the entire colony. As a colonel of a battalion of minute men he engaged the Tories in 1775. The following year he was appointed Brigadier General. He took part in a number of battles against the British and Tories during the Revolution. He was captured by the British in 1781 but was released and continued to fight till the end of the war. He also was successful in a major campaign against the Cherokees. By the end of the war his reputation had become national.

After the war Rutherford became interested in the fertile lands across the mountains. In 1783, he joined with William Blount, Richard Caswell, John Donelson, Joseph Martin and John Sevier in the creation of a company for the establishment of a colony in the Mussel Shoals region. A land office was opened and a settlement attempted but the Indians forced its abandonment. In 1784 he was surveying land for North Carolina in middle Tennessee. He later owned land in Sumner, Maury, Davidson, Williamson, Rutherford and Dyer Counties.

In 1790 the Rutherford family consisted of four free white males over 16 years of age and one under 16, three free white females and eight slaves.

After disposing of his North Carolina lands, Rutherford moved to Sumner County. In 1793 Tennessee had a population sufficiently large to justify the establishment of a territorial legislature. Accordingly, thirteen delegates to the House of Representatives were elected. This body then submitted the names of ten men from whom five were to be chosen by President Washington for a legislative council. Rutherford was one of the five chosen and became chairman of the body. It might be added that Rutherford was a personal friend of Washington. In 1791 at a dinner in honor of Washington at Guilford Court House given by Rutherford and others, Rutherford was presented with a silver snuff box by the President.

In 1793 Rutherford was instrumental in establishing the Shiloh Presbyterian Church in Sumner County. He later became a member of the La Gardo Church in Wilson County, a few miles from his home. He was probably buried in the La Gardo church yard, although there is no marker to indicate his resting place.

No portrait or likeness of this sturdy pioneer remains for posterity. One must be satisfied with the few following quotations from a book on the Rutherford family by Minnie Rutherford Long, one of his descendents.

He was "about five feet eight inches tall, and was compactly formed." "When he formed an opinion he was not easily driven from it." "He was of a pleasant and social turn."

Rutherford at his death in 1805 had three living children, John, Griffith W., and Elizabeth. He has many descendants in middle Tennessee today.

Not only was Rutherford County, Tennessee named after Griffith Rutherford, but Rutherford County, North Carolina and its seat of government, Rutherfordtown honor his name.

THE ESTABLISHMENT OF A SEAT OF GOVERNMENT

In 1804, the first session of the county court met, according to provisions of the Legislative Act, at the home of Thomas Rucker, near where the Veterans' Hospital now stands. The members of the court named in the commission were, James Sharp, Colonel John Thompson, Peter Legrand, Thomas Rucker, John Howell, Charles Ready and John Hill. They were sworn in by William Nash, a member of the Davidson County Court who was reinstated as a member of the Rutherford County Court. Only early meetings were held in the home of Nimrod Menefee. In 1804 a committee composed of John Hill, Frederick Barfeald, Mark Mitchell, Alexander McKnight and Peter Legrand was authorized to fix a permanent seat for the government. They chose Jefferson, at the forks of Stone's River. The town was named in honor of Thomas Jefferson.

The land at the forks of Stone's River originally was part of a grant of 4,800 acres by North Carolina to Reading Blount. Blount, however, never occupied the land. Later, part of this land came into the possession of two real estate men, Robert Weakly and Thomas Bedford. They were instrumental in getting the county seat located at Jefferson. The first town lot they sold brought $29.00.

The courthouse, begun in 1804 and completed in 1806, was constructed of logs. A jail, stocks and a whipping post were also erected. The cost of these buildings was between two and three thousand dollars.

In 1805 an overseer was appointed and all able-bodied males were required to work the streets of the town. In 1807 an act of the Legislature further regulated the town, while in the same year, the court appointed patrollers for militia companies and also for the county seat.

By 1811 the southern and eastern parts of the county had developed to a point where Jefferson was not the population center of the county and there was considerable agitation for moving the county seat. The legislature accordingly appointed a committee consisting of Charles Ready, Hugh Robertson, Hans Hamilton, James Armstrong, Owen Edwards, Jesse Brashear and John Thompson, Sr., to decide upon a permanent seat of government. The sites considered were the William Lytle land, the Rucker place, the Black

Fox Camp and the Ready place. Although the county line at that time was several miles east of the Ready place, that location was far from the center of the county and probably would not have been considered at all, but for the fact that Colonel Ready entertained the members of the committee with both food and drink in a most royal manner. Soon, however, the contest was narrowed to the Lytle place and Rucker's. By a four to three vote, the Lytle tract was selected.

The original act named the sight to be chosen Cannonsburg in honor of Newton Cannon of Williamson County who was later governor of the state. Colonel William Lytle, however, offered to give the county sixty acres of ground upon which to erect a courthouse if his location was accepted. According to members of the Murfree family, the commission suggested that the new town be named after Lytle. Lytle in turn suggested that the town be named after a former friend of his, Colonel Hardy Murfree who had recently died in Williamson County and whose heirs owned land south of the Lytle tract. His request was granted and the legislature immediately passed another act naming the town Murfreesborough. The spelling was not changed until after the Civil War.

In 1812 a courthouse was begun in Murfreesboro. Provisions were also made for a jail, stocks, and a whipping post. The whipping post was first located on the square, but was later moved to the jail yard. In 1811 the legislature named commissioners for the town of Murfreesboro while two years later the people of the town were authorized to elect their commissioners. The courthouse was completed in time for the January meeting of the court in 1813. Murfreesboro was given a charter in 1817.

LIEUTENANT COLONEL HARDY MURFREE

Lieutenant Colonel Hardy Murfree, son of William Murfree, was born on June 5, 1752 on a tract of land in Hertford County upon which the town of Murfreesboro, North Carolina, was later built. Both Tennessee and North Carolina in addition to having counties named Rutherford also have towns named Murfreesboro. The North Carolina town, however, was not named after Colonel Hardy Murfree but in honor of his father.!

Before Colonel Murfree was of age, he was a captain in the Hertford militia. When the Revolutionary body, the Provincial Congress of North Carolina, met in 1776, two regiments were organized and placed under the control of the Continental Congress.

1. Much of the information in this sketch was furnished by Misses Mary Roberts Murfree and Libbie Morrow Murfree, descendants of Colonel Murfree and by Judge Samuel C. Williams.

Such troops were thereafter referred to as the "Continental line." In the Second Regiment of the Continentals young Murfree was named a captain. He was sent north and served first under Colonel Howe, who soon became a general, and later under Washington. He participated in the battles of Brandywine, Germantown, Stony Point and Monmouth. He is often referred to as the hero of Stony Point. He soon became a major and, a year later, was raised to the rank of lieutenant colonel. He was then shifted to the First Regiment under Colonel Thomas Clark. In that regiment were several officers who later became prominent Tennesseans: Captain Tillman Dixon, Lieutenants Dixon Marshall and Robert Hayes and Ensign John Lipscomb. It is interesting to note that Murfree succeeded as Lieutenant Colonel, William L. Davidson, after whom Davidson County, Tennessee, was named, while Davidson succeeded as Brigadier General, General Griffith Rutherford for whom Rutherford county was named.

In addition to being a gallant soldier, Colonel Murfree displayed such executive ability that he was placed in charge of supplies, was presiding officer in court marshal trials, and was on the board for reorganizing the forces of North Carolina.

Although he seemed adverse to a political career, he served in the legislature of North Carolina in 1784 and With General Rutherford, was a member of the committee which considered the bill to reform the reservation in the west for the soldiers of the Continental line. He was also a member of the Convention which ratified the Federal Constitution.

The remainder of his life was devoted chiefly to repairing his fortune and to aiding Continental soldiers in proving their claims to western lands. He, as a lieutenant colonel, was entitled to a large acreage. He visited middle Tennessee as early as 1784 for the purpose of locating good lands and acquired tracts in Williamson, Rutherford and other counties.

In order to look after his immense holdings in Tennessee, he moved to Williamson County in 1806 and settled on Murfree's Branch of West Harpeth River, where he planned to duplicate the beautiful colonial mansion in North Carolina from which he had moved and which today is still in a good state of preservation. Unfortunately, he died before reaching old age on April 6, 1809. His funeral oration was delivered by Felix Grundy. His remains were interred on his estate near Franklin. This true and fitting sentence is engraved upon the slab: "In war the soldier; in peace the citizen; reverential to God; respectful to man."

The Tennessee Historical Society held a meeting in Murfreesboro on December 8, 1885, and to it Major D. D. Maney, on behalf of

himself and other descendents presented the sword of Colonel Murfree. Major Maney delivered an eloquent address dealing chiefly
with Colonel Murfree's heroism during the night attack on Stony
Point. He closed with the following words:

"I have no doubt, Mr. President, that the sword this day presented to the Society was worn by Colonel Murfree on that memor-
able night, as well as on many other fields of the Revolution."

Colonel Murfree was married to Sarah Brickell, daughter of
Mathias and Rachel Noailles Brickell of Hertford County, North
Carolina. Colonel Murfree left two sons and five daughters:
William Hardy who married Elizabeth Maney, Fanny N. who married
David Dickinson, Mary N. who married Isaac Hilliard, Matthias
Brickell who married Mary Roberts, Sallie Hardy who married Dr.
James Maney, Lavinia who married Colonel Frank Burton, and
Martha L. who married Major William Maney. Prominent mem-
bers of the Murfree family who have lived in Murfreesboro are
sketched in later chapters.

No steps have been taken to pay honor to the hero for whom the
city of Murfreesboro was named. It is suggested that at some appropriate time a celebration be held in his honor and a bronze plaque
in his memory be placed in the city hall, perhaps a new city hall.

PIONEER INSTITUTIONS AND LIFE

By far the most important governmental institution in the life
of the early citizens of Rutherford, as well as other counties in the
state, was the county court made up, as today, of the justices of the
peace.

The Constitution of 1796 made no provision for the establishment of civil districts. The first subdivision of the county in its
early history was the captain's company. The early pioneers had
to be on the alert at all times, chiefly because of the Indians. The
organization of a militia was absolutely necessary. The Constitution of 1796 included extensive provisions for the creation of a state
militia. It was organized on a rather democratic basis. Each
county was divided into captains' companies. Each captain's
company was entitled to two justices of the peace, except the company including the county seat, which had three. Justices of the
peace were appointed for life by the legislature. The Constitution
of 1796 also made provision for the appointment of a constable for
each company.

At the first meeting of the Rutherford County Court there were
six justices present. At the January meeting of the court in 1810,
thirty-seven were recorded as being present. An examination of

the minutes of the meetings of the early Rutherford County Court not only shows the importance of the court as a governmental agency, but also gives the best picture to be found of the early life of the county.

Prior to the Constitution of 1834 county officers were appointed by the county court. The first holders of the important officers were: Samuel McBride, Sheriff; Joseph Herndon, County Court Clerk; William Mitchell, Register; John Howell, Ranger; Alexander Mc Culloch, Trustee. Other officers filled by the court were coroner, constable, solicitor, cotton and other inspectors, patrolmen for captains' companies, and election officials.

One of the most important duties of the court which it still exercises today was the assessment of taxes. Justices were appointed to make out lists of taxable property for each captain's company. The court then fixed the rates. The rates for the county in 1804 were: Each 100 acres of land, 6¼c; each town lot, 12½c; each free poll or indentured servant, 6¼c; each slave, 12½c; each stud horse, ⅛ of season price. The amount of money spent by the county was indeed small.

The law at this time required certain official papers, as powers of attorney, deeds, bills of sale, and indentures of apprenticeship, now sworn to before a notary, to be proven in open court before they were recorded. Many such documents were presented to the court at every session.

The court also registered stock marks. Sparsely settled areas have always let cattle run at large. Such cattle, therefore, must be marked for identification. For example, at an early session of the court, Joseph Nevins was authorized to mark "with a half crop in the underside of each ear,"—a pioneer coat of arms, shall we say.

The county court had supervision over highways and bridges. It appointed jurors for laying off new roads. Overseers were appointed for supervising the construction and repair of roads and able-bodied males were required to work the roads. In 1811 the court authorized $9.25 for the purchase of a crow bar and sledge hammer to be used on the roads. Large bridges appear not to have been constructed in the county till the advent of toll roads. Ferries were used earlier. The following rates for ferries were authorized by the county court in 1811: Foot passenger 6¼c; horseback 12½c; two wheel carriage 50c; four wheel carriage $1.00 (drivers included). Our individualist, freedom-loving, pioneer ancestors had no scruples against price ceilings for public utilities.

The court also licensed ordinaries or taverns and required the operators to give bond. The rates for ordinaries fixed by the county court in 1804 were: Dinner 25c; supper and breakfast 20c; corn and oats 8_ _c per gallon; stabling a horse 24 hours with corn and fodder or or oats 33_ _c; peach brandy, ½ pint, 12½c; French brandy and wines, ½ pint, 50c.   Apparently many citizens of the county were born too late.

Other powers of the court included recognizing that colored people had been granted their freedom, paying bounties for wolf scalps, appropriating money for the poor, releasing individuals from double taxation and discharging individuals from working public highways.

The judicial powers of the early county court included, for the most part, those now exercised by the monthly county court, as well as part of those exercised by the circuit, including the criminal court, and the chancery court.   Single justices, as today, heard minor civil cases.

An important function of the early county court which that court still exercises was the appointment of guardians and the administrators of estates.   The first estates administered by the court were those of John Cummings, Thomas Bedford, Richard Searcy, William Marlin, Isaac Barr and John Miller.

The administrators for the Cummins estate, in 1804, reported the following personal property: Three negroes, five horses, one wagon and harness, one jackscrew, twenty head of cattle, thirty head of hogs, four feather beds, two sets of curtains, six bedsteads, two tables, one beaufett, one writing desk, one bureau, one pair of money scales, five pots, three chairs, one dutch oven, one kettle, with other household furniture, two sets of plow irons, two hoes, two axes, two wedges, one rifle gun, one shot gun, three saddles, twenty thousand feet of plank, debts due the estate, one hundred and forty-one dollars, good, and one thousand three hundred and fifty dollars, bad . . ."

The court also appointed juries, both grand and petit, heard lunacy and bastardy cases, and tried by jury both civil and criminal cases.   When the quarterly court was set up in Washington County, there was no superior court west of the mountains.   That court, therefore, tried felony cases and punished with fines, imprisonment, and by whipping.   When Rutherford County was established, it was placed under the jurisdiction of the superior court of the Mero district.   The superior court heard felony cases and appeals from the county courts.   The records of the Rutherford County Court do not show the nature of the criminal cases tried, but since the fines usually ran from one cent to a few dollars, it is assumed that they were misdemeanors.   An examination of the civil cases before the Rutherford County Court indicates that most of the suits were for debt or damages.   Some of the judgments ran as high as $2,000.

Apparently in pioneer days when people fought, they did not neglect to make use of all weapons available. Witness the following quotation from the records of the court: "John Taylor, the fifth day of January, 1810, came into court and then proved by the oath of William Coldwell that a part of the right ear of the said John Taylor was bitten off by him, the said William Coldwell." Another case of ear biting is found in the minutes for 1811. During the same year the court guaranteed the fee of a local physician for services to a pauper. The court also appropriated $150 for the poor. John Coffee who was soon to win fame as a general under Jackson at New Orleans was appointed road overseer in 1810.

One of the first lawyers to be admitted to practice in the Rutherford County Court was Thomas Benton who later ably represented Missouri in the United States Senate. In 1812 the court ordered that three dollars be paid to Jeremiah Ward for a wolf scalp. An early law authorized county courts to pay bounties for the scalps of wolves, squirrels and crows. In 1813 the election precinct at Black Fox Camp was moved to Murfreesboro. In 1815 certain magistrates complained that the court house was not clean. The following order was entered on the minutes: "It is ordered by the court that Blackman Coleman be and is hereby appointed to keep this courthouse cleaned and to attend to the same for which this court will allow him the sum of twenty-five dollars per year." Since that time courthouse sanitation has not kept pace with the increases in the salary of the janitor.

Back taxes apparently plagued the early courts since from time to time lists of delinquents were ordered published in the Nashville and Knoxville papers. Murfreesboro did not have a paper until 1814.

Pioneer life in Rutherford County differed somewhat from that of the Watauga Settlement in the 1770's or the lower Cumberland in the 1780's. These settlements were what might be called primary while Rutherford was secondary or merely an expansion of an earlier settlement. The first settlers in the Rutherford area therefore were spared many of the hardships of the earlier immigrants, especially attacks by the Indians.

The first houses in the Rutherford area were log, but soon more modern types, including brick, were to be found. By 1815 the wealthier families in the region had large homes and many slaves, and were entertaining in typical southern style.

Skins of animals were first the most important material from which the pioneer made clothing. They were also used for money. By the time Rutherford County was organized in 1804, cotton was being planted extensively and a variety of textiles were used. Fishing and hunting were widely indulged in by the early settlers in the county, partly for acquiring food and partly as a sport. Domesticated animals played an important part in the economy of the county from the start.

Little is recorded of the recreation in the early life of the county. We have good reason to believe, however, that it resembled that of the area generally of which much is known. In addition to hunting and target practicing, the men wrestled (rassled as it was commonly called), boxed with bare fists, attended cock fights and horse races. Some time before the Civil War two wagon loads of dead cocks (an exageration no doubt) were reported to have been removed from a local pit. Bradley had a race track near Murfreesboro before 1820. Andrew Jackson is said to have won and lost small fortunes betting on the races. The enmity between him and Newton Cannon was aggravated, if not started, by a wager on a race which, according to rumor, cost Cannon all of his slaves.

The inns were the night clubs of the pioneers and there were no curfews. Young men (and often the old) would gather here and drink. Brawls were frequent to the discomfiture of the landlord. Log rollings and corn shuckings were also popular.

The women had quilting parties and other forms of entertainment. Parties and dances in which both sexes participated were common. The house party lasting a week or more became popular with the upper classes as soon as substantial homes were built.

By 1815 Rutherford County had established itself as one of the rapidly developing counties in Tennessee, while Murfreesboro was soon to be the capital of the state.

CHAPTER II

Rutherford County from 1815 to 1946

Before presenting a series of chapters on Rutherford County's contributions to the state and nation in the major fields of human achievement, a summary of her general history with emphasis on political trends will be given. The chapter will be organized around the following periods: 1. The County's Preeminent Position in State Affairs, 1815-1860; 2. The Civil War and Reconstruction, 1860-1870; 3. Period of Slow Recovery, 1870-1900; 4. The Picture Brightens, 1900-1946.

THE COUNTY'S PREEMINENT POSITION
IN STATE AFFAIRS

From the War of 1812 to the close of the Mexican War few states, if any, occupied a more prominent place in the national scene than Tennessee, while Rutherford County claimed a similar place in the life of the state. Tennessee not only experienced outstanding population growth and economic development but her contributions in war and politics were surpassed by none.

During this period Tennessee was the heart of the west and settlement was rapid. The population of the state rose from 105,602 in 1800 to 681,904 in 1830 when it was eighth among the states. By 1840 with a population of 829,210 it had attained fifth place which it retained in 1850 with 1,002,717 inhabitants. It was during this period that middle Tennessee far outstripped east Tennessee in population and wealth. By 1830 middle Tennessee had a population of 389,395 to 196,474 for its eastern rival. The middle section more than doubled the eastern in manufacture and commerce. West Tennessee which had been opened to settlement by a treaty with the Indians in 1818 was also making rapid strides and was beginning to drain population from both of the older sections.

The growth of Rutherford County somewhat paralleled that of the state. Its population rose from 10,265 in 1810, the first year in which a census was taken, to 26,134 in 1830 when it attained fifth place among the counties of the state, exceeded only by Bedford,

Davidson, Maury and Williamson in the order named. Soon after 1830 the county reached the saturation point for the type of economy prevalent in the area. By 1840 it had declined to 24,280. This was due, in part, to many residents going further west, especially to west Tennessee. It is also partly explained by the creation of Cannon County which included the eastern part of Rutherford. In 1850 the population rose to 29,122, while in 1860 it dropped to 27,918.

Tennessee first achieved prominence in the national picture by her contributions in the Creek War and the War of 1812, where her soldiers under Jackson surprised the military world. Rutherford County contributed General John Coffee and Colonels John H. Gibson and Robert H. Dyer in addition to a number of militiamen. Later, in the war with Mexico the state clinched the name "Volunteer State" which had been applied earlier. Rutherford County furnished two companies to this war.

It was in the field of politics, however, that Tennessee made its greatest contribution to the nation. That outstanding stalwart, "Old Hickory", has given his name to one of the most important developments of modern times, the rise of the common man, called almost universally by historians "Jacksonian Democracy." The most outstanding president from Jackson to Lincoln, James K. Polk, was also a Tennessean.

In addition to two Presidents, Tennessee furnished one of the Whig candidates, Hugh Lawson White, in the election of 1836 and John Bell, the Constitutional Union Candidate, in 1860. Other outstanding offices held by Tennesseans during this period include two speakers of the United States House of Representatives, Polk and John Bell; six cabinet members, Return J. Meigs, Postmaster-General under both Madison and Monroe, John H. Eaton, Secretary of War under Jackson, Felix Grundy, Attorney-General under Van Buren, John Bell, Secretary of War under Harrison, Cave Johnson, Postmaster-General under Van Buren, and Aaron V. Brown, Post-master-General under Buchanan; two diplomats, Neil S. Brown, minister to Russia and William Trousdale, minister to Brazil. John Catron was an Associate Justice of the United States Supreme Court, while Hugh Lawson White declined a similar post under Jackson. Tennessee also furnished Sam Houston and Davy Crockett, among others, the cause of Texas independence.

During the period before the Civil War, Rutherford County furnished three of the Congressmen to represent her district. They were Charles Ready, Junior, David Dickinson and Parry W. Humphreys. A dozen other men who held seats in Congress from other districts in Tennessee or from without the state, in addition to many prominent in other fields, were either born in Rutherford County or lived there for a time. Rutherford County has an indirect claim to Polk and Bell both of whom chose wives from Murfreesboro.

Tennessee and Rutherford County present an interesting study in politics from 1830 to the Civil War. Prior to 1835 the state went consistently Republican (Jeffersonian Democratic). With a rise of the Whig Party, however, the state found itself rather equally divided between the two major parties, the Democrats and the Whigs. In state elections Tennessee went back and forth from one party to another. Newton Cannon, a Whig, served two terms from 1835 to 1839; Polk, a Democrat, served from 1839 to 1841. He was succeeded by Jones, a Whig, who served for two terms. Aaron V. Brown, a Democrat, then served one term followed by Neal S. Brown, a Whig, who also served one term. Trousdale, a Democrat, served from 1849 to 1851, and was succeeded by Campbell, the last of the Whig governors, who served from 1851 to 1853. He was succeeded by Andrew Johnson, a Democrat.

In the presidential elections of 1828 and 1832 the state and county went overwhelmingly for Jackson. In the elections from 1836 to and including 1852 the state went Whig though the vote was very close in 1844 and 1852. The county did not go Democratic in a national election from 1836 till after the Civil War. It even voted against Polk in 1844. Many in the county blamed Polk for the failure of Murfreesboro to become the permanent capital of the state.

In state elections the county went from one party to the other with such regularity that the slogan "As Goes Rutherford so Goes Tennessee" became popular. Both parties shared in the county's representatives in the legislature.

It is difficult for many to understand why the Whigs were so strong in Jackson's state after he retired. This can be explained partly by the following facts. Many people who disliked Jackson voted for him because of fear or of local pride. He was the type of man to make many bitter enemies as well as stanch friends. When Jackson cast his mantle upon Van Buren, it was too much for many southern Democrats. The Whig conception of nationalism appealed to many in the west and south. This party favored internal improvements and most of the west approved such a policy. Some Tennesseans, especially the wealthy, favored the United States bank. Many cultured southerners were none too fond of Jackson's rough and ready habits and, for that reason, joined the Whig party which leaned toward the aristocratic concept of life. Some State's Rights Southerners were against Jackson because of his attitude toward Calhoun and South Carolina. Since the Whigs had made no official pronouncement on slavery many southern planters found themselves at home in this party.   When Hugh Lawson White, probably second only to Jackson in popularity in the state, broke with Jackson and became for all practical purposes a Whig, the position of that party in the state was well established.   In view of these facts one can understand why so many of the outstanding families in Rutherford County were Whigs.

The industrial revolution struck the United States with full force after the War of 1812.   This development combined with westward expansion created a demand for internal improvements. Such an important issue could not long stay out of politics and soon heated arguments arose as to the agency responsible for financing these projects.   The various agencies suggested were federal, state and local governments, and private companies, or, sometimes various combinations of these.   When the federal government, after long discussions and many battles, finally decided not to finance internal improvements, with the exception of rivers and harbors, pressure was brought to bear upon the states, most of which succumbed. Tennessee in 1836 adopted the so-called "Pennsylvania Plan" whereby the state agreed to subscribe to a part of the capital stock of railroads and turnpike companies.

Politically the position of the state on this question is difficult to analyze.   The Whigs generally favored internal improvements by the federal government.   When the issue was before the state, party lines were not always followed because of localism.   East Tennessee favored internal improvements financed by federal or state or both governments.   West Tennessee leaned in the same direction.   Middle Tennessee, however, which had become the most wealthy section of the state and.did not have the difficult transportation problems of east Tennessee, was generally opposed to a state policy of improvements.   Rutherford County usually followed party lines on this issue.

Senator Rucker, a Jeffersonian Democrat from Rutherford County, as early as 1827, opposed the spending of state money for internal improvements although at this very time an attempt was being made to make Stone's river navigable for steamboats.   He pointed out that the three geographic divisions of the state made a unified system of internal improvements impossible.   He also stated that every member of the legislature had "some favorite river to be opened, some canal to be made and some mountain to be leveled." On the other hand Charles Ready, an outstanding Whig from the county, made a long and able speech in the State Legislature, which was printed in full by one of the Nashville papers in 1836, favoring the use of state funds derived from the federal government for internal improvements and education.   Senator Henderson Yoakum, a

Democrat, in 1840 took the lead in the fight to repeal the state-aid
acts which he had opposed at a previous session.

From 1819 to the Civil War Murfreesboro was exceeded in political importance by few towns in the state.   In addition to being
the capital of the state, many other important political meetings
took place there.

Knoxville had been the capital, with the exception of a one day
session at Kingston, until 1812. It was transferred to Nashville
until 1817 when the legislature again met in Knoxville.   From 1819
to 1826 the legislature met in Murfreesboro.

During the period in which the capital was located in Murfreesboro, attempts were made by the friends of Murfreesboro to make
that site the permanent location. The friends of Nashville made
similar efforts for their city.   In 1826 the capital was again moved to
Nashville.   One reason for making the change at this time seems to
have been that many thought that the legislature should meet in
Nashville in order to exercise proper supervision over the new State
Bank.

The question was not argued again until the Constitutional
Convention in 1834 where many hours were consumed in an attempt
to find a permanent location for the capital.   The friends of Nashville, Murfreesboro and other cities made attempts to have their
favorite town declared the permanent seat of the government.

It was at this time that the geographical center of the state,
which was frequently discussed in the convention, was determined.
A resolution was passed directing the Secretary of State to find,
as nearly as possible, the true geographical center of the state.   The
Secretary referred the matter to James Hamilton, Professor of
Mathematics at the University of Nashville.   His conclusion was
that the center of the state was about a mile and a half east of Murfreesboro.

The Convention, being unable to agree upon a permanent location for the capital, incorporated a compromise in the schedule of
the Constitution.   It provided that the General Assembly of 1943
"shall within the first week after the commencement of the session,
designate and fix the seat of government."   It further provided
"that the first and second session of the General Assembly under
this Constitution shall be held in Nashville."

In 1840 the question of the seat of government again was presented to the legislature.   Murfreesboro, by a close vote, was chosen
as the capital.   Dr. Robert H. White, who has made an exhaustive
study of Tennessee's four capitals, gives the following summary of
the contest:

"The legislative snarl with reference to the removal of the Seat of Government from Nashville to Murfreesboro may be stated thus: Resolution XI, providing for the removal of the capital from Nashville to Murfreesboro, had been adopted by both Houses on January 29, 1840. Subsequently, the House rescinded its action on the above resolution with which the Senate refused to concur. On the other hand, the Senate had passed a resolution supplementary to the resolution concerning the capital removal which provided that the Governor and other State Officials might remain in Nashville until September, 1841. This Senate supplementary resolution was declared out of order by the Speaker of the House and no action was taken thereon. And so as matters then stood, the Seat of Government had been removed from Nashville to Murfreesboro by passage of the resolution of January 29."

Yet, Murfreesboro did not again become the seat of government for the state. The friends of Nashville refused to concede defeat. Furthermore, the opposition charged that while Governor Polk wanted the capital moved to Murfreesboro, he did not want to move his office from Nashville for political reasons. When the Appropriations Bill came before the Senate, that body added an amendment appropriating $100 for moving state records from Nashville to Murfreesboro. When this amendment reached the House, that body substituted another which was accepted by the Senate, declaring that Nashville "be the seat of government until otherwise directed by the law." According to an unverified rumor the House of Representatives would not have objected to moving the capital to Murfreesboro had that city been willing to pay the one hundred dollars necessary for transferring the state records. The city, however, declined and lost the capital.

In 1843 the question was again taken up in the legislature for final settlement according to the schedule of the Constitution of 1834. Dr. White sums up the action of this session in the following words:

"On October 4, 1843, the House had selected Murfreesboro and the Senate had selected Kingston as the permanent capital of the State. In an effort to work out a compromise, the House struck Kingston from the Senate Bill, forgot its own first choice of Murfreesboro, and inserted Nashville, which had twice been voted down by its own body. When the amended Senate Bill was returned to that body for consideration, Nashville was finally accepted, although on a former occasion it had been voted down by 13 to 9. Incidentally, the Senate had, at no time, voted favorably for more than two cities, namely, Kingston and Nashville; whereas the lower House had upon various occasions voted favorably for six different towns, Murfrees-

boro, Chattanooga, Taylorville, McMinnville, Columbia, and Nashville. However, the vote upon four of these places was rescinded
immediately, namely Chattanooga, Taylorsville, McMinnville and
Columbia."

While the legislature was meeting in Murfreesboro, Andrew
Jackson was rapidly becoming the chief political figure in the state.
His name, therefore, frequently appears in the preceedings of that
body. Swords were presented to him and to General Gaines for
gallantry in the War of 1812. In 1822, by a unanimous vote of both
houses, the legislature indorsed Jackson for the presidency in the
coming national election. In 1823, he was elected to the United
States Senate, and two years later, resigned. The legislature chose
his friend, Hugh Lawson White as his successor. In the same year,
the legislature with only one dissenting vote again indorsed Jackson
for the presidency.

The composition of the last legislature to sit at Murfreesboro
was as follows: 38 farmers, 12 lawyers, 5 doctors, and 5 merchants.
The birthplace of the members was: Virginia 21, North Carolina 16,
Tennessee 14, Kentucky 3, Pennsylvania and Maryland 2 each, South
Carolina and Rhode Island one each.

In addition to being the capital, Murfreesboro was politically
alive in other ways. In January 1828 a banquet was held in the
interest of General Jackson's candidacy for the Presidency. Dr.
Dr. William Rucker presided. While Van Buren was President he
visited Tennessee. Rutherford County was not neglected by him.
He was entertained at the Ready home and a gala gathering at Murfreesboro in his honor was attended by many from adjoining counties.
In 1838, Polk at a dinner in his honor at Murfreesboro, announced
his candidacy for the office of governor. On April 11 of the following
year he and Cannon began their famous series of joining debates in
the same city. In 1841 the first Whig convention held in the state
met at Murfreesboro. Polk and Jones chose this popular city as
the starting point for their series of joint debates in the gubernatorial campaign of 1841 and as the closing place for their debates
in 1843. In 1844 the Whigs opened their campaign with a gathering
at Murfreesboro. Charles Ready of Murfreesboro was elected
chairman of the meeting, while William L. Murfree submitted reso-
lutions adopting the platform of the Whig convention at Baltimore.
John Bell was the chief speaker. In 1854 the Prohibitionists chose
this city as the place for holding a state convention, while in 1855
Johnson and Gentry began their gubernatorial campaign with a
joint debate at Murfreesboro.

Another gala day for Murfreesboro was on July 4, 1851 when the
first successful run of a train in the state took place from Nashville

to Murfreesboro. People gathered from miles around and many interesting incidents are told of the reaction of people upon seeing their first locomotive. The first macadamized toll road completed in the state was also from Nashville to Murfreesboro.

Developments of a more local nature will now be taken up.

Prior to the Civil War a number of prosperous towns and communities sprang up in the county. The Tennessee Gazette of 1834 lists the towns of Murfreesboro, Jefferson, Readyville, Milton, and Fosterville. The following description is given of Murfreesboro.

"In 1830 it contained a population of 786 and in 1833 about 1,000· It is well laid out and handsomely situated near the west branch of Stone's River, surrounded by a body of rich farming land under a high state of cultivation. It has an academy and two shools, three churches, four clergymen, ten lawyers, four physicians, a printing office, two cotton factories, two cotton gins, one carding machine, one grist mill, four blacksmiths, four bricklayers, three hatters, one painter, three saddlers, five shoemakers, one silversmith, four tailors, one tinner, two taverns, and ten or twelve stores."

The other communities were naturally overshadowed by the county seat. These villages usually consisted of one or more general merchandise stores which carried in stock everything from cucumbers to castor oil, a blacksmith shop and perhaps a church, an inn or cotton gin. A grist mill could often be found in the vicinity.

For a time after the moving of the seat of government to Murfreesboro, Jefferson continued to prosper. It was a port of importance for flat bottom boats. It had one or more warehouses and was an inspection center for cotton, tobacco, meat, and other products of the county. It had an academy and was on the mail and stagecoach route from Knoxville to Nashville. The development of the steamboat, followed by the coming of turnpikes and railroads left Jefferson an inland town and by 1850 its hopes for becoming a large town had vanished.

There is a story in circulation that Colonel Ready, who apparently was angered by the choice of Murfreesboro as the permanent county seat over Readyville, decided to transform his village into a rival of Murfreesboro. It already had a grist mill. He planned the erection of a fine brick home, which, however, was not completed till after 1830. The town did not develop as rapidly as he hoped. In 1836 the county line between Rutherford and newly created Cannon County cut Readyville into two parts. Since that time Readyville has been only a prosperous village.

The next community to come into prominence was Milton. This section of the county appears to have had some ambitious citizens and real estate dealers who would shame a modern chamber of commerce. The Tennessee Gazette of 1834 states that Milton, a post town, was established in 1820. Although an act of the legislature in 1820 authorized the establishment of the town by laying off of lots on the land of Gideon Thompson, and set up a voting place at Thompson's home, it appears that the project was not successful for in 1826 another act stated that lots in Milton were to be taxed as other lands in the state and not as town lots. After the Civil War the Act of 1820 was repealed.

The next town authorized by the legislature to incorporate was Fosterville, in 1832. In 1838, a group of interprising citizens, Leonard H. Sims, John M. Watkins, William Grey, John S. Cooper, Joseph Clough, Alsea Harris, James P. Shepport, John Patterson and Thomas Edwards received a charter for the establishment of the Fosterville Steam Mill Company. This part of the county had no water power sites and turned to steam. Fosterville, however, failed to maintain a sustained growth and remained a village.

The building of the Nashville and Chattanooga Railroad brought Smyrna into being. The Stewarts Creek settlement, one of the oldest in the county, was by-passed by the railroad. Some of the business establishments made the best of it by moving to the railroad. The new town took the name Smyrna, which had long been used by the Presbyterian Church in the vicinity. It was incorporated in 1854 and today is the second town in the county in importance. Eagleville and Christiana were incorporated for a time after the Civil War.

A few changes worthy of mention were made in the government of the city of Murfreesboro between 1815 and 1860. In 1817 Murfreesboro was formally incorporated. The mayor and alderman type of government was set up. The aldermen were elected by popular vote and they in turn chose a mayor. The first town officers were: Aldermen: Burrell Gannaway, Nicholas Tilford, Thomas G. Watkins, William Barfield, Charles Niles and George A. Sublett. Burrell Gannaway was treasurer; William Ledbetter, recorder; and Benjamin Blankenship, town constable. Joshua Haskell was the first major. He resigned before the end of the year and was succeeded by David Wendell. Although the charter was amended by the legislature from time to time, no important changes were made until after the Civil War, while the basic structure was not changed till the manager plan was adopted in 1921. It is interesting to note that the budget for Murfreesboro during the 1820's was between three hundred and four hundred dollars per year.

In 1822 while Murfreesboro was the capital of the state the court house burned. The legislature was forced to meet in the Presbyterian Church. A commission consisting of David Wendell, John S. Jetton, Samuel P. Black, Benjamin McCollough and John Hoover was appointed by the legislature for the purpose of supervising the erection of a new court house. The commissioners were authorized to borrow six thousand dollars from the branch of the Nashville Bank at Murfreesboro. The building erected at this time was used until 1859 when the present structure was completed.

By 1860 the residents of Rutherford County and Murfreesboro could well be proud of the position of their county and city in state politics. Advances made in other fields will be elaborated upon in later chapters. The Civil War, however, was soon to cause the county to lose much of its former prestige.

THE CIVIL WAR AND RECONSTRUCTION 1860-1870

In a study of the period of American History from 1815 to 1829 the development of American nationality is usually stressed. The period also marks the rise of sectionalism which eventually engaged in a death struggle with nationalism culminating in the Civil War.

In the early days of the Constitution various sections of the country preached the doctrine of States' rights. After 1815, however this issue found support chiefly in the south, first in connection with the tariff question and later over slavery. The west, however, developed a somewhat different point of view from the south. The western states were creatures of the central government and not creators of it. Tennessee and Kentucky as well as other sections of the west relied more heavily on the Federal government than the older states. The important part played by Tennessee in the settlement and independence of Texas was motivated more by the spirit of nationalism and manifest destiny, in all probability, than by the desire to expand slavery.

Tennessee therefore showed little enthusiasm for South Carolina's nullification of the federal tariff law. This loyalty to the union caused Tennessee to cast her vote for the Constitutional Union candidate, John Bell, in 1860 instead of the pro-slavery candidate, Breckenridge. Rutherford County although it grew much cotton and had many slaves supported Bell.

Furthermore Tennessee did not believe that the election of Lincoln was sufficient ground for secession and took the lead in trying to effect a compromise on the issue. On January 19, 1861, the legislature decided to submit to the people the question of a convention to vote on secession. The state was not ready to secede. On April 12, the convention was voted down by a vote of 69,675 to 57,798.

The delegates to the convention (if called) favoring secession received only 24,749, while those against secession received 88,803. The "Rutherford Telegraph" of Murfreesboro appears to have expressed the prevailing sentiment of the county and state with the following words: "Under the circumstances that now exist, there is no cause whatsoever for disunion, and he that favors it can be guilty of nothing short of treason to his country."

The firing on Fort Sumpter changed the situation. On May 6, the legislature passed an act to organize and equip a provisional force. On the same day, it again voted to submit the question of secession to the people. The members of the Rutherford delegation in the legislature voted for these measures. The state voted for secession by a vote of 104,913 to 47,238. Only in east Tennessee was there pronounced opposition to secession. In Rutherford County the vote was, for secession 2,392, against 73. Professor Hamer quotes a citizen of Murfreesboro who wired to Nashville: "All excited and aroused. All united. Secession flag waves over us. All for war."[1] Similar expressions were voiced from other parts of the state.

From 1861 to 1865 the Civil War overshadowed other issues in the nation. Tennessee was the site of many important battles during the war. The part of the county in the Civil War is discussed in a later chapter. In reconstruction, Tennessee did not conform in many ways to the general pattern for the south. It was the last state to secede and the first to be readmitted to the union. Andrew Johnson was appointed military governor in 1862 and political affairs were under his control and that of his successor for most of the state until the close of the war. In 1865 William G. Brownlow, a Republican, was elected governor. He served until 1869 when the Democrats again took control of the state. During the military occupation of Tennessee, the city council of Murfreesboro was suspended during the years of 1863 and 1864.

The Rutherford County Court was also suspended during the Civil War as is evidenced by the following quotation from its minutes:

"At a county court begun in holden at the courthouse in the town of Murfreesboro, state of Tennessee, Rutherford County, on the first Monday in May, 1864, it being the second day of said month and being the first court holden since the March term, 1862, owing to the military *imbarisment* of the county—justices present, the Worshipful Joseph Lindsay, former chairman, M. L. Fletcher, former assistant and G. W. Smith and William Bradley, justices pro temporore present and presiding . . .

1. P. M. Hamer, *Tennessee: A History.*

"In accordance with a proclamation of Andrew Johnson, Governor, an election was held in the county of Rutherford, state of Tennessee, on the fifth day of March 1864 for the election of county officers."

In the Brownlow regime those loyal to the south were for the most part disfranchised. In the presidential election of 1868 Rutherford County gave Grant, the Republican candidate, 957 votes to 841 for Seymour, the Democrat. After the voting restrictions were removed, the election of 1872 showed a very large increase in the number of votes cast. Greely, the Democrat, received 2503 to 2326 for Grant. Early in the Brownlow regime, many whites who had been loyal to the union rejected the extreme view taken by the state administration and were often spoken of as Conservatives. They supported the position of Andrew Johnson in national politics. The Brownlow followers were usually called Radicals. During this period there was considerable rioting in Tennessee. The Ku Klux Klan which originated at Pulaski had a strong organization in Rutherford County. The county, however, did not escape the disorder of the day. Professor Hamer gives the following description of a riot which took place in Murfreesboro:

"Late in February a riot developed in Murfreesboro, the details of which throw light on conditions in 1868. A meeting was being addressed by a white Radical who grew violent in his denunciation of the Conservatives. The audience became disorderly, the Conservatives yelling for Andrew Johnson and the Radicals for Brownlow. When order had been partially restored a negro, known as Free Jack, insisted on making a conservative speech. The Radicals objected and the town constable attempted to arrest Jack, but the crowd prevented this. Then John Cockerill, a Nashville negro, mounted the stand, denounced all Conservatives, white and black, and declared that 'the rebels should all have ropes about their necks and be dragged to the Cumberland River, and that he would be glad to aid in such an interprise.' A bystander broke in with the declaration: 'If you were a white man, you would be taken down.' Cockerill answered that even though he was black, he was whiter than any rebel; and he declared that he would not be taken down. A negro in the audience yelled: 'That's right, give 'em hell.' At this a white veteran of the Union army knocked Cockerill down, and was immediately attacked by a number of negroes. Some one fired a pistol. The fighting became general; bricks were thrown and other pistols were fired."

One negro was reported killed in this riot. After 1869, when the better class of white people took over the government, disorders gradually subsided.

As a result of the fighting in and near Rutherford County during the war, that region was laid in waste. A correspondent for a Boston newspaper quoted by Professor Hamer wrote in 1864:

"Let this point (Murfreesboro) be the center, and then make a circumference of 30 miles, and with me, we will stay a week in the womb of destruction. Whether you go on the Salem, the Shelbyville, the Manchester, or any other pike for a distance of 30 miles either way, what do we behold? One wide, wild and dreary waste, so to speak. The fences are all burned down: the apple, the pear, and the plum trees burned in ashes long ago: The torch applied to thousands of splendid mansions the walls of which alone remain."

The economic problems faced by the county after the war were similar to those in many other regions where much fighting took place. Readjustment was slow and painful. During the Brownlow administration much state money was spent on internal improvements, most of it unwisely. Many envisioned a rapid economic development characterized by an expansion of manufacturing. Charters were issued by the legislature to many manufacturing companies including several in Rutherford County. Most of the companies either were never organized or operated only for a short time.

During the Brownlow regime there was some special legislation affecting the city of Murfreesboro. In 1865 an act of the legislature extended the boundaries of the city to the distance of three quarters of a mile from the square. A recorder's court was established and provision was made for dividing the city into six wards of as equal size as possible. An act of 1869 required each alderman to live in the ward he represented.

In 1872 a bill was filed in the chancery court to define the power of the city board. So many acts had been passed from time to time that much confusion existed. This procedure amounted to a codification of the laws governing the city. Some ordinances in effect in the years following the war protected gas lights, prohibited disturbing the peace by "loud and unusual noises", and regulated gambling and the sale of liquor. Some of these problems are still with us.

PERIOD OF SLOW RECOVERY 1870-1900

From 1870 to 1900 national economy underwent a great change. Industry developed to an unprecedented height. Corporations were combined into trusts. Problems never before faced by a people, made their appearance. Although production increased rapidly and standards of living improved for many, large segments of the

SNAP SHOT OF A FEW LOADS OF COTTON ON THE SQUARE. ONE LOAD 11,030#.

Scene on Murfreesboro Public Square about 1910

The Rutherford County Courthouse and the Confederate Monument

population claimed that they were being discriminated against. This resulted in the rise of labor unions and farm organizations.

Tennessee and Rutherford continued largely agricultural during this period. Labor unions, therefore, played an insignificant part in the development of the county. Agriculture, however, raised its voice. Farmers, especially in the south, were anything but prosperous during a greater part of the period. They were forced to borrow money at high rates of interest. Transportation rates were high and taxes were rising at a rapid rate. The use of machinery and improved methods increased production. The tariff was holding down the price of some farm products while raising the price of many goods which the farmer purchased. There is little wonder that the farmer frequently expressed dissatisfaction, especially when it was necessary for him to pay back what he had borrowed. Sometimes the dollar which he paid back represented greater purchasing power than the dollar which he had borrowed. The western farmer, though radical at times in at least some lines of thinking, usually voted the Republican ticket, because of the late war, while his southern brother in suffering was chained to the Democratic party. The farm vote continued to control state and county elections in Tennessee.

In all presidential elections from 1870 to 1900 the state went Democratic though the Republicans offered some opposition and a few elections were rather close. The county was safely Democratic in all of these presidential elections though the Republicans cast a substantial vote. The highest vote cast by the Democrats was 3,855 in 1880, while the lowest was 2,511 in 1892. The highest Republican vote in the county was 2,482 in 1880 while the lowest was 1,202 in 1892. Third parties as the Prohibition, Socialist, Populist and Greenback polled few votes in national elections in either the state or the county.

In the gubernatorial elections the Republicans were more fortunate. In 1880 Hawkins, the Republican candidate, was elected as a result of a split in the Democratic party over the state debt issue. He was opposed by John V. Wright, a state credit Democrat who received 78,783, S. F. Wilson, a low tax Democrat, whom some accused of favoring repudiation of the state debt, who received 57,080, and R. M. Edwards, a greenback man, who received only 3,459. Hawkins' vote was 103,564. In the county, Hawkins received 2,371, Wilson 2,944, and Wright 1,035.

The most heated question in state politics for some years was the debt question. The debt in 1871 amounted to about $35,000,000. About $3,000,000 was incurred in bank bonds, the purchase of the Hermitage and the building of a state capitol. In addition the state had extended its credit to internal improvements prior to the Civil War and many of these ventures proved unsound. This part of debt amounted to about $14,000,000. Another $14,000,000 had been incurred chiefly in aid to the railroads during the Brownlow administration. The remainder was unpaid interest. Some wanted to cancel the Brownlow debt while others wanted to pay the state debt in full.

In 1879 an agreement was reached with most creditors to settle at fifty cents on the dollar with four per cent interest. This was submitted to the people and was voted down by a vote of 76,755 to 46,704. Rutherford County opposed the proposition by a vote of 2,311 to 1,648. This vote, taken in connection with the county's vote for Governor in 1880, indicates that Rutherford County either did not consider the state debt as a just and binding obligation, or welcomed an opportunity to penalize the wealthy bondholders, perhaps both. Others, no doubt, wanted to pay the debt in full. Many southern states repudiated their reconstruction debts.

An act of legislature to settle the debt at par was voided by the Supreme Court. The issue was finally settled in 1883. The old debt was settled in full, while the rest was paid fifty cents on the dollar with three per cent interest.

In the gubernatorial election of 1890 the Farmers' Alliance group got control of the Democratic Convention and nominated John P. Buchanan, a citizen of Rutherford County and a leader of the Alliance. Buchanan was elected by a vote of 126,348 to 70,081 over his Republican opponent. The county went for its native son by a vote of about two to one. In the election of 1892 Buchanan was not nominated by the Democrats. Many, especially farmers, had been disappointed because they had received little from the administration. Peter Turney was nominated by the Democrats and was elected. Buchanan ran as an independent candidate, but received only 29,918 votes in the entire state. Rutherford County, as usual, went Democratic.

In 1894 the complete returns showed that H. Clay Evans, the Republican candidate had won over Turney by a small majority. The Democratic legislature, however, made an investigation and declared that many illegal votes had been cast. After throwing out the vote of certain areas, Turney was declared elected by a vote of 94,620 to 92,266. The vote in Rutherford was close, but not contested. Turney received 1,958 votes to 1,781 for Evans. Both the state and county supported Bryan and free silver enthusiastically in 1896.

The population of Tennessee was 1,109,891 in 1860 and 2,020,616 in 1900. This represents a decennial increase ranging from 13.4

to 22.6 per cent.   The county was not so fortunate.   The population
of the county increased till 1880 when it was 36,714, the highest ever
attained.   By 1900 it had declined to 33,543.   The negro population
during this period averaged between 11,000 and 12,000.   The population of Murfreesboro in 1900 was 3,739.

Although there were no important changes in the government
of the city or the county in the latter part of this period, many improvements in ways of living came to the town.   Gas was introduced
for lighting the streets soon after the Civil War.   Before 1900 the
city had electricity, waterworks, and a street car system.   A railroad
was surveyed to Woodbury but was never begun.

THE PICTURE BRIGHTENS, 1900-1946

American democracy has been characterized by alternating
periods of liberalism and conservatism.   From the close of the Reconstruction period to the nineties conservatism prevailed, for the
most part.   About the turn of the century a wave of liberalism,
which approached radicalism at times, began to sweep the country.
Some of its results in the political field were the extension of the
merit system to state and local government, the commission and later
the manager form of government for cities, the initiative, referendum
and recall, direct primaries for the nomination of party candidates,
popular election of United States senators, a graduated income tax,
further curbing of trusts, regulation of public utilities and banking,
and a lower tariff.   Some of the more radical were still advocating
inflation in some form.   The leaders in this liberal movement were
to be found in both of the great national parties with wuch men as
Bryan, La Follette, Theodore Roosevelt, and Woodrow Wilson
occupying the spotlight.   Tennessee and Rutherford County, during
this period, were by nature conservative as most of the south had
always been.   History and hard times, however, combined to cause
both the state and county sometimes to favor liberalism, occasionally
radicalism.

In politics, Tennessee remained democratic in most elections
from 1900 to 1946.   The state gave a majority to the Republicans
in the presidential elections of 1920 and 1928.   It also elected a
Republican, Ben W. Hooper, as governor in 1910 and 1912, and
Alfred Taylor, another of that party in 1920.   The county, however,
went Democratic in all presidential and gubernatorial elections.   The
closest the Republicans came to winning the county in a presidential
election was in 1928 when the vote was 2,115 to 1,429.   Many people
did not vote in this election.

Since 1928 the county has been overwhelmingly Democratic in both state and national elections. The same is true for the state. The Republicans of east Tennessee have found it more profitable to trade with democratic candidates than to attempt the almost hopeless task electing one of their number. Furthermore, the Republicans in the state have been badly split in recent years. Finally, the New Deal, while holding most Democrats, except a few with a real or supposed financial background, heavily invaded the ranks of the low income Republicans, especially Negroes.

In Rutherford County the Republican party is now almost non-existent. In 1944 Mr. Dewey polled only 871 votes to 4,730 to Roosevelt, while a very promising young Republican, John W. Kilgore, polled only 332 votes to 4,439 for Jim McCord, the Democrat. McCord, however, had the support of all Democratic factions in the state. In addition to the causes listed above for the decline of the Republicans in the state, one other might be given for the county. The group of citizens that have for some years been business, social and political leaders in the county have been mostly Democrats. While this group has been open to some criticism, it contained some men of ability who knew politics, several of them being prominent in state affairs. During the same period, the Republican leadership has been confined chiefly to office seekers. There are many conservative Democrats in the state and county who would gladly join a rejuvenated Republican party if it were moderately conservative and if it could convince them that it would not lead the county into a repetition of the follies of the 1920's. Otherwise, the county will, no doubt, remain a Democratic stronghold.

Two very important issues that have frequently been before the state and naturally the county, are the liquor question, and the problem of amending the state constitution. Both will be briefly discussed.

Primitive man learned to get drunk before he mastered the art of writing. Many of our pioneer ancestors drank with or without restraint. Stills were established along with grist mills. The regulation of liquor was one of the first acts of the Rutherford County Court.

In 1827 a temperance society, said to be the first of its kind in America, was organized at the Presbyterian Church at Murfreesboro. From that time to 1900, many state acts regulated liquor in some form. The ordinances of the City Board for Murfreesboro also record various attempts to regulate the problem. In 1877, the legislature prohibited the sale of intoxicating liquors near a schoolhouse, and ten years later broadened the scope of the law. In 1884 the prohibitionists met in convention in Nashville and proposed an amendment to the constitution outlawing liquor. Such an amendment was submitted to the people by the legislature in 1887 but was defeated by a vote of 145,237 to 117,504. In the county, however, the amendment lost by a much larger vote, 4,300 against the proposal and only 1,451 favorable.

From 1899 to 1907 a series of local option acts were passed which resulted in all cities in the state being "dry" except Memphis, Nashville, Chattanooga, and La Folette. Since these cities served as oases for the rest of the state, a movement was initiated for a state-wide law. Rutherford County went "dry" in 1903.

In 1908 the question became so heated that a state-wide primary election was held within the Democratic party for the purpose of nominating a candidate for governor. Ex-Senator Edward Ward Carmack favored a state-wide law while Malcolm R. Patterson championed local option. Patterson won the nomination and of course the election. The vote in the county for Carmack was 1720, for Patterson 1831. In November of the same year, Carmack, who was then editing the *Nashville Tennessean*, was assassinated on the streets of Nashville by two friends of Patterson, who resented an editorial written by Carmack. When a prison sentence imposed upon one of the assassians was upheld by the State Supreme Court, Patterson pardoned him.

Seldom has there been a more heated issue in the state. In 1909 the state passed a state-wide law. Patterson vetoed it, but the legislature repassed it. In the next election the Democratic party split into two factions. The regular group prevailed upon Senator Robert L. Taylor, the most popular man in the party, to leave his duties at Washington long enough to become a candidate for the governorship. The "state-wide" Democrats bolted the party and voted for Ben W. Hooper, the Republican candidate. Hooper was elected in 1910 and again in 1912, but was defeated in 1914. Rutherford County, however, voted the straight Democratic ticket in all of these elections. The closest vote was in 1912 when Hooper received 2,268 to 2,630 for his Democratic opponent.

In the vote on the repeal of the eighteenth amendment, the state voted for repeal by a vote of 126,951 to 120,154. The county, however, voted against repeal by the close vote of 1,722 to 1,737. After the repeal of the eighteenth amendment, the sale of beer was permitted in both Murfreesboro and the county. In 1945 the city council banned the sale of beer within the corporation. A petition was immediately filed with the council demanding a referendum on the subject. The act of the council was sustained by a close vote

At the April 1945 session of the county court, the sale of beer within one thousand feet of a church, school or lodge was prohibited. Furthermore, beer could not be sold in dance halls or places equipped with music machines. In August, 1946 a petition permitting the sale of liquor in the county was defeated by a two-to-one majority.

Another much discussed question in the state and county has been the movement for a new constitution. Although this question has frequently been before the voters of Tennessee, no changes have been made in that document since it was ratified in 1870. All other states in the union have changed their constitution one or more times since 1912. There are two reasons for Tennessee's failure to act in this respect. The people of Tennessee are among the most conservative in the nation. Furthermore, the method of amending the Tennessee constitution is most difficult. Two methods are outlined. An amendment may be initiated by two successive legislatures. It must be passed the first time by a majority of each house and two years later by a two-thirds majority of each house. The amendment must then be ratified, not by a majority of the people voting in an election therefor, but by "a majority of all the citizens of the State voting for representatives . . ." An amendment may receive a ten-to-one majority and yet fail to pass because a sufficient number of people did not vote. Amendments may not be submitted more often than once in six years.

The legislature may submit to the people the question of a constitutional convention at any time. Seven times have the people voted on the question of a convention for revising the constitution of 1870 and, in all cases the proposition has been voted down.

Amendments have been submitted to voters in four different years. In 1887 the question of prohibition amendment was voted on but was defeated by a substantial majority in the state and an overwhelming majority in the county.

In 1904 seven amendments were submitted, the most important being extending the term of office of the governor from two to four years. All were defeated, the vote being extremely light.

In 1922 the legislature voted to submit to the people the question of modifying the tax clause but bacause of a technicality the amendment was not placed on the ballot in most localities.

In 1935 an amendment to increase the salaries of members of the legislature was overwhelmingly defeated. Again, the vote was very light.

In 1940 two amendments were submitted to the voters. One was to increase the pay of legislature, while the other was for a four year term for the governor. Both amendments received a majority of the votes cast, the vote in the first case being 158,216 for and 77,614 against, while the vote for the second was 171,209 for and 68,506 against. Yet, neither amendment was adopted since neither received a majority equal to the majority of the votes cast for members of the legislature. The total vote cast for members of the legislature in 1940 was 377,111. This meant that a vote of 188,556 would have been necessary to ratify either amendment. Rutherford County favored raising the pay of the legislators by a vote of 1,446 to 1,238. The vote for a four year term for the governor was 1,796 while 987 votes were cast against this proposition.

In voting either for a convention or for amendments the counties with large cities, especially Shelby, have usually favored constitutional change, while the rural counties have almost always opposed change. The vote also shows that Rutherford although one of the moderately large counties of the state has been more opposed to changing the Constitution than the state average. The conclusion reached is that Rutherford is one of the most conservative counties in the most conservative state in the union as far as constitutional change is concerned.

Murfreesboro and Rutherford County have experienced considerable economic development since 1900 though agriculture is still the basic industry. During the First World War, though no camps or war industries came to the county, the powder plant near Nashville, the Muscle Shoals project and others caused an increase in wages. Farmers experienced a period of prosperity for a time. Many, however, who tried to expand their holdings, suffered heavily in the liquidation period immediately after the war.

In the so-called prosperity period following the First World War, the county conformed to the general pattern of the nation. Murfreesboro experienced considerable growth and began to take on the aspects of a city. The streets were improved, a modern hotel was erected, a modern filtration plant was installed, and a sewage system completed. Bus and truck lines were put into operation and new industries came to town.

Another important gain for the community during the thirties was the location of the Veterans' Facility near Murfreesboro. This institution has brought to the area a large number of high class professional and technical experts.

By the time of the outbreak of the recent war the county was, relatively speaking, in good shape. Its cultural institutions, manufacturing establishments, and transportation facilities tended to equalize the uncertainties of agriculture and produced a rather well balanced economy that many counties of the state did not enjoy.

From 1900 to 1940 the county remained almost stationary in population, increasing from 33,543 to 33,604. The city of Murfreesboro during the same period, increased from 3,999 to 9,495, an increase of over 5,000. This meant that the agricultural area lost population. Not only was this true, but most of the loss was in Negroes. The Negro population in 1910 was 11,357 and had shown no marked decline to that time. In 1940 it dropped to 6,780, a decline of almost 5,000. Most of the departing Negroes went to the cities, a large number going to the north.

The Second World War caused considerable activity in the Murfreesboro area. Many officers at Camp Forrest made their homes in Murfreesboro which caused a demand for rental property. The Smyrna Air Base, Air Utilities at the old Sky Harbor, and smaller industries caused a war boom. Although many new houses were built, the rent situation remained serious. As the camps and war industries began to leave the area the Veterans' Facility began an expansion program. Returning veterans also increased the demand for homes. The city now claims a population of over 12,000.

At present, the city of Murfreesboro, with its railroad, many bus and truck lines, cheap power, and excellent supply of water, might well take advantage of the decentralization movement in industry and become a manufacturing center. The building of the proposed dam on Stone's River at Stewart's Ferry in Davidson County would make one of the finest recreation lakes in the state. If the dam is equipped with a lock and several auxilliary locks and dams are placed on the river, Murfreesboro might realize a dream over a century old and become an inland port of some importance.

The governments of both the county and the city have undergone important changes in recent years. While the functions of all counties have increased, those of Rutherford have expanded more than the average county. This expansion has been in the areas of agriculture, education, highways, health, social security, and others. This has necessitated the addition of new departments and the reorganization of others. The county now has an agricultural agent, a home demonstration agent, a purchasing agent, a budget commission, a highway board and a superintendent, a board and superintendent of education, a health department headed by a full time health officer and a veterans' service officer.

The county also has a county judge instead of a county chairman. The advantages of a judge over a chairman are that the judge is paid a regular salary, devotes his full time to the office and is usually a lawyer. The greatest need of county government in recent years has been a responsible chief executive. The office of judge, while not carrying with it all of the functions of a chief executive, is a decided improvement over that of chairman, and the larger counties with a wide range of functions could hardly operate under a chairman.

In 1909 a special act of the legislature created the office of county judge for Rutherford County. The incumbent died and Governor Hooper appointed a Republican in his place. This was too much for the Democrats of the county, and in 1911 an act was passed repealing the act of 1909. Although the Supreme Court of the state had ruled that the office of county judge could not be abolished during the incumbent's term, the judge gave up the office. In 1931 the legislature again established the office of county judge. It was first held by John Wiseman. Wiseman was succeeded by Harold Earthman, who resigned in 1945 to take his seat in Congress. Hoyte Stewart, appointed by Governor McCord to fill the vacancy, was elected by the voters of the county in 1946 for the remainder of the term.

The justice of the peace courts have, in recent years, come in for so much criticism that the demand for a general sessions court, such as exists in more than twenty counties in the state, was heeded by Representative Holden, who sponsored an act establishing such a court during the 1947 session of the state legislature. The first judge was Andrew L. (Jack) Todd. He soon resigned and Alvin Collins was appointed in his place. There has also been some discussion in favor of reducing the number of the magistrates in the court as well as for a commission or manager form of government for the county.

The most important change in city government has been the adoption of the manager form of government. This popular form of government is especially suited for cities of from 5,000 to 100,000 population. It was adopted by Murfreesboro in 1921. The people elect a five man council chosen at large from the city. The council chooses one of its number as mayor. The administration of the city's business is placed in the hands of a manager who holds at the will of the board. The first manager was Edd Lowe. He was succeeded in 1928 by Sam Cox. Hubert McCullough succeeded Cox in 1947.

Preceding the city elections of 1946 the city council had for years been composed of W. A. Miles, W. T. Gerhardt, T. J. Dement, G. B. Sawyer and Beecher Horton. The office of mayor had alternated between Miles and Gerhardt. In 1946 the younger men of the city sponsored a ticket and elected John Holloway, Herbert Young and Clyde Fite in place of Miles, Gerhardt and Horton. Holloway was chosen mayor. A group of younger men also have been appointed to the city board of education.

There are several other issues of a local nature that have come up for discussion in recent years. Murfreesboro is one of the few cities of its size and wealth which until recently did not have a public park and playground. Neither does it have a public library. All attempts to get a park and playground for the last twenty years ended in failure until recently when a movement was inaugerated to equip a playground on the Tennessee College campus purchased for the high school. The city is now building and equipping one of the finest playgrounds in the state. A former citizen of Murfreesboro, Mr. Linebaugh, before his death, gave five thousand dollars towards the establishment of a public library for the town. Steps are under way for a public library on the high school campus.

Another question that raises its head periodically is the cleaning up of the "bottom." The buying of the land and wrecking of the houses presents no insurmountable obstacles, but what to do with residents has never been successfully answered. The proposed re-routing of Highway 41 through the city will partly solve this problem.

Although Rutherford County has not attained the place it held in state and national affairs before the Civil War, progress since the turn of the century has been pronounced. Murfreesboro is today known primarily as a residential city with a cultural background flanked by schools, writers, and churches discussed elsewhere in this work. It has an active Chamber of Commerce, Kiwanis, Rotary and Lions Clubs, a woman's club, several garden clubs, and in addition, veterans, patriotic, and fraternal organization too numerous to mention.

The next chapter will point out interesting places and views in the county. This will be followed by a series of chapters on the county's contributions in the major fields of human experience.

CHAPTER III

Monuments and Other Interesting Places

In bronze and native limestone, in pillared mansions and humbler dwellings made of virgin cedar, Rutherford Countians have their reminders of the county's storied past. Born of that western surge of colonization that followed the Revolution, the county is today indexed with markers that recall its stately growth from a land-grant wilderness to a typical modern community and comprise a key to its history.

TRAILS AND ROADS: The trails over which the pioneers made their way by oxcart or horseback to settle the cedar-covered land of what in 1804 was to be known as Rutherford County were first made by the buffalo, then used by the Indian, and today are rather closely followed by modern paved highways, which may be said to be markers in themselves. The most ancient of these is the famous War Trace, which led from the lower Cumberland to the Indian settlements near Lookout Mountain, and which is now sketchily followed by Federal Highway 41 and, for a distance, by the Nashville, Chattanooga and Saint Louis Railroad. The town of Wartrace in Bedford County got its name from this trail. Goodspeed says that the Indians held their gatherings and tribal dances in a natural amphitheatre just off the old trail south of Murfreesboro, but no one today knows the exact spot to which the historian referred.

The present Federal Highway 70 South, from Readyville to Murfreesboro has markers designating it as a part of the Immigrants' Trail and though not quite as old as the Walton Road which passed further north, it brought many pioneers into the county. It was also an early stagecoach and mail route between Knoxville and Nashville.

The first road from Nashville to Rutherford County was by way of Jefferson. This road was later extended to Murfreesboro and was used by stagecoaches to Knoxville as well as by those to Alabama. Later a road was built farther west which eventually became the present highway from Nashville to Murfreesboro and is today one of the most heavily traveled highways in the nation.

55

The period from 1840 to 1920 was the toll road era in highway transportation. These pikes, as they were called, were macadamized or gravel roads with a toll gate usually every five miles. Rutherford was one of the last counties in the United States to discontinue the use of toll gates. The only evidence today that toll was once charged on these roads, most of which are now paved, is an occasional toll gate house still standing on the very edge of the road.

MILLS: The song "Down by the Old Mill Stream" might well have originated in Rutherford County. Next to springs, water-power sites were most in demand along the rivers and creeks by the early settlers. By 1812 the county court had authorized the erection of more than twenty mills. Nothing tangible remains of this early attempt at civilization except an occasional millrace which carried water to an overshot water wheel. This picturesque type of wheel was long ago replaced with the more modern turbine.

Among these early mills, or the immediate successor to them, is that one located on Stone's River near the community of Florence, known today as Nice's Mill, but more familiarly known as Ward's Mill. The exact date of its origin is unknown, but the mill is believed to be one of the oldest industries in the county, and its beginning is thought to have been near 1800. The original foundation of limestone still stands.

MONUMENTS AND PARKS: The earliest known date commemorated in a public monument is September 7, 1794. On that date Orr's expedition sent out by General Robertson from Nashboro against the Indians paused for the night at Black Fox Spring, three miles southeast of Murfreesboro. On Flag Day, June 14, 1933, the Captain William Lytle Chapter, Daughters of the American Revolution, placed a large native limestone base with an iron marker at the mouth of the road leading to Black Fox Camp Spring on Federal Highway 41, with the following inscription: "Road to Black Fox Camp Spring, Orr's expedition sent out by Gen. Robertson camped near this spring, Sept. 7, 1794. Erected by Captain William Lytle Chapter, Daughters of the American Revolution, 1933."

The one tangible evidence that Rutherford County's seat of government was also once the capital of the State is a bit of limestone and iron placed at the northwest corner of Murfreesboro's old city cemetery on East Vine Street, amid weathered tombstones. The inscription reads: "Presbyterian Church of Murfreesboro was organized in April, 1812, under the name of the Murfreesboro Spring Church with 18 members; Joseph Dickson, Susanna Henry, Margaret Jetton, Isabella Smith, Margaret Wasson, Grace Williams, Mary Stewart, John Smith, John Henry, Margaret Dickson, James C.

Smith, Abagail Baird, Elizabeth Kelton, Frances Henderson, Mrs. Samuel Wilson, Robert Wasson."

"In 1818 the name of the church was changed to the First Presbyterian Church and a brick building was erected. The legislature sat here in 1822 during the time when Murfreesboro was the capital of Tennessee. The church was demolished by the Federal Army in 1864. This tablet is placed by the Col. Hardy Murfree Chapter of the National Society of the Daughters of the American Revolution September, 1933."

The passerby, if he has eyes to see such things, will pause to read this inscription. If he is historically minded, he may take pleasure in the thought that here passed to and fro the young James K. Polk (who earlier had attended the old Bradley Academy here) busy with his duties as clerk of the senate; or Sam Houston, then the state's adjutant general, or Andrew Jackson who was rapidly becoming a national political figure.

Of the county's part in the War Between the States there is abundant commemoration. A beautiful national cemetery established in 1867, and a three hundred and sixty acre park, established in 1932 commemorate the bloody Battle of Stone's River (sometimes called the Battle of Murfreesboro) fought northwest of the city on the dates of December 31, 1862 to January 2, 1863.

Distinctive among the many markers and monuments of the park and cemetery—and, in fact, distinctive among those of their kind throughout the nation—are the Hazen's Brigade and McFadden's Ford or Artillery monuments.

The Hazen's Brigade monument has been said by the National Park Service to be the first monument ever erected to a battle of the War Between the States. Soldiers of this brigade, the Union detachment which withstood the terrific onslaughts of the Confederates in that three-day battle, erected the monument of native limestone while in winter quarters in Murfreesboro in January, 1863. Later they added inscriptions in memory of comrades that fell at Chickamauga and Chattanooga.

Standing on a spot especially set apart, partially surrounded by graves of fallen soldiers, the monument speaks eloquently, in letters cut out of the stone, of a great and terrible battle-one of the six decisive engagements of the war:

"Hazen's Brigade to the memory of its soldiers who fell at Stone River, December 31, 1862.

"Their faces toward heaven, their feet to the foe.
"The blood of one-third of its soldiers

"Twice spilled in Tennessee
"Crimson the battle flag of the Brigade
"And inspires to greater deeds."

"Erected in 1863 upon the ground where they fell by their comrades."

Of Shiloh the inscription reads:

"The veterans of Shiloh have left a deathless heritage of fame upon the field of Stone River."

At the close of the war, the two significant words "Chickamauga" and "Chattanooga" were added.

Several hundred yards away, on an eminence overlooking a curve of the quiet river, stands the Artillery monument. This shaft of whitewashed concrete, erected by the Nashville, Chattanooga and Saint Louis Railway, marks the spot where on January 1, 1863 fifty-eight guns rained grapeshot and canister over the heads of the retreating Union troops to pour bloody death into the Confederate ranks as they advanced across the river. This incident is said to mark the first time in history that an army had ever fired long-range over the heads of its troops, and the maneuver so caught the Confederates by surprise, that some 1800 of them were mowed down by the concealed emplacement of guns. Survivors of that engagement have described how the river "ran blood" at McFadden's Ford for several days following the battle.

These monuments and other points of interest in the park have been viewed by thousands of visitors and tourists who have been escorted through the park by guides in the past few years.

Rutherford County's courthouse, with its tall Corinthian columns, is in itself a monument to historical events, pratically the famous raid of General Nathan Bedford Forrest described in a later chapter. The passerby may pause as he enters the east door to read a marker, placed at a spot where a Confederate soldier fell mortally wounded during this raid. The inscription reads: "Erected to the memory of Gen. Nathan Bedford Forrest by the Daughters of the Confederacy for heroic services to the citizens of Murfreesboro on July 13, 1862— July 13, 1912."

In the northeast corner of the public square stands the famous bronze Confederate soldier on a base of limestone, "built of a people's love", as its inscription says. The monument was first placed at the intersection of East Main Street and the square, but was removed to its present location when the street was paved.

On the northwest corner of the courthouse lawn is the monument recently erected in memory of General Griffith Rutherford for whom the county was named. This memorial, a part of the Tennessee Sesquicentennial celebration, was the result of a joint effort by the Tennessee Historical Commission and the local Daughters of the American Revolution, not to mention the untiring efforts of Judge Samuel C. Williams. The local committee was composed of Mrs. C. F. Partee, Chairman, Mrs. James Patterson, Mrs. Annie Youree and Mrs. J. J. Edwards. The money was furnished by the state of Tennessee, Rutherford County, the city of Murfreesboro and by private subscriptions. The monument was dedicated in an impressive ceremony on August 29, 1946. Collier Critchlow was master of ceremonies and E. W. Carmack the chief speaker. The monument was unveiled by Mrs. Mary Purseley Baum, a great-great-granddaughter of General Rutherford, and a resident of Murfreesboro. A number of other descendents of the General was also present.

The home of Sam Davis, near Smyrna, the martyred Confederate boy hero, is also a monument in itself. Purchased by the State in 1927, the home is now a public shrine, with its museum of war relics, its furnishings in typical colonial style, and its cemetery where Sam Davis lies buried.

OLD HOMES: The old homes of the county that have survived the passing of time are evidence of its gracious mode of living that evolved out of the county's rich lands. Of these it is possible in the space here allotted to name only a few.

Built sometime between 1805-1809, "Springfield", stands today in magnificent decay on the banks of Overall's Creek just off the Manson Pike. The builder was "General" John Smith, and the present owner is the Washington family, descendants of "General" Smith through his daughter, Julia. It was at this home that a romance of the War of 1812 was written. Overton Washington Crockett and his brother, Fontaine Posey Crockett, sons of Colonel Anthony Crockett of Revolutionary fame, stopped for the night at the Smith home on their way from their home in Kentucky to join Tennesseans at the Harpeth River, from where they were to proceed to New Orleans to join General Andrew Jackson's forces. After the war, the brothers returned to the Smith home, and on November 25, 1815, Overton married Evalina Smith. Five years later Fontaine married Julia Smith, and their daughter Sara Katherine Crockett was married years later to Francis Whiting Washington, a fourth cousin to George Washington. Their son, John Hall Washington, inherited the place. In 1857 John Washington had the home remodeled, adding the portico and tall columns and lengthening the windows. During the War Between the States Federal officers were quartered in the west side of the house, while on the east side, the family sheltered a wounded Confederate soldier.

The home of Charles Ready near Readyville is one of the earliest and most imposing brick structures in the county. Tradition has it that the home was originally a three-story structure, and that the Colonel kept a colony of silk worms on the third floor. The old house is noted for having been the place where Forrest's cavalrymen were given a hasty supper as they passed along the road to Murfreesboro. Hazen's Brigade later made the house its headquarters. Among those who are said to have visited the house are Presidents Andrew Jackson, Martin Van Buren and James K. Polk, William Cooper, the famous Tennessee artist, and William Haskell, "the silver-tongued orator of Tennessee." The evergreens near the entrance are said to have come from the yard of John Sevier. Present day owners are Mr. and Mrs. Lawrence Barker.

So old that the date of its building is lost in history, the home of Absalom Scales near Eagleville is remarkable for its silver doorknobs, its carved mantels and casings. The home once sheltered Doctor Wyeth, a biographer of General Forrest, during the war. It is still owned by descendants of the builder.

Andrew Jackson was often a visitor to the home which, Moses Ridley, a Revolutionary soldier, built on the main stem of Stone's River at the northwest corner of the county. Ridley and his nephew, Moses Ridley Buchanan, operated one of the early mills of the county. The 2,800 acres of land granted to Ridley must have been a favorite hunting ground of the Indians, as is evidenced by the arrowheads and tomahawks which still may be found on the place. The present owners are Mr. and Mrs. Alton Wade of Nashville.

Oak Manor, or Oaklands, as it was called by its builder, Doctor James Maney, dates from the 1820's. It was here that Jefferson Davis was a guest when he came to make his own investigation of the Tennessee campaign in 1862, and here also that the Federal troops under Colonel W. W. Duffield surrendered to Forrest.

Perhaps the most widely publicized mansion in the country is Marymont, built near Salem by Hiram Jenkins in 1864. A feature of this stately home is the original goldleaf papering, imported by Jenkins from France and still in good state of preservation on the south parlor walls. The tall Ionic columns and bracketed cornice of the portico were added by Doctor J. J. Rucker, who in 1878, married Nimmie Jenkins, niece of the builder. During the War Between the States, a Federal garrison was stationed at Marymont.

Though it has been replaced by a modern industry, the site of the home of William Lytle, son of Captain William Lytle, Revolutionary officer, bears mention here. The house built in the early 1800's, was one of elegance in every detail, with its broad hall papered

Home of Major John W. Childress where President Polk
often visited

"Oaklands," built by Dr. James Maney before the Civil War

in scenes from "The Lady of the Lake," and with its rich furnishings. All that remains today is one wing of the structure. Following the death of the builder, his widow married Captain Carter Harrison, a cousin of President Benjamin Harrison, and the home became known as the Harrison place. The grave of Captain William Lytle is in the old family cemetery on the place. Its time-worn stone slab bears the following epitaph: "Sacred to the memory of Captain William Lytle, an officer of the War of the Revolution. He was born in Pennsylvania the 17th of February A.D. 1735 and died on this farm September 1807." "Universally beloved for his honesty and firmness in all the relations of life."

"His youngest son on whom his name was bestowed placed this tablet in his memory."

"Bloomfield", the widely known home of the Ordway family, is part of the Lytle grant. Famous for its acres of daffodils, tradition has it that the bulbs were brought from England and planted in a plot which became known as "Government Garden."

In the Wendell home on the sight of which a doctor's clinic now stands, President James A. Garfield, then a Brigadier General, had his quarters during the war when he was chief of staff to General W. S. Rosecrans.

Other interesting homes in Murfreesboro worthy of mention are the Hooper home on East Main Street, built by James Newton Clark and now a doctor's clinic; the Faircloth residence on East Lytle Street, where Jean Faircloth McArthur was reared; the home of General Joseph B. Palmer on East Main Street; the Perkins home on East Bell Street which formerly housed Eaton College; the Eaton home on the Tennessee College campus where the first president of Union University lived; the Childress home on North Academy Street where James K. Polk frequently visited; and the Ewing home on North Highland now occupied by Mr. and Mrs. George Nelson.

Just out of the city on the Woodbury road is located the Arnold home, now the residence of the Harrells. On the Manchester road near Murfreesboro stands "Bellwood" the home of Mr. and Mrs. Robert Bell. This home was built by Colonel Frank Burton on land granted by the state of North Carolina to Colonel Hardy Murfree. Colonel Burton called the place "Uxor Hill" which meant "wife's hill." A few miles further out on the pike is the Henderson home famous in the history of the War Between the States and now the residence of Mrs. William A. Snell.

Still other famous old home in the county are "Evergreen" on the Lebanon highway, built by Doctor Thomas C. Black and owned by Thomas Brandon, one of Black's decendants; "Riverside," the Randolph home near Walter Hill; the Jenkins home on the Manson pike; the King home near Jefferson; the Tucker home at Smyrna; "Elmwood," home of the Hords, on the Nashville highway; the Buchanan residence on the Manchester pike, where Governor Buchanan lived; the Gregory home near Smyrna which as an early inn was frequented by Andrew Jackson and other notables; "Castlewood," home of Mr. and Mrs. James Haynes and the Turner home on the Salem road owned by Mr. and Mrs. Jesse Brown, noted for its boxwoods brought to the county at an early date in a powder horn. (Editor's note. For a full description of famous Rutherford County homes see "Hearthstones" by Mary B. Hughes, author of this chapter.)

Other interesting landmarks include a log house near Jefferson which was built by Joseph Herndon, Rutherford's first County Court Clerk, and a cedar-log smokehouse in the same vicinity built by General John Coffee about 1812.

OLD JEFFERSON: In driving from Walter Hill to Smyrna one passes through a village called "Old" Jefferson. And old it is. Its appearance today, however, would not suggest that it was the first seat of government for Rutherford County, that it was once the leading trade town of the area, that its warehouses were places for inspecting various farm products and that it was a port of some importance for flat bottom boats. All that remains of the courthouse, stocks and whipping post is a grass-covered mound in the yard of Ben Ward, the spot where the courthouse chimney stood.

GRAVEYARDS: One who has an inclination for such things might well spend a few hours in some of the old burying grounds of the county. Here one finds a variety of stately old gravestones, an occasional vault and epitaphs that all but run the entire scale of human emotions. The simple faith expressed by many of these is heartening to read in a world now so inclined toward materialism. In many of these cemeteries the stones are so old that it is impossible to read the inscriptions. Others like the old Bradley ground on the Halls Hill pike have long ago disappeared.

The best known graveyard in the county is the Old City Cemetery on East Vine Street on the block where the Presbyterian church once stood. It is the resting place for members of many pioneer families including the Hendersons, Burtons, Bairds, Maneys, Currins, Kings, Searcys, Jettons, Childresses, Holmes, and others. Although Samuel Wilson, said to have been the first settler in the county, was buried on his farm near the National Cemetery, his stone was removed to this cemetery by the Captain William Lytle Chapter, Daughters of the American Revolution in 1937. During the same year markers were erected here in memory of several Revolutionary heroes who died in the county.

Evergreen, in Murfreesboro, founded before the War Between the States, is also the resting place for many notables including Carter Harrison, General Joseph B. Palmer, Congressman Charles Ready, Junior, David Wendell, Doctor J. B. Murfree and Mary Noilles Murfree.

Probably the oldest marker in the county is in the Searcy graveyard near Walter Hill. It is dated 1804. The stones in the Ready cemetery at Readyville where, no doubt Charles Ready, Senior, is buried, are so weatherbeaten that it is impossible to read them.

The Woodfin ground near Fosterville is a very large cemetery with stones dated as far back as 1815. Another large graveyard is the Sims ground near Barfield with many stones erected long before the War Between the States. The Black family ground on the Lebanon pike is the resting place of Samuel P. Black and Dr. Thomas P. Black. The Campbell graveyard on the Midland road is also very old and is the resting place of Reverend William Eagleton who served as pastor of the Presbyterian church in Murfreesboro from 1829 to 1866. His wife is buried beside him. Congressman David Dickinson, son-in-law of Hardy Murfree and father-in-law of John Bell, is buried in the family ground near the Nashville pike about a mile out of the city limits.

Other interesting graveyards dating long before the War Between the States include the Jackson and the Carlton grounds near Rockvale, Lillard near Salem, Taylor near Eagleville, Mulloy near Murfreesboro, Beesley six miles west of Murfreesboro, Miles seven miles from Murfreesboro just off the Nashville highway, Haynes on the Franklin road, Gannaway on the Midland road, McKnight near Milton and Youree on the Bradyville pike.

Many counties, in addition to old cemeteries, have one or more very old church buildings of which they are justly proud. The early church houses in Rutherford County, however, were either soon outgrown and replaced, or were destroyed by fire, tornado or by the invading armies of the north. The only church buildings in Murfreesboro that were constructed before the Civil War are the Methodist just south of the present church which is used as a store and the Cumberland Presbyterian building that is used as the city hall.

INSTITUTIONS: Should a stranger visit Murfreesboro he would no doubt be shown by his host the campus of the Middle Tennessee State College with its farm and airport, and the campus of what was formerly Tennessee College for Women but which was recently purchased by the county and city for a high school and play ground. The Bristol-Nelson School for children on North Highland

Street has more than a local reputation. Another spot of interest is the Veterans' Hospital on the Lebanon road. This institution, built by the federal government at a cost of several million dollars is on land originally granted by the state of North Carolina to Isaac Shelby as payment for surveying land in middle Tennessee. It is interesting that government officials and engineers, over a century later, were impressed with the possibilities of this site just as was the early Revolutionary surveyor and Indian fighter who had seen most of middle Tennessee. This spot also missed by one vote becoming the permanent seat of government for the county. In addition to a group of large and attractive buildings the hospital grounds are fast becoming a spot of beauty.

NATURAL PHENOMENA: There are a few points of natural interest in the county that deserve to be mentioned. In the eastern part of the county near Readyville stands Pilot Knob, the highest hill in the county. The peak is over eleven hundred feet high. It was used by the Indians as a lookout post in the early history of the state, and for the same purpose by both sides in the War Between the States. Its base was the scene of a skirmish during that war. From its crest one can see most of Rutherford and parts of several adjoining counties. The view of the hills to the east, is especially impressive in the fall of the year when the leaves begin to turn.

Another most interesting and peculiar formation is Snail Shell Cave, in the western part of the county. Here it appears that some prehistoric giant might have taken a huge auger a hundred or two feet in diameter and bored a hole a hundred feet deep through solid rock for the most part. If one is careful a trip to the bottom is possible and profitable. Here are large trees growing on the floor. One also finds a subterranean stream of clear, cold water that comes from a cave to vanish into another a few yards away. In the stream are minnows which are said to have no eyes. Even on the hottest days of summer the air is cool and bracing. The floor and walls are dotted with a variety of wild flowers and ferns and, of course, with snail shells. As interesting as the spot is, few residents of the county have ever seen it.

The county is also noted for its large springs, some of which have a daily flow of over a million gallons. While they sometimes rise at the foot of a hill, one should not be surprised to find water bubbling up out of comparatively level ground. One of these, the Murfree spring in Murfreesboro, until recently, supplied the city with water. The most famous spring from the historical point of view is the Black Fox Spring frequently referred to in this work and located three miles southeast of Murfreesboro. It was used by the Indians as a camp site for hunting expeditions as well as for attacks on the early Cumberland settlers. There was also an early trading post near it where the Cumberland settlers and the Indians exchanged wares. It got its name from a chief, Black Fox, who often camped there. There is an interesting legend with several versions about the chief's death. He was said to have been surrounded by his enemies and all his followers slain. His body was not found among the dead. He is said to have jumped into the spring. One story has it that he escaped through the Murfree spring while another says that his bones were later found there. This is interesting in view of the fact that the waters of the Black Fox spring enter the ground and are thought to come out again at the Murfree spring.

Rutherford County has no mountains to rival east Tennessee or lakes or other large bodies of water that add so much to the beauty of many parts of the country. Man and nature, however, have combined to give middle Tennessee, including Rutherford County, a simple beauty that changes with the seasons leaving a lasting impression on visitors as well as residents. In the spring of the year hills of tender green buds with a darker background of evergreen cedar are not soon forgotten. Soon the combination of redbud and wild plum yields its glory to white hills of dogwood. If one will take the trouble to enter the woodlands, the reward will be a variety of wildflowers including violets, ferns, columbine, anemone, shooting star, pink root and others too numerous to mention. To many, however, the most attractive feature of the countryside is where man and nature have become partners and pastures of blue grass and fields of alfalfa are dotted with grazing herds of cattle and sheep.

In May, fields of crimson clover followed by summer's waves of golden grain and cotton blossoms add to the ever changing panorama. In the fall, the coloring forests present another lasting impression with red dogwood and maple ranging from brilliant red to pastel yellow, and with the cedar again forming a background which causes many to think this the most beautiful season of the year. The cultivated fields white with cotton, shocks of corn, and yellow pumpkins rival the hills and pastures. Even bleak winter is occasionally interrupted with a snow which perhaps shows the cedar at its best.

Under the leadership of various garden clubs and individuals, plantings of trees, shrubs, daffodils, iris, and scores of other flowers have made the homes and highways of the county rival the natural beauty of the woods. Nature, man, and a rich historical background have all combined to make Rutherford County a wholesome place in which to live.

CHAPTER IV

Statesmen, The Bench And The Bar

Since her formation in 1803, Rutherford County has served as the birthplace, living place, or burial spot for many important statesmen who have contributed largely to the growth and development of Tennessee and the nation. Colonel Robert Weakley figured prominently in the beginning of the county. When he came to Tennessee he settled near Nashville in Davidson County which included Rutherford County. He lived near Smyrna for a short time after the establishment of Rutherford County. He helped to draw the boundary line between Rutherford and Davidson Counties and was instrumental in having Old Jefferson chosen as the first county seat upon the land which he and another land speculator, Thomas Bedford, owned. He was a candidate for governor in 1815 and later represented his district in the Federal House of Representatives.

James C. Mitchell was born in Augusta County, Virginia on March 10, 1786, and received his early education in that county. As a young man, he moved to Rhea County, Tennessee and began the practice of law. He served as Solicitor-General of the Second Tennessee District from 1813 to 1817, and was elected to the lower house of the state legislature in 1819, serving in the Thirteenth and Fourteenth General Assemblies which convened at Murfreesboro. It was during his years in Murfreesboro as representative that he formed an attachment for the town and its people and was led to become a citizen six years later.

In 1825 Mitchell was elected to the Nineteenth Congress where he served four years in the lower house. Mitchell, along with Adam Alexander of Jackson, Tennessee and James K. Polk opposed the bill for extending the Cumberland Road. He wrote his constituents that the extravagance of national appropriations for internal improvements was "truly alarming." He depreciated the policy of "some politicians" to get Congress "at some unthinking moment" to make an appropriation of considerable magnitude, and then come back repeatedly asking for additional appropriations on the ground "that it will never do to lose the money already expended". Such, he said, has been the history of the Cumberland Road. Mitchell asserted many times, however, that he was not unfriendly to the national program of internal improvements as a whole and considered it very necessary at many places. His record as a congressman consistently bore out this statement of fact.

Contemporary with Congressman Mitchell in the lower house were such able statesmen as James K. Polk, John Bell, and David Crockett, and serving in the Senate were John H. Eaton and Hugh Lawson White from Tennessee.

Following his retirement from Congress in 1829, Mitchell moved to Rutherford County and established residence, and in 1833, he was appointed by the General Assembly to fill the office of circuit judge, which office he held until 1836.

Judge Mitchell was a large and imposing personality and would often place a fine on lawyers and spectators alike for wearing creaking boots in the court room where he was trying a case. For this and other court practice, he was more feared than loved by lawyers of his circuit.

Upon retiring from the bench in 1836, and being seized by the "Mississippi Fever", he moved to that state during its flush era and became a candidate for the legislature and also the governorship, but since he was a Whig, he was never elected to an office there. He died in Jackson, Mississippi on August 17, 1843.

One cannot read the early history of Rutherford County without realizing the great contributions made by the Ready family which settled in the county about 1800, and in the community which now bears the name of Readyville. Charles Ready, Sr., was one of the seven justices of the first county court, organized in 1804.

Colonel Charles Ready, Jr., was born in Readyville, December 22, 1802, and later attended the common schools of the county. After studying law with a practicing attorney in Murfreesboro, he was admitted to the bar and began practice there. In 1835, he was elected to represent Rutherford County in the lower house of the Twenty-First General Assembly, serving one term.

In 1853, Colonel Ready was elected on the Whig ticket from the Fifth District to serve as a representative in the Thirty-third Congress of the United States, and through one of the stormiest periods in American history, he served for three consecutive terms. Unsuccessful in his race for reelection in 1858, he resumed the practive of law in his home community, Murfreesboro. There he lived the last twenty years of his life without further effort at politics. Death came to him on June 4, 1878.

From September 26, 1819 to October 15, 1825, Murfreesboro was the capital of Tennessee; during this period many of the leading statesmen met in the little city, where their brilliant minds clashed in the meetings of the state legislature.

As a young man, James K. Polk attended Bradley Academy in Murfreesboro, and while a student there, he met Miss Sarah Childress; when he returned to the-then capital as clerk of the Sixteenth General Assembly in 1824, he and Miss Childress were married at her home. While Murfreesboro cannot claim James K. Polk, the Governor, or James K. Polk the President as a native son, his wife, the first lady of both the state and nation is Rutherford County's own daughter. An English authoress in her book, *AN ENGLISH WOMAN IN AMERICA*, speaks in the most flattering terms of Mrs. Polk's poise, her literary taste, and her brilliant repartee.

On Polk's return to Nashville at the close of his presidency, he was a sick man, and according to his diary which is published in four volumes, he felt an urge to visit his old home in Columbia and his wife's home in Murfreesboro. So it was that the former President and Mrs. Polk visited in the home of Dr. William Rucker, a brother-in-law of Mrs. Polk. In the diary account of his visits to Dr. Rucker's home, he refers to several friends he knew in former years who called to see him.

Another prominent Tennessean who chose a Rutherford County wife was John Bell of Nashville who served as Congressman, Secretary of War in William Henry Harrison's cabinet, United States Senator, and nominee for the Presidency on the Constitutional Union Party ticket in 1860. During his period of service, Bell supported Clay's historic Compromise of 1850, and opposed the Kansas-Nebraska Act. He married Miss Sally Dickinson, daughter of David Dickinson in December, 1818. Thus, John Bell often visited in Murfreesboro where he had many warm personal and political friends.

Mrs. Sally Dickinson Bell was the granddaughter of Colonel Hardy Murfree, for whom Murfreesboro was named. Her father, David Dickinson was a brilliant lawyer and statesman. He was born in Franklin, Tennessee, June 10, 1808, and received his early school training there; later he attended and graduated from the University of North Carolina. Following his graduation from the university, he studied law and was admitted to practice in Rutherford County. Elected in 1831 to represent his adopted county in the lower house of the Nineteenth General Assembly of Tennessee, he served one term; then he was elected on March 4, 1833, on the Democratic ticket, to the lower house of the Twenty-eighth Congress of the United States. In 1843 he was again elected to Congress but this time as a whig.

Following his retirement from Congress, due to ill health, he lived for a short time on his father's farm, "Grantland," until his death on April 27, 1845.

No Rutherford County statesman has had a more colorful and varied career than Parry W. Humphreys. Born in Lexington, Kentucky, he later moved to Tennessee where he studied law and was licensed to practice in Nashville in 1801. When the government of Rutherford County was put into operation in 1804, Humphreys became the first solicitor for the county. In 1805, he was elected to the lower house of the State Legislature, and in 1807 to the State Senate where he served until appointed a special member of the State Supreme Court. He remained on the high bench until 1809 when he was chosen judge of the Fifth Judicial Circuit, sitting with credit and ability until 1813, at which time he was elected to the lower house of the Thirteenth Congress of the United States from the Sixth District. After completing one term in the lower house of Congress, he made the race for the United States Senate on the Whig ticket against John H. Eaton, but lost by two votes. In 1818, he was again chosen judge, this time from the Fourth Judicial Circuit, and served until 1836, when he retired from the bench and moved to Hernando, Mississippi.

The contributions of Parry W. Humphreys are recognized in his varied public service and by the gift of his son, West H. Humphreys, to many important offices in the state and national government.

Few men ever achieve distinction in more than one field of service, but Samuel Hogg was one of those rare exceptions who rose to prominence in two service areas. Born in Halifax County, North Carolina on April 18, 1783, he was brought by his family to Sumner County, Tennessee some years later where he studied medicine in 1804. He moved to Lebanon, Tennessee and began the practice of his profession; then when the First Regiment of Tennessee Volunteer Infantry was established, Dr. Hogg became its chief medical officer and surgeon. In the winter of 1814 when General Andrew Jackson set out on his campaign against the Creek Indians, Hogg became hospital surgeon on his staff. He also served as medical officer under General William Carroll at the Battle of New Orleans.

In 1817, Samuel Hogg was elected as a Democrat to the lower house of the Fifteenth Congress where he served one term. After voluntary retirement from the United States Congress, he returned to Lebanon, Tennessee and resumed the practice of medicine, continuing until 1828, when he moved to Nashville and practiced until 1836, then moving to Natchez, Mississippi for a stay of two years. In 1838, Hogg returned to Nashville for resumption of his medical practice until 1840, at which time he was chosen president of the Tennessee Medical Society. After his presidency of the Medical Society, he moved to Rutherford County, where he resided until his death on May 28, 1842.

Of all the statesmen from Rutherford County in the era before the Civil War, in eloquence, none was ever the equal of William T. Haskell. In fact, Tennessee never produced an orator more famous than he. Born in Murfreesboro, July 21, 1818, he was the son of Joshua Haskell, a well known and popular circuit court judge and the first mayor of Murfreesboro. He attended the University of Nashville, but never graduated; in fact, he was a very poor student, except for the things which interested him. He was spoken of by his teachers and companions as a dreamer, poet, sparkling conversationalist, and orator.

In 1836, Haskell enlisted in the Seminole War and served with credit, returning to Jackson, Tennessee where his father was judge of the circuit. He was admitted to the bar in 1838, then drifted into politics and was elected to the lower house of the Tennessee Legislature from Madison County in 1844. During this year, he also canvassed the state for Henry Clay's Presidency, making a very favorable impression upon his hearers with his pleas of eloquence.

In the spring of 1845, William Haskell enlisted in the Mexican War and was made colonel of the Second Tennessee Regiment of Volunteer Infantry. Returning from the Mexican War, Haskell was elected as a Whig to the lower house of the Thirtieth Congress from the Eleventh District of Tennessee. After serving one term, he declined a second nomination because he did not find the work interesting.

During the Whig era from 1836 to 1856, no man of the party fought its battles with more ardor than William T. Haskell. His best political addresses were made in the campaign of 1856, and the greatest of this campaign was delivered in Knoxville during the first week of September of that year. This week saw one of the last demonstrations of vitality in the Whig Party. Three days were given in an attempt to revive the party in Tennessee. A great crowd of twenty thousand people gathered to hear the orator, and for more than four hours Haskell spoke, and he spoke as the people had never heard man speak before. Women shrieked and fainted during his address. This occasion brought him a reputation of being Tennessee's greatest orator, and one of the nation's best.

Following his retirement from the United States Congress, he suffered a mental breakdown and never recovered. On March 12, 1859, he died in an institution in Hopkinsville, Kentucky.

During the "Whig Era" in national politics, Edwin H. Ewing played a rather prominent part both in Tennessee and in the Congress of the United States. Born in Nashville, December 2, 1809, he graduated from the University of Nashville in 1827, and was admitted to the bar in that city in 1831. He served as a Whig in the lower house of the Tennessee Legislature from 1841 to 1842. Throughout this term of office in the state legislature, Ewing was reputed for his able addresses made on important issues of the time.

While in Congress, he took part in the disputes over the Oregon question, the tariff issue of 1846, and the Mexican War controversy. He was one of the best students of tariff problems in the Congress during his term of service. Since Mr. Ewing was a close friend and staunch admirer of Daniel Webster, he was chosen to deliver an eulogy on the Great Contender in Nashville in 1852. This address brought him more fame than any which he delivered.

Edwin H. Ewing was married in Nashville in 1832, and practiced law there without a break from 1831 to 1851, except for the two years of service in the Twenty-ninth Congress.

In 1856, Ewing moved to Murfreesboro where he practiced law until 1859, then he removed to Nashville, remaining there for less than a year. Then he moved back to Murfreesboro in 1860 to live with his son, Josiah W. Ewing, also a prominent attorney of Murfreesboro.

In 1861, Edwin H. Ewing spoke for the Union and urged Tennessee not to secede; but when the sword was drawn in conflict between the sections, he supported the South with all his energies, and was under close surveilance of Federal troops because of his sympathy for the South. After the Civil War, he resumed the practice of his profession in Murfreesboro with E. D. Hancock as partner, but the partnership was dissolved in 1869.

Mr. Ewing was interested in the cause of education in Tennessee and served for a time on the State Board of Education. He was also a trustee of the University of Nashville for several years.

He was nominated for the United States Senate in 1875, but failed to be elected. Death came to him in Murfreesboro, April 24, 1902.

In the period preceding the Civil War, Rutherford County furnished many famous statesmen to other parts of the state and nation. William Henry Sneed was one of these. Born in Davidson County, August 29, 1812, he was later brought to Rutherford County by his father who settled there.

In 1839, Sneed formed a partnership with Judge Charles Ready, Junior of Murfreesboro. This business union lasted until 1843, when Sneed was elected to the state senate from Rutherford and Williamson counties. He served until 1845, during which time he waged a valiant fight to keep the state capital at Murfreesboro.

At the end of his term of office in the state senate in 1845, William Henry Sneed moved to Greenville, Tennessee, where he married the daughter of Doctor Alexander Williams of that place. There he formed a law partnership with Judge R. J. McKinney and practiced for about a year. Moving then to Knoxville, he practiced successfully until the Civil War, and he continued to live there until his death in 1869.

In 1855, Sneed was elected as a Whig to the lower house of the United States Congress, where he served one term, but he did not seek reelection. In Congress, he was a pronounced Union man up to the secession of the southern states from the Union; then he went with his state. He, however, never ceased to advocate the return of the seceded states to the Union. In 1858, at a Southern Commercial Convention in Knoxville, he declared that it was inexpedient and against public policy to re-open the question of African slave trade.

William Henry Sneed was one of the most successful lawyers East Tennessee ever had. Doubtless his reputation was heightened by the publication of the Sneed Reports, with which every lawyer in the state is familiar. He had a son, Joseph W. Sneed who was a well known lawyer and circuit judge of Knoxville.

Another distinguished sojourner in Murfreesboro was John Cummins Edwards. Born in Frankfort, Kentucky, June 24, 1804, he graduated from Black's College in the same state. Edwards studied law, and was admitted to practice in 1825, in Murfreesboro, Tennessee where he remained for about three years. Then he moved to Jefferson City, Missouri.

From 1830 to 1835, Edwards served as Secretary of State in Missouri, and again in the same position in 1837, following a two-year term as District Judge of Cole County. He served as Secretary of State for only a few months in 1837, when he was elected to the Missouri House of Representatives. He served one term in the legislature when he was appointed to fill out an unexpired term as judge of the State Supreme Court, but he did not seek reelection to that office. In 1841, he was elected to the Twenty-seventh Congress, and served one term without seeking reelection. He was governor of Missouri from 1844 to 1848. Later he moved to Stockton, California, where he died October 14, 1888.

On May 25, 1817, Sydenham Moore was born in Rutherford County, Tennessee. He attended the University of Alabama from 1833 to 1836. After studying law he was admitted to the bar in

Greensboro, Alabama. From 1840 to 1846, he served as judge of the Green County Court, and again from 1848 to 1850. In 1857, he was made judge of a circuit court, but he served for only a few months due to his election to the Thirty-fifth Congress. As a member of the lower house from Alabama, he served two terms in Congress when the Civil War ended his career in this body in 1861.

Sydenham Moore experienced a brilliant career as a soldier. While a member of Colonel Caffey's Alabama Infantry Regiment, he served as captain. Later he was made brigadier-general of the Alabama Militia. During the Civil War, Moore served as colonel of the Eleventh Alabama Regiment in the Confederate Army. He died in Richmond, Virginia from wounds received in the Battle of Seven Pines, Virginia, May 31, 1862.

William Barksdale was born in Smyrna, Tennessee, August 21, 1821. Attending the public schools of the county, and later the University of Nashville, he studied law, and was admitted to the bar in 1839, beginning his practice in Columbus, Mssisssippi. He served as Quartermaster of the Mississippi Volunteers during the Mexican War. In 1852, he was chosen as a delegate to the Democratic National Convention in Baltimore. In 1853, he was elected as a States Right's Democrat to the lower house of the Thirty-third Congress, and served four consecutive terms of the Congress until 1861, when Mississippi seceded from the Union.

William Barksdale was a strong and zealous advocate of secession for the southern states. He received some reflected notoriety by accompanying Representative Preston S. Brooks of South Carolina to the Senate chamber when the latter attacked Charles Sumner, Massachusetts Senator, with a cane. This episode was a climax to the ardent anti-slavery Senator Sumner's criticism of a South Carolina Senator in his "Crime Against Kansas" speech in 1856. Barksdale made himself conspicuous by preventing interference of others present at the scene.

Entering the Confederate army during the Civil War as colonel of the Thirteenth Regiment of Mississippi Volunteers, William Barksdale was promoted to the rank of brigadier-general on August 12, 1862. Commanding a Mississippi brigade in Longstreet's Corps, he was killed in the Battle of Gettysburg, Pennsylvania on July 2, 1863.

Ethelbert Barksdale, a brother of William Barksdale, was also born in Smyrna, Rutherford County, January 4, 1824. While he was quite a young man, he moved to Jackson, Mississippi where he later took up journalism as a profession. He edited the official State Journal from 1854 to 1861, and again from 1876 to 1883. In

1861, he was elected as a member of the Confederate Congress, serving until 1865, when that body was dissolved. Later, he served as a delegate to the National Democratic Conventions of 1868, 1872, and 1880; he also served as President of the State Electoral College of Mississippi. As a high point in his successful career, he was elected to the Forty-eighth and Forty-ninth Congresses of the United States as a Democrat, serving from 1883 to 1887. He died in Yazoo City, Mississippi, February 17, 1893.

Winfield Scott Featherston was among the men who left Rutherford County before the Civil War, to find their places of service in other states. He was born four miles from Murfreesboro, Tennessee, on August 8, 1819, the youngest of seven children. Like many other Rutherford Countians he moved to Mississippi where he studied law and was admitted to the bar. His successful legal career, which began in 1840, was interrupted by his election to the Thirtieth Congress in 1847, where he served the lower house of that body until 1851. After failing to be elected for a third term, Featherston remained in private life until the beginning of the Civil War. As secession became imminent, he was sent from his state of Mississippi in December, 1860, to negotiate with Kentucky authorities regarding their seceding from the Union. Being a man of commanding presence—more than six feet tall—he was chosen colonel of the Seventh Mississippi Regiment. On March 4, 1862, he was promoted to brigadier-general—this honor coming after he was wounded while serving in the Virginia Army. At the close of the war, Featherston returned to Holly Springs, Mississippi and took up his law practice there. He became an important factor in the overthrow of the corrupt Ames regime in Mississippi.

Serving in the lower house of the Mississippi Legislature from 1876 to 1878, and again from 1880 to 1882, as Chairman of the Judiciary Committee, Featherston assisted in the revision of the code of that state in 1880. He was a delegate to the National Democratic Convention which met in Cincinnati in 1880. In 1882, he became judge of the Second Judicial Circuit of Mississippi, serving until 1890, a term of eight years. He became a member of the State Constitutional Convention of 1890. His death occurred on May 28, 1891, in Holly Springs, where he had spent his last years.

Many states have been recipients of the energies of Tennesseans. It is a common expression that Tennesseans made Texas. So it was that during the Texas struggle for independence, Henderson Yoakum played a considerable part.

Yoakum was born in Powell's Valley, Claiborne County, Tennessee, on September 6, 1810. He entered the United States Military Academy in 1828, graduating in 1832. He moved to Murfreesboro, Tennessee the following year. In 1838, he was made a colonel of a Tennessee Infantry Regiment. In 1839, he was elected to the Tennessee State Senate and was active in politics until 1845. During this period he moved to Huntsville, Texas where he practiced law. He was an ardent advocate of the annexation of Texas to the United States and worked hard to see this realized. He was a strong partisan of James K. Polk and probably influenced President Polk to devote his energies to annex Texas to the Union.

A History of Texas in two volumes published in 1855 is the work of Henderson Yoakum. This history deals with the period from the first settlement in 1685, to the annexation to the United States. This work has long been used as a trustworthy record of the early development of Texas.

In 1803, Joseph Dickson moved from North Carolina to Rutherford County. He took part in the Battle of King's Mountain in 1780 as a major in the Lincoln County, North Carolina Army, later being elevated to brigadier-general. Afterwards he represented his native state in Congress. After coming to Rutherford County, Dickson was made Speaker of the lower house of the Seventh Tennessee General Assembly, serving from 1809 to 1811. He is buried on a plantation northeast of Murfreesboro, which he owned during his residence in the county.

Other statesmen who held residence in Rutherford County and served their state and country prior to the Civil War are: Leonard H. Sims who was born in North Carolina, later coming with his family to this county about 1830, where he lived for several years, serving in the State Senate from Rutherford and Williamson Counties, then removing to Springfield, Missouri. He held several local political positions, and in 1845 was elected to the lower house of the Twenty-ninth Congress of the United States, from that state, serving one term. Joseph Philips was a captain of artillery in the War of 1812, and at its close, settled in Illinois, and became the first Secretary of the territory of Illinois. He afterwards served as judge of the Supreme Court for the State of Illinois. After the death of his first wife, he came to Tennessee and married again. He died in Rutherford County in 1857, at the age of seventy-three. Colonel Robert H. Dyer moved with his parents to Rutherford County in 1807, and was commissioned a lieutenant in a cavalry regiment of the Fifth Tennessee Brigade in this same year. In the correspondence of Andrew Jackson, a copy of a letter to James Monroe, Secretary of War, tells of Robert H. Dyer's being wounded in the Battle of New Orleans. The Duke of Orleans, later King Louis Philippe of France, was often entertained in the home of Joel H. Dyer, father of Robert H. Dyer, when the Dyers lived in Grainger County, Tennessee. Robert H. Dyer served one term in the State Senate from Rutherford and Williamson Counties. Dyer County in West Tennessee, was named in his honor. He died in May, 1826. Edmund Rucker of Rutherford County was in Baltimore during the convention which nominated Martin Van Buren in May, 1835. He found it greatly "regretted" by the delegates that there were no representatives from Tennessee. He was requested to cast Tennessee's votes, which he did, and the supporters of Judge Hugh Lawson White made much of this "Ruckerizing" of the convention.

George W. Smith moved from Rutherford County to the Republic of Texas in 1828 and there he assisted in setting in operation the Texas State Constitution. He was a signer of the Texas Declaration of Independence of 1836. Becoming a congressman from that state in 1853, he served one term.

Edwin A. Keeble an outstanding Murfreesboro lawyer was Speaker of the lower house of Tennessee's Legislature as well as a member of the Confederate Congress during the Civil War.

The following is a list of Rutherford Countians whose contributions to Tennessee entitle them to be classed as statesmen: William Ledbetter, who served in the State Senate during the Twenty-first and Twenty-second General Assemblies. General William Brady, one-time candidate for Congress, many times served his county in the Legislature; and he was Speaker of the lower house. Others are; Robert Jetton, John W. Richardson, Samuel Anderson, William Searcy, W. Y. Elliott, Joseph B. Palmer, and B. F. Alexander.

Among Rutherford County's contribution of statesmen to the state and nation since the Civil War is William Robert Moore, who was born in Huntsville, Alabama on March 28, 1830. When he was less than a year old his parents moved to Beech Grove in Coffee County, and when he was six they again moved, this time to Fosterville in Rutherford County. There young Moore attended the common schools of the county for about ten years; then the family moved back to Beech Grove for a short time, later going to Nashville.

William Robert Moore was elected to the Forty-Seventh Congress on the Republican ticket serving from 1881 to 1883. In 1890 he declined the nomination for Governor of the State. He died in Memphis June 12, 1909.

William Henderson Cate was born in Rutherford County November 11, 1839, later graduating in 1857 from East Tennessee University which is now the University of Tennessee. When his service in the Confederate Army was complete, he settled in Jonesboro, Arkansas where he was admitted to the bar in 1866. His political career consisted of service in the lower house of the Arkansas Legisla-

Governor John P. Buchanan

James D. Richardson

ture; state prosecuting attorney; and circuit court judge; and finally he served as a member of the national Congress from that state from 1889 to 1899.

Haywood Yancy Riddle was born in Hardeman County, Tennessee, June 20, 1834. He attended Union University at Murfreesboro and graduated from that institution in 1854. As assistant professor of mathematics and languages he served his alma mater for fifteen months, then resigned to study law in Cumberland University, Lebanon, Tennessee. After graduating from the law school in 1857, he went to Ripley, Mississippi where he was admitted to law practice. He remained there less than a year when he removed to Smith County, Tennessee where he practiced law until the Civil War. Serving in the Confederate Army until the end of the war, he moved to Lebanon, Tennessee practicing his profession there until he was elected as a Democrat to fill a vacancy in the Forty-fourth Congress, caused by the death of Samuel M. Fite. He was reelected to the Forty-fifth Congress and served till 1879. His death occurred in Lebanon on March 28, 1879 just at the close of his second term in Congress.

Philip Doddridge McCulloch, Jr. was born in Murfreesboro, June 23, 1851 and moved with his parents to Trenton, Tennessee shortly after his birth. His education was received in the common schools and at Andrews College in Trenton. He studied law and was admitted to practice in Gibson County, Tennessee in 1872. In February 1874 he moved to Marianna, Arkansas where he continued the practice of law until his election as Prosecuting Attorney for the First Judicial District of Arkansas in 1878, serving three successive terms which ended in 1884. He served as presidential elector on the Democratic ticket of Cleveland and Thurman in 1888. In 1893 McCulloch was elected to the lower house of the Fifty-third Congress from the First Arkansas District where he served for five consecutive terms which ended in 1903. Death came to him at Marianna November 26, 1928.

Of all the men from Rutherford County who served in the national Congress, James D. Richardson has the longest and most distinguished record. Born March 10, 1843 he received his early education in his native Rutherford County. He attended Franklin College near Nashville but left without graduating to enter the Confederate Army where he served with distinction, retiring as Adjutant of the 45th Tennessee Volunteer Infantry. He married Miss Allie Pippen of Greene County, Alabama in 1865, and two years later after studying law with Judge Thomas Neal Frazier, he began his legal practice in Murfreesboro. His election in 1871 to represent Rutherford County in the lower house of the State Legislature marks the beginning of his political career. When the Legislature convened

Richardson was chosen speaker. Then he was only twenty-eight years of age and probably the youngest speaker on record to that date. In 1873 he was elected to the State Senate where he served as a member of the Judiciary Committee.

In 1885 James D. Richardson was elected to the Congress of the United States from the Fourth District, and he was reelected ten successive terms ending in 1905. He was a Reformed Whig in political thought, but never cast any vote except for the Democratic Party. He served as a delegate to many Democratic National Conventions and was made permanent chairman at Kansas City in 1900. By resolution of Congress in 1893, he was chosen to publish a "Compilation of the Messages and Papers of the Presidents," in ten volumes; this he did during the period from 1896 to 1899. In 1900 by another resolution of Congress, he was authorized to publish the State Papers and Diplomatic Correspondence of the Confederate States. This was published in 1905 in two volumes entitled a "Compilation of the Messages and Papers of the Confederacy."

In 1883 James D. Richardson was elected Grand High Priest of the Tennessee Royal Arch Masons. In that same year, he published his *"Tennessee Templars"*, a biographical account of the Commandery and its membership in Tennessee. In 1884 he was elected to active membership in the Scottish Rite Supreme Council, Southern Jurisdiction, and during the remainder of his life, he missed but three of its regular sessions. In 1901 he was elected Grand Commander and served until his death.

After his retirement from Congress in 1905 he devoted his entire time to Masonry. His commandership was notable for its promotion of international good will, and the construction of the imposing Scottish Rite Temple in Washington, generally considered to be the finest specimen of Masonic architecture, stands as a monument to his ideal.

James B. Frazier who served the state as governor and United States Senator lived for a time in Rutherford County. He was born in Pikeville, Tennessee on October 18, 1858, the son of Thomas Neal Frazier. In 1863 the father moved to Rutherford County, where his son James B. grew up and attended the public schools of that county and Davidson County. Records are vague as to how long the Frazier family lived in Rutherford County, but it must have been for a short time, probably three or four years. He attended Franklin College near Nashville but graduated from the University of Tennessee in Knoxville in 1878 with the A. B. degree. He was married to Miss Louise Douglas Keith of Athens, Tennessee on January 10, 1883. In 1891 he became a law partner in the firm of DeWitt, Shepherd and Frazier in Chattanooga.

In 1900 James B. Frazier was chosen elector-at-large on the Democratic ticket. Two years later he was elected governor of Tennessee by the largest plurality given to any candidate since the Civil War—or ever, up to that time. A second time he was elected to the governorship without opposition in 1904. His administration was strictly a business one.

In 1905 Frazier was elected to the United States Senate to succeed William B. Bate and served until 1911. During his senatorship, he advocated federal aid to the states for public highways; honesty in elections; and federal income taxes. He opposed federal encroachment upon states' rights and the Payne-Aldrich Tariff Bill.

John Price Buchanan was another of Rutherford County's gifts to the governorship of Tennessee. He was born in Williamson County, October 24, 1847 and attended the public schools in that county. After serving in the Confederate Army during the Civil War, and while quite a young man, he moved to Rutherford County. In 1887 he was elected to represent his adopted county in the lower house of the State Legislature. Becoming active in the organization of the Farmers' Alliance, in 1888 he was elected the first president of the State Alliance. The following year he was reelected, and when the Agricultural Wheel, the Farmers' and Laborers' Union, and the Alliance joined into one body in 1889, Buchanan became the president of the consolidated organization. This gave him great political power in the state and caused him to be nominated to the governorship in 1890. Four opponents entered the race against him and it was one of the most spirited contests ever held in Tennessee. The platform of the Democratic Party denounced the Republican Party as the party of Wall Street, and a high protective tariff. The Democrats demanded cheaper money by advocating the free coinage of silver. They favored better schools, better roads, economy in government, and equitable taxation. Buchanan was elected and began to serve as governor of Tennessee in January, 1891.

The Buchanan administration was marked by one of the stormiest industrial insurrections the state ever experienced. The seat of the trouble was the coal miners of East Tennessee; the cause was the convict lease system by which convict labor was brought into direct competition with free labor. The trouble cost a number of lives and the loss of thousands of dollars in property, and led to the abandonment of the labor lease system.

The most important pieces of legislation enacted during Buchanan's short tenure of office were: the establishment of secondary schools; the lengthening of the term of the free school; summer institutes for teachers; and the Confederate soldiers' pensions.

The work of Andrew L. Todd did not extend beyond the borders of his native state, but few men have had greater influence on the legislation of their day than he. Born in Rutherford County, July 27, 1872, he attended his county's public schools and also Union University which was located in Murfreesboro at the time. Mr. Todd later taught in the above named institution and in Woodbury College. He was superintendent of Rutherford County Schools from 1900 to 1907, and Assistant State Superintendent of Education from 1907 to 1911. For five years, 1905 to 1910, he served as Chairman of the Tennessee Textbook Commission. Governor James B. Frazier appointed him to the State Board of Education in 1905 and he continued to serve until 1915.

Andrew L. Todd served two terms as a member of the lower house of the State Legislature in 1913 and again in 1921, as Speaker of that body; and he also served two terms in the State Senate—in 1915 and again in 1919, as Speaker of that body. He is the only man in Tennessee ever to serve as Speaker of both House and Senate. To him is due much credit, while serving in the Legislature, for the Compulsory School Law of the state; creation of the School Board Law; creation of the Workman's Compensation Act of 1919; the Inheritance Tax Law; and the ratification of the 19th Amendment to the Federal Constitution.

John E. Miles was born in Rutherford County and educated in her public schools, but left the state while a young man to seek his place in Oklahoma. After spending only a few years there, he went to New Mexico and soon entered state politics. He rose to the governorship of that state, serving two terms from 1938 to 1942.

The last name which may be added to the illustrious roster of Rutherford County's statesmen, is that of Harold (Doc) Earthman who was elected to the National Congress in 1944 from the Fifth District of Tennessee.

THE BENCH OF RUTHERFORD COUNTY

The County Court of Rutherford County was established on January 4, 1804, and the first meeting was held in the home of Thomas Rucker who lived about four and one half miles north of Murfreesboro on what is now known as the Lebanon Pike.

In 1809 a higher court, known as the circuit court, was created by an act of the Legislature, which divided the state into five judicial circuits. Davidson, Rutherford, Wilson, Giles, Williamson, Maury, Lincoln, and Bedford Counties were grouped in the Fourth Judicial Circuit. It is difficult to determine the number of times the Legislature regrouped the judicial circuits of the state from 1809 to the

Civil War, but one is safe in saying that several times this was done. In 1817 the Sixth Judicial Circuit was established from Smith, Wilson, and Rutherford Counties; then in 1830, the state judicial system was reshuffled so that the Eleventh Judicial Circuit was formed from Warren, Franklin, Bedford, Wilson, and Rutherford Counties. The General Assembly reshuffled the judicial circuits again in 1835, putting Wilson, Bedford, Franklin, Coffee, and Rutherford into the Fifth Judicial Circuit.

The Chancery Court was set up in Rutherford County in 1836, with Judge J. M. Bramblett as its first chancellor. He presided over the Fourth Chancery Division until 1842, when he was succeeded by Judge Bromfield L. Ridley of Rutherford County, who served with exceptional ability until the court was suspended by the Civil War. Judge Ridley then entered the Confederate Army, serving with distinction. After the war, he resumed the practice of law in Murfreesboro and continued until his death in 1869.

Judge Ridley was involved as a party to one of the most famous trials in Tennessee history in August, 1866. Under the brow-beating tactics of Governor Brownlow a new franchise law was passed on May 3, 1866 which provided for the "perpetual disfran-chisement of all citizens, otherwise qualified, who had voluntarily borne arms against the government of the United States in the late rebellion; all who had sought, or voluntarily accepted any office, or attempted to exercise the function of any office under the authority of the so-called Confederate States; and all who had voluntarily supported any government, power, or authority hostile or inimical to the authority of the United States, by persuasion, influence, or in any other way whatsoever." The radicals had triumphed in the Legislature; only the judiciary remained to check them. The ad-ministration of Brownlow signified its determination to enforce the franchise law.

With such a condition prevailing it was inevitable that an at-tempt would be made to defeat the operation of the franchise law in the courts. This attempt was made in the case of Ridley vs. Sherbrook. Bromfield L. Ridley of Murfreesboro applied to Freeman Sherbrook, the Commissioner of registration for Rutherford County on August 1, 1866 for a certificate of registration. The applicant affirmed that he was fifty years of age, a free white man, and a citizen of Rutherford County for more than twenty years, and had been accustomed to exercising the voting privilege. He stated that he had taken part in the rebellion, but had received pardon from President Johnson on July 26, 1865 for all offenses committed against the United States and the State of Tennessee, and that he had com-mitted no crimes since receiving the pardon. He demanded the right to exercise the franchise under the state constitution. Sherbrook refused to issue the certificate unless Ridley could qualify under the Elective Franchise Act of May 3, 1866. Ridley then made application to Judge Henry Cooper of the circuit court for a writ of mandamus compelling Sherbrook to issue the certificate. The case came to trial on the question of the constitutionality of the Franchise Act. Judge Cooper granted the mandamus and held the act unconstitutional. Sherbrook then appealed the case to the Supreme Court, which was at that time made up of radical appointees of Governor Brownlow. Ridley was represented by Edwin A. Keeble, Charles Ready, Jr., Edwin H. Ewing, Murfreesboro Lawyers, Robert L. Caruthers, M. S. Frierson, A. O. P. Nicholson, and James E. Bailey.

The case came to the Supreme Court in January, 1867, and the decision was in favor of Sherbrook. This decision showed that the radicals were now in control of the judicial as well as the executive and legislative, branches of the state government.

Among the most prominent jurists from Rutherford County prior to the Civil War, many of whom have already been mentioned as statesmen, were: Parry W. Humphreys who served in the Supreme Court of Tennessee from 1807 to 1809, and was judge of the Fifth Circuit from 1809 to 1813, and again from 1818 to 1836. William E. Anderson was chosen the first chancellor for west Tennessee which at that time included most of middle Tennessee, in 1827, and became judge of the Fifth Judicial Circuit in 1835 and served continuously until 1851. John Cummins Edwards served as district judge of Cole County, Missouri, 1832-37, and as judge of the Missouri Supreme Court, 1837-39. James C. Mitchell served as circuit judge in middle Tennessee from 1833 to 1836. Syderham Moore was county judge of Green County, Alabama, from 1840 to 1846, and again from 1848 to 1850, and he was judge of an Alabama circuit court from 1857 to the Civil War. Joseph Philips settled in Illinois at the close of the War of 1812, afterwards becoming judge of the Illinois Supreme Court. Joshua Haskell in 1821 was appointed judge of the newly created Eighth Judicial Circuit of Tennessee, where he served until 1836. Haskell once tried John A. Murrell, noted outlaw of middle Tennessee, for stealing Negroes. Samuel Anderson was appointed judge of the Fifth Circuit of Tennessee in 1835 to fill out a vacancy caused by the resignation of James C. Mitchell; he served continuously until 1851.

Among the great judges after the Civil War who were born in, or sojourned in Rutherford County, was Thomas Neal Frazier who was elected circuit judge from Bledsoe County, Tennessee in 1861; but before he took office, Tennessee seceded from the Union. In

1863 he moved to Rutherford County, and soon afterwards Governor Andrew Johnson appointed him criminal judge of Davidson and Rutherford Counties. He held this place until he was impeached by a radical legislature in 1867. A constitutional convention, however, restored him to full political rights in 1870, and he was re-elected to the judgeship of his old district the same year. Upon retirement from the bench in 1878, he made his home in Davidson County until his death. Other prominent jurists who served with credit are: Winfield Scott Featherston who was judge of the Second Judicial Circuit of Mississippi; Horace Palmer who served as judge of the Court of Appeals for several years in Tennessee; William Henderson Cate who served five years as judge of the Second Judicial Circuit of Arkansas, beginning in 1884; John W. Burton who served as special judge of chancery, and as special judge on the State Supreme Court of Tennessee from 1878 to 1883; E. D. Hancock, chancery court judge in Tennessee from 1883 to 1886; G. S. Ridley who served as criminal court judge from Davidson and Rutherford Counties; John E. Richardson who was appointed judge of the Eighth Judicial Circuit by Governor James D. Frazier, served continuously until 1944. He was a classmate of President Woodrow Wilson in Princeton University, and was a member of the Notification Committee when Wilson was nominated for his second term. Also in this group are William Hunter Washington who served as special judge of the Tennessee Court of Appeals in the noted case of Kiger v. the Mayor of Nashville; Fletcher R. Burrus who served as special judge of the Fourth Chancery Division, 1880-81; Joseph L. Cannon special circuit court judge, and chancellor in Tennessee several times; Thomas B. Lytle who was chosen in 1919 to fill out the term of Judge Walter Bearden as chancellor, and served until his resignation in 1944. Judge John D. Wiseman is the latest Rutherford Countian to serve on the bench of the Eighth Judicial Circuit to which he was appointed by Governor Jim McCord in 1945.

THE BAR OF RUTHERFORD COUNTY

Many members of the Rutherford County bar are listed among the statesmen and judges in other portions of this chapter, and therefore, it will not be necessary to do more than mention them in this connection. Among the visiting lawyers at the Murfreesboro bar in the early history of the county are the wellknown names of John Bell, John H. Eaton, Andrew Jackson, Felix Grundy, Robert Butler, and Thomas H. Benton who began his practice of law at Old Jefferson, the first county seat of Rutherford County.

Most prominent among those who lived in Rutherford County and practiced at the bar before the Civil War were: David W

Dickinson, Charles Ready, Sr., Charles Ready, Jr., William Henry
Snead, Parry W. Humphreys, Samuel Anderson, William Brady,
Edwin H. Ewing, John W. Childress, brother-in-law of President
Polk, Joshua Haskell, Joseph Dickson, James C. Mitchell, John C.
Edwards, Bromfield Ridley, Sr., John Easter Dromgoole, of whom
William H. Seward said while Secretary of State, "Dromgoole's
legal papers were the best prepared of any I received during my
service in the Department of State," Andrew Childress, S. A. Laugh-
lin, S. R. Rucker, Ned Keeble, J. P. Burrus, General Joseph B.
Palmer, Andrew J. Hoover, E. W. Keeble, S. D. Rowan and E. D.
Hancock.

Outstanding lawyers since the Civil War include, J. C. Cannon,
G. S. Ridley, Sr., B. R. Lillard, Richard Beard, J. M. Avent, John
E. Richardson, Horace E. Palmer, John W. Burton, James D.
Richardson, Sr., William Hunter Washington, who was prosecuting
attorney for his district for eight years, B. R. Alexander, Frank Avent,
William Henry Williamson, Pleasant J. Mason, John Bell Keeble,
who served as dean of the Vanderbilt Law School, John C. Ferress,
Jesse W. Sparks, William M. Carter, Darwin Hancock, Edgar P.
Smith, who served as Attorney-General for the Eighth Judicial
Circuit, Andrew Todd, Sr., Thomas B. Lytle, E. C. Holloway, Sr.,
James Jetton, James D. Richardson, Jr., who now resides in Kansas
City, J. H. Warden, E. L. Whitaker, Hoyte Stewart, Sr., Attorney-
General for the Eighth Judicial Circuit, and W. B. Knott who was
also Attorney-General for this district.

The Murfreesboro bar at present consists of John D. Wiseman,
Andrew L. Todd, Jr., John Holloway, Wiley Holloway, John Jewell,
formerly Attorney-General for the Eighth Judicial Circuit, Alfred
Huddleston, Alvin Collins, Judge of the General Sessions Court,
Ewing Smith, Hoyte Stewart, County Judge, Harold Earthman,
Winston Price, Howell Washington, George Buckner, John Rucker,
Granville S. Ridley, Jr., Ben F. Kerr, Howard Massey, M. A. Hines,
Clarence Cummings, Barton Dement and Jesse Huggins.

CHAPTER V

Rutherford County's Military Contribution Through The Years

When the "embattled farmers" at Concord Bridge fired the shot heard round the world, the 600 odd square miles now known as Rutherford County was a land of big timbers and wild animals. Here the Cherokee, Chickasaw and other Indian tribes held undisputed and even undisturbed sway. But in the early life of the nation heroes of the Revolutionary War began coming west on land grants from North Carolina. By an act of North Carolina passed in 1782 each private in the Continental army was given 640 acres, each captain 3800 acres, and other officers were given acreage in proportion to their rank. The land first set apart for these veterans was the northern half of middle Tennessee. Since the territory later to become Rutherford County was included in the military reservation, many Revolutionary soldiers received grants in the area. While many soldiers sold their land without ever seeing it, many others actually occupied the land granted to them while still others bought land in the area to become Rutherford County.

In many parts of the country are more or less well preserved homes of colonial style that in a proud and stately language testify to the Revolutionary age of their builders. Many of these homes have already been described in an earlier chapter. Markers in many old cemeteries in silent majesty testify that over thirty Revolutionary heroes are sleeping in Rutherford soil. A partial list of these heroes, includes William Lytle, Samuel Henderson, John Bradley, Robert Smith, William Searcy, Archibald Lytle, William Batey, Charles Ready, John Etter, and Thomas Bedford. Two large and active chapters of the Daughters of the American Revolution, one named after Colonel Hardy Murfree and the other honoring Captain William Lytle, testify to the numerous descendants of Revolutionary veterans now residing in the county.

When middle Tennessee was settled the pioneers had to be on the alert at all times because of frequent Indian attacks. An organized militia was a necessity. When Tennessee became a state

85

the constitution of 1796 made provision for organizing the militia. One of the earliest laws of the state required all ablebodied men, unless over age, to enlist in one of the companies of militia. The first companies were mustered in Rutherford County in 1805, the year following its organization. The minutes of the county court for that year show that Justice John Hill listed Captain John Smith's company; William Nash listed Captain Samuel McBride's company; W. M. Searcy listed Captain John Johns' company; William Smith listed Captain O. M. Venge's company; and Charles Ready listed Captain Alexander McKnight's company. As the population of the county increased from year to year the number of the militia companies increased. The companies seemed to be distributed somewhat along the lines of civil districts. This practice continued until 1833 when there were thirty-six companies in the county. The Knox, R. Ready, Henry McCoy, Nimrod Jenkins, William Robertson, W. A. Sublett and other such familiar Rutherford County names as Webb, Miller, Doak, Ganaway, Cook, Morris, Thomas, Fox, Todd, Moore, Haley, Elliot, McGregor, Stevens, Sanders, Ridley, Blair, Ferguson, Hicks, Edwards, Osborne, Lillard, Newman, Youree, and Hoover. Muster grounds were established at various places throughout the county where the militia would assemble at stated times for military training. According to the historian these occasions were more often recreation affairs than training periods. However picnic-like the meetings at the muster grounds might have been, the defense against the Indians was strengthened by the existence of the companies for there was organization and there was leadership.

While Revolutionary land granters were concerning themselves with spacious homes on wooded hills, the younger men were heeding the call to arms for the War 1812. While it is clear that Rutherford County furnished Andrew Jackson with a comparatively large number of volunteer troops, no exact number can be found. The present County Court Clerk of this county, Mr. J. P. Leathers, has in his possession a manuscript that gives the names of 115 Rutherford County men in one outfit that took part in the War of 1812 and were in the Battle of New Orleans. They belonged to Captain George Barne's company of Col. John Cocke's regiment. Other officers were: David M. Knight, 1st. Lt.; James Berry, 2nd. Lt.; John Ray, 3rd. Lt.; Daniel Lovell, Ensign; William Venson, 1st. Sgt.; Loamy Potts, 2nd. Sgt.; Larken Newton, 3rd. Sgt.; James McEwin, 4th. Sgt.; George Brandon, 5th. Sgt.; William Rogers, 1st. Corp.; Herman Howell, 2nd. Corp.; William Adams, 3rd. Corp.; Buckner Adams, 4th Corp.; Jonathan Rucker, 6th. Corp.; John Gillespy, Fifer; Aaron Turpin, Drummer. Col. James Henderson of Rutherford County was killed in a skirmish near New Orleans and Andrew

M. Alexander, Sr., was killed in the Battle of New Orleans. Other high ranking Rutherford Countians with Jackson in the War of 1812 were Major Samuel McClanahan, Major John H. Gibson, Col. John Coffee and Lt. Col. Robert Henry Dyer.

The last three names were of special distinction.[1] While Coffee was yet a colonel, living about two miles from Old Jefferson in the upper part of the County, his regiment of cavalry was called on by the Governor of Tennessee and General Jackson to march overland to Natchez to meet a threat of the Spaniards. General Jackson and two regiments of infantry went to Natchez by the water route, in boats constructed for the transportation of the two regiments, their equipment and supplies. Coffee's regiment rendezvoused at Franklin and from there began the march along the Natchez Trace. Dyer was lieutenant-colonel and Gibson was major.

On January 19th this regiment, 670 strong, began the march and on February 16th all of the troops of General Jackson united at Natchez, where, after a month of waiting for orders, they were disappointed when an order came to disband, the plan of President Monroe to occupy West Florida having been abandoned. The troops had a toilsome march back to their homes in Tennessee. Ever since, this has been called the *aborative* Natchez campaign—abortive because of no fault of Jackson or his troops.

The next call of Coffee's regiment was to march south again; this time to avenge the massacre by the Creek Indians at Fort Mims in the Alabama country. Coffee's command now numbered above 1300 mounted gunmen. Its rendezvous was at Fayetteville and the first destination was Huntsville, in Alabama. At the latter point an advance guard was ordered out under Gibson to scout and ascertain the movements of the Indians. One of the scouts was Davy Crockett. As the second section of the regiment moved towards Huntsville, intelligence was received that Gibson had been killed by the Indians. The desire of the troops for a rapid march forward "was strengthened by the information just received." "They mended their pace" but on reaching Huntsville it was learned that the information was erroneous.

Soon what is known in history as the Creek War was flagrant. On a reorganization of the army, Coffee was made a brigadier-general, Dyer a full colonel, and Gibson a lieutenant-colonel. The brigade and regiment took a gallant part in all the main battles against the Creeks.

In the decisive battle of Tohopeka or the Horse-Shoe, Coffee's command did effectual fighting that resulted in a pronounced victory and the Creeks' submission.

1. Most of the information on these three heroes was furnished by Judge Samuel C. Williams.

The Tennessee troops returned home, widely acclaimed as heroes. But Coffee's was a short stay on his Stone's River plantation. When the British made their first appearance on the Gulf Coast 2,500 troops from Tennessee were called to march once more southward. Jackson made a request that all of them be led by General Coffee; and on October 5th his command, including his old regiment left Fayetteville and joined General Jackson at Mobile. The push against Pensacola was taken in November. On returning to Mobile, Jackson suspected that the British would attempt to land and cross by land to the Mississippi and attack New Orleans from the north. He sent Coffee's command to Baton Rouge to frustrate such an attempt. Soon came an urgent order to Coffee from Jackson to make a forced march to New Orleans. In about three days Coffee and his forces covered the distance of over one hundred and twenty-five miles and reached the city on December 20th, just in time to take a leading part in the weird and bloody night battle of December 23rd, in which Lieutenant-Colonel Gibson was wounded, but not so gravely as to prevent his participating in the great victory of January 8, 1815.

The details of the battle of that day are well known. Coffee's command holding the left troop, took a leading part.

In 1818 Colonels Dyer and Gibson of the Rutherford County trio were again in their saddles, this time to fight in Florida against the Seminole Indians under General Jackson. Pensacola was once more captured. The final result was the acquisition of East Florida by the United States.

In view of these campaigns, all within a period of less than six years, we find ample reason for the naming of Coffee, Dyer, and Gibson Counties for these men.

A wealthy and influential near-neighbor of General Coffee, Thomas Bedford, of Old Jefferson, had been earlier honored in the bestowal of his name on Bedford County, and Humphreys County bears the name of another resident of Rutherford, Judge Parry W. Humphreys.

When the Mexicans under Santa Anna attacked the Alamo in San Antonio and massacred its defenders, including the celebrated Davy Crockett and "his Tennessee boys," a feeling of bitter resentment ran through Tennessee. "Remember the Alamo" became the war cry. And when the call came for volunteers to go to Texas, two companies were raised in Rutherford County. "The Mustered Men" sixty-four in number had the following officers: Captain J. W. Jetton; 1st. Lt. E. C. Norman; 2nd. Lt. Henry McCullock; Ensign William Prewett; and "The Murfreesboro Sentinels" sixty-four in number had the following officers: Capt. H. Yoakum;

1st. Lt. John B. Maclin; 2nd. Lt. A. B. Morris; Ensign James Watts. The movement came to an end when Gen. Sam Houston so completely defeated the Mexicans at San Jacinto.

Prior to these events many young men from Rutherford County had gone to Texas, notably George C. Childress, who became an outstanding leader. Childress is credited with helping to draft the Texas Declaration of Independence. And it is said of him that he was second only to Sam Houston.

It was in 1847 that Tennessee got its name as the Volunteer State. The occasion was Governor Brown's call on May 26, 1847 for 2800 Volunteers for the war with Mexico. In a very short time more than 30,000 men had volunteered. And again the courageous little county in the very middle of the state answered with more than its allotted number. Two full companies were raised in Rutherford, one under Capt. Mitchell and the other under Capt. Childress. It is understood that many of these men saw little or no service for the war was short lived.

After the men returned from the War with Mexico, there was little more than a decade when life in Rutherford County meant peace and prosperity. And the people liked it and would have kept it so. They did not want secession and they did not want war. The people believed in State's Rights but hoped for a position of neutrality on the part of Tennessee. But with the fall of Fort Sumpter and the call for troops on the part of the Federal Government the thinking reversed itself. Rutherford County voted for secession by a count of 2392 to 73. Most of the counties in middle and west Tennessee had similar counts. Rutherford County became "The Little Theater" of war for the Civil War. No area of Tennessee and probably no equal area of the entire South can point to as many finger prints of the war as can Rutherford County. War came time and time again not only to the doors but to the very firesides and dining tables of Rutherford County families. The section west and northwest of Murfreesboro bore the brunt of the burden though no area escaped the ravages of war. Homes were used for headquarters for officers, for hospitals, for fortresses and for barracks. Barns and even smokehouses were also used for barracks and fortresses. These conditions were especially true along the railroad and turnpike between Nashville and Murfreesboro. Geographically, Rutherford County is in the exact center of the state, for that reason Murfreesboro and the surrounding county afforded a strategic position in the control of the state. Moreover, good roads radiated in every direction from the town and the Nashville and Chattanooga Railroad, a most vital artery, bisected the county. The eyes of both armies were upon Rutherford County. During the late summer and fall of 1862 the Confederate Army hoped to hold the county. And even in the early winter of that year when Jefferson Davis, Commander in Chief of the Confederate Army, visited the army at Murfreesboro, the prospects for the reorganized and heavily reinforced Confederate Army of Tennessee looked rather good. General Braxton Bragg was in charge of this army. This was the army that was to fight the three days battle of Stone's River against the army of General Rosecrans.

Although the Battle of Stone's River is, by and large, the most important military engagement that took place in Rutherford County during the Civil War it has been described so many times in other works that only a brief summary will be given here so that little known events can be more fully described later.

The first day of the battle began at daybreak with the Confederates on the offensive. Historians list the first day as a victory for the Confederates. On the second day, January 1, 1863, there was little activity except for occasional engagements by cavalry units against supplies and wagon trains. General Bragg was intoxicated with joy over the success of the first day's fighting. He is said to have flashed a message to Richmond exclaiming "God has granted us a Happy New Year." But the next day's battle was another story. Bragg again took the offensive. And to this very day there are those who question the wisdom of his choice. He had noticed a Federal detachment that had been thrown across the river and determined to dislodge it. At first success seemed his. The Federals fell back and finally fled across the river. The Confederates pushed on crossing the river and scrambling up the banks on the opposite side on the west continuing the rapid advance until they found themselves in an open field unprotected by cavalry or artillery. On an elevation some three hundred yards away there were fifty-eight Federal guns. These guns boomed forth in protest and rained a withering fire into the advancing ranks. Line after line was decimated, until a retreat was ordered. And now the Confederates fell back across the river, shattered and demoralized, leaving over seventeen hundred men dead and dying. Undoubtedly this was the decisive conflict of the three days battle. The next day, January 3, 1863 Bragg withdrew his army from Murfreesboro and retreated. The significance of the outcome of that battle is greater than many historians have indicated. Vance in his *Stone's River* expressed it in this manner:

"It was at Stone's River that the South was at the very pinnacle of confidence and war-like power, and it was there that she was halted and beaten back, never again to exhibit such strength. It was a battle that marked the turning point of the war. To the

The Sam Davis Home

Stone's River National Park

people of two sections it seemed at times but another Shiloh—horrifying, saddening, and bitterly disappointing."

Both the infantry and the cavalry were active in the Battle of Stone's River. Some historians feel that it was at this battle that the cavalry came into full bloom. No mention can be made of the cavalry in Rutherford County without calling up the story of Joe Wheeler at Lavergne. Lavergne is a small village on the northwest border of the county. It lies at the crossing of the old Nashville or Murfreesboro Turnpike and The Nashville, Chattanooga, and St. Louis Railroad. This made it an important position because it was a key to communication along the two lines of movement.

A strong Federal garrison had been stationed there to guard the point. Wheeler and Wharton with cavalry units were backing up the Confederate line. They were attacking the rear of the enemy, capturing wagon trains and picking up stragglers from Rosecrans' army. When notice was taken of the garrison at Lavergne, Wheeler with about three thousand men was dispatched to dislodge the garrison and reopen communication. The Federals had taken position on a slight elevation near the rear of the village. The barricade they were using was improvised of cedar brush and only shoulder high. Wheeler stormed up the little incline and demanded an immediate surrender. This was curtly refused and Wheeler's men charged the position. The charge was repulsed. Again and again a charge was made and repulsed. At length the dauntless Confederates dashed their horses against the brush fence in an attempt to destroy it. Again they were repulsed. Finally Wheeler despaired and ordered a retreat. The cavalry quickly rode away into a near cedar thicket, leaving about fifty men and horses dead and wounded.

Another outlying point definitely connected with the Battle of Stone's River is Pilot Knob near the eastern margin of the county.

After Rosecrans had won the battle, he turned his attention to establishing signal stations over the surrounding country. The cupola of the courthouse at Murfreesboro was selected as the central station with auxiliary posts at Lavergne, Triune and Pilot Knob. The signal platform at Pilot Knob was placed on limbs of a large elm tree that towered above all other trees on the knob. The wigwag flags spelling out the code to the courthouse eight miles away became a familiar sight to the people of the neighborhood. And Pilot Knob remained a signal station throughout the remainder of the war.

To most readers of American History the Battle of Stone's River and the Battle of Murfreesboro are one and the same. But to the people of Rutherford County and at one time to a goodly number of Federal soldiers, the Battle of Murfreesboro was a very distinct and separate event, having a very different outcome.

The following account of the Battle of Murfreesboro was written from an article carried in the Nashville Tennessean in 1907. It was published in the Murfreesboro, Tennessee's issue of the *Rutherford Courier*, in 1935. Other writers have given us the same story under the title of *Forrest Birthday Party*. July 13 is the birthday of General Forrest and it is said that he used the idea of a birthday celebration in Murfreesboro when he urged his men to give every atom of their energy in support of the undertaking. The Battle of Murfreesboro or skirmish of Murfreesboro is one event when success came to the valiant Forrest, although, he did not get there "firstest" or "with the mostest."

On July 13, 1862, Murfreesboro was occupied by the Ninth Michigan and the Third Minnesota regiments. There had been friction between the commanding officers and there seems to have been little communication between the regiments. The Ninth Michigan, commanded by Colonel Parkhurst, was encamped in Maney's Grove, just within the corporate limits. The Third Minnesota, Colonel Leslie commanding, had taken a position on Stone's River, one mile from town. Colonel Leslie, with the eye of a trained soldier, had chosen his position well, a position almost impregnable, from which Forrest with his inferior force never could have driven him.

Forrest and his command arrived in the vicinity of Murfreesboro a little before dawn, coming from the direction of Pikeville.

Forrest's scouts had apprised him of the presence of a strong picket guard on the road from Woodbury to Murfreesboro, and it was necessary for the success of his plans that this guard be captured. A detail of picked men was sent out with orders to get between the guard and the main body of Federals. This was accomplished and as the detail approached from one direction, Forrest and his entire company confronted the surprised pickets. They were captured without the firing of a gun.

Forrest's horsemen then galloped pell mell with drawn sabers into the midst of Parkhurst's camp. The regiment was scattered and demoralized; but few prisoners were taken. Forrest could not spare from his little command a detail strong enough to guard a regiment of prisoners. Besides, there was more work for him. He hoped to surprise the Third Minnesota on the west side of town. But Colonel Leslie's men were ready to receive him. They had heard the firing and were drawn up, awaiting the assault upon their positions. The rear rested on the river bluff; a long stretch of open field would have to be crossed by an attacking enemy, and Colonel Leslie had planted Hewitt's battery of six guns in such a position as to sweep the open space. Two charges were repulsed with heavy loss, after which Forrest withdrew to the town.

It was then that one of the most thrilling scenes of the entire Civil War took place in the heart of the city of Murfreesboro.

The courthouse, sitting in the center of the public square was occupied by a strong detachment from the Federal regiments, stationed there as a provost guard. To Forrest's demand for surrender, the officer in charge of the troops in the courthouse sent a curt refusal. They refused to permit a man to approach under a flag of truce. Several citizens and soldiers were shot from the courthouse.

To reach the courthouse from any point the attacking party would be compelled to pass through an open space under the deadly fire of the men within the building. A man could not show his head without danger of having it filled with lead.

Forrest sat on his horse on the corner of Church and College streets, protected from the rifle fire by a row of low buildings. After a consultation with Colonel Wharton, the Confederate leader decided upon a simultaneous attack on the courthouse from two quarters.

Orders were given that axes be procured. Forrest, taking one of the axes in his hand, called for a Georgia company. They were drawn up along the sidewalk. Placing the axe in the hands of the first man, Forrest gave an order in a low tone—an order that meant inevitable death to many. The soldier who took the axe from the hands of Forrest was seen to reach his breast pocket and pass something down the line to his comrade. It was a letter to his mother. The order was to advance single file toward the courthouse. When the first man fell, the axe was to be picked up by the next man and carried forward. And so on until the survivors reached the courthouse. The company attacking from the east had no sooner come into the open than the man bearing the axe fell. It was picked up by the second, who was shot down. And the third. But by this time the column was under the protection of the walls of the courthouse. An attacking column from the west side was already hammering at the doors of the courthouse. Both doors were soon down and the Confederates swarmed into the lower halls of the building. But the men on the upper floors were undismayed. Forrest's men had entered the courthouse but they had not captured it. It meant certain death for every man who attempted to ascend the steps. There was a cessation of firing—minutes of anxious suspense for the dauntless riflemen above and the determined hearts below. A score or more of the attacking party were dead, dying or wounded on the square and under the walls of the courthouse. Suddenly from the windows of the building came smoke. The Confederates had fired the building. "Come down, Yanks, and leave your guns behind you!," was the command called up by the Confederates. The Federals had no choice but to surrender or be burned to death. They came down and surrendered.

While the courthouse was being taken by Forrest, Colonel Parkhurst had gathered about 100 members of his scattered regiment, the Ninth Michigan, and prepared strong fortifications of bales of hay. After the courthouse was captured, Forrest turned his attention back to Parkhurst and sent a demand for the surrender of the command.

Colonel Parkhurst turned to his men, and told them: "You may surrender if you wish, if not, we will defend our position."

With the consent of Colonel Parkhurst, a citizen who was among the Federals raised a linen duster on a pole as a signal that the little garrison had surrendered.

Having captured the provost guard and a part of the Ninth Michigan, Forrest now planned another attack on the Third Minnesota. Colonel Leslie still occupied his strong position from which the Confederates had failed to drive him earlier in the day.

Forrest sent a message to Colonel Leslie, demanding his surrender, and informing him of the capture of the Ninth Michigan and the provost guard and of the capture of Colonel Duffield, who had arrived only the day before. Colonel Leslie asked for time to confer with other officers, and then surrendered.

Thus, Forrest, in one of the most daring raids of his brilliant career, captured Murfreesboro from a superior force of Federals.

The accounts of the conflicts within the borders of the county by no means tell the full story of Rutherford County and the Civil War. Rutherford County is said to have furnished more men to the cause of the Confederacy than any other county in the state in proportion to its population. Her sons felt the sting of battle within whistling distance of their homes and in areas far distant from their home. Rutherford County furnished infantrymen to twenty different regiments and cavalrymen to more than a dozen different regiments.

The first regiment raised in the county was the Second Tennessee in 1862. Two of its companies, A and F, were made up almost entirely of Rutherford County men. The captains of these companies at one time or another were; S. N. White; John A. Butler;

Thomas G. Butler; James T. C. McKnight; Thomas D. White; W. D. Robinson, and William H. Newman.

To General Joseph B. Palmer of Rutherford County, goes the credit for raising the 18th Regiment. Three companies of the regiment were made almost entirely of men from this county. Captains from the county were B. G. Wood; B. F. Webb; R. M. Rushing; W. R. Butler. The 24th Regiment was raised at Camp Anderson near Murfreesboro and contained several companies with a large number of enlistments from Rutherford County. The 45th regiment was another having many Rutherford County men.

One of the most outstanding companies from Rutherford County was Company I of the First Tennessee Regiment. This was often spoken of as Captain William Ledbetter's Company. The Company participated in many of the most important battles of the war.

Among the military leaders not already mentioned may be listed: Gen. George Maney, Commander of 1st Tennessee Infantry, with Lee in Virginia and with Johnston at Shiloh; Col. D. Robinson of First Middle Tennessee; Col. Robert Jetton; Col. Joel Battle of the 20th. Tennessee; (Col. Battle had been a Captain in the Second Seminole War), Col. Richard Keeble of the 22nd. Tennessee; Col. John H. Adkerson of the 4th. Tennessee; Col. William Patterson. Presiding Judge of The Cavalry Court under General Kerby Smith; Col. Thomas Benton Smith of Bragg's Army; Lt. Col. John S. Gooch of 20th. Tennessee; Lt. Col. Jesse W. Sparks of 4th. Tennessee Cavalry; Lt. Col. E. F. Lytle of the 45th. Tennessee; Capt. William Ridley with the 20th. Tennessee; Capt. Frank Battle with Wheeler's Scouts; Capt. Jack Lytle, with General Morgan's Cavalry; Capt. Richard Beard, with the 5th. Tennessee; Capt. Thomas Hollowell, with the 21st. Tennessee Cavalry; Capt. William Killough with the 45th. Tennessee; Capt. Charles F. Vanderford with 18th. Tennessee; Capt. Isaac H. Butler with Carter's Cavalry; Capt. William Sykes with the 45th. Tennessee; Capt. Robert H. Young with the 18th. Tennessee; Capt. Thomas D. White and Capt. William H. Newsome with the Middle Tennessee Infantry; Capt. Thomas G. Butler with 2nd. Tennessee; Capt. J. E. Coleman with Cavalry Scouts. Capt. Charles Sheafe, with the Federal force, moved into Rutherford County in 1872 and spent the remainder of his life in this county. Thomas Frame was another Federal captain who came to Rutherford County to live.

The rank of Lieutenant seems to have been used rather sparingly during the Civil War, but records show a few Rutherford County men with this rank. There was Lt. Frank White with the 4th. Tennessee Cavalry; Lt. Moses A. Nelson; Lt. Joseph P. Hale with the 45th. Tennessee; Lt. Thomas B. Fowler; Lt. John W. Farris

with the 24th. Tennessee Cavalry; Lt. Charles King with Capt.
Ledbetter's Company; Lt. Crosswaite, who was killed in the Battle
of Murfreesboro and Lt. Peyton, who was killed at Chickamauga.

Rutherford's Civil War Service Roster would include Josiah
W. Ewing, Provost Marshall; James D. Richardson, adjutant of the
45th. Regiment, and Lt. Broomfield Ridley of the staff of A. P.
Stewart, and a long list of doctors. The doctors identified with
the Army include: Dr. Samuel P. Black with the 4th. Tennessee
Cavalry; Dr. Henry H. Clayton with the 45th; Dr. John N. Dykes
with Company G; Dr. Thomas J. Elam with 45th. (Dr. Elam had
been a soldier in the War of 1812 and fought in the Battle of New
Orleans); Dr. Robert B. Harris with the 23rd.; Dr. A. W. Manier
with the 24th.; Dr. William H. McCord with the 8th. Tennessee
Cavalry; Dr. James B. Murfree with Company I of the First Tennes-
see; Dr. Joseph Warmuth with the 17th. and 18th. Texas Regiments;
Dr. Robert S. Wendel, hospital surgeon in Georgia and Mississippi;
Dr. Bartley N. White with Company F of the Second Tennessee; Dr.
William Whitson with the 45th. Tennessee.

It is without pride that an unreconstructed "rebel" mentions
that the 10th. Union Regiment of Tennessee Infantry organized in
Nashville, July 1862, was recruited partly in Rutherford County.
In the beginning this company was known as The First Governor's
Guard. On January 27, 1863 four companies B, C, D, and E of the
3rd. Union Regiment of Tennessee Cavalry were mustered into service at Murfreesboro. These companies did much scouting and
skirmishing throughout the section.

The enlistments for the Confederate Army cover such a wide
span of years that it is no wonder we find Veterans of other wars
on the muster rolls. The names, Jetton, Lytle, Mitchell, Childress,
Murfree and Nichols appear on the rolls of intermittent wars for
a full half century.

No figure in the military history of Rutherford County seems
to have had a longer or more varied military career than did Col.
James Moore King. James Moore King who came to this county
from Sampson County, North Carolina in 1807 served in both Seminole Wars, in the War of 1812 and in the Civil War. He was a corporal in the War of 1812; and he and his brother Henry were both
with Gen. Coffee on the first day of fighting at New Orleans, December 23, 1814. Due to exposure Henry King contracted pneumonia
and died in New Orleans just a few days before the famous 8th of
January battle. But Corporal James Moore King took part in
this battle and remained on duty in New Orleans for several months
afterwards. Some time during the 1820's he was elected Colonel

of the State Militia and served efficiently at that post but declined to announce himself for Brigadier-General. Colonel King was not regularly enlisted in the Confederate Army, but during the latter part of the war spent much time with the army and took part in several battles.

Although Tennessee was the last of the states to secede from and first to return to the Union, one still sometimes finds an "unreconstructed Southerner" in Rutherford. And it is no wonder that such is true for the county bears so many scars of the War Between the States. The history of the county abounds in stories of patriotic heroes and martyrs for the Southern cause. The next few pages carry the stories of four such martyrs. These stories were furnished by a thesis written by Homer Peyton Pittard, a graduate of Peabody College.

Dewitt Smith Jobe's life parallels that of many others during the War Between the States of 1861-65. During this period when passions were high and "glorious death" was accepted with a flourish, many young men went to their graves with an enemy curse. Scouting in and behind the enemy line was precarious work and if the soldier was unlucky enough to be captured, the natural procedure was to exact, if possible, any information that he might be carrying. If the captors were unsuccessful, the soldier was executed, usually in a macabre manner. Jobe shared his fate with fellow countians including John Bowman, Dee Smith, N. N. Dillard, and Sam Davis, the latter the best known of the group.

Dewitt Smith Jobe was born June 4, 1840, at Mechanicsville in Rutherford County. He enlisted in 1861 at College Grove in Williamson County, ten miles from his home. The company that Jobe joined later became Company D of the Twentieth Tennessee Regiment. He served with this company until after the Battle of Murfreesboro. He was wounded and captured at the Battle of Fishing Creek and after his exchange participated in the Battle of Murfreesboro.

In the spring of 1863, while Bragg's army was at Shelbyville, General W. J. Hardee had Jobe detailed for service in which he did a great deal of dangerous work. He did this work for General Hardee until Bragg's army fell back into Georgia, when he was transferred to the Coleman Scouts. This was a very responsible position and necessitated working behind the Federal lines.

In the summer of 1846, D. S. Jobe, Tom Joplin, and others came into middle Tennessee and were scouting about in the area of College Grove, Triune, and Nolensville, in Williamson County. These villages were about seven miles apart and connected by the Nolensville Pike. The scouts, when in danger, would separate.

On the night of August 29, 1864, Jobe rode all night and about sunrise the next morning called at the home of Mr. William Moss, who had two sons in Company B, Twentieth Tennessee Regiment, and got his breakfast. Mr. Moss lived about halfway between Nolensville and Triune, on the pike. His home was about two hundred yards west of the pike which ran between some very high hills.

After Jobe ate his breakfast he went about one mile west of Mr. Moss's house into a cornfield on the Sam Water's farm. Here he concealed himself and his horse. At this time a party of Yankees, fifteen in number, were scouting in the same neighborhood under the command of Sergeant Temple of the 115 Ohio Regiment, and to them Jobe's presence in the community was made known. They tracked his horse to the field, surrounded and captured him; and when Jobe saw that he would be captured or killed, having on his person some very valuable papers that would comdemn himself and others (some thought these papers were procured by a sweetheart of his in the neighborhood), he destroyed these papers by tearing and chewing them up. After they had captured him, they tied him and tried to make him tell the contents of the papers, but he would not. The Yankees told Jobe that they would kill him if he did not divulge the contents but still he refused. Then they tied a leather strap around his neck and began to choke him to death; but the brave boy in gray, who was alone, disarmed, and both hands tied, with fifteen of his armed enemies standing over him thirsting for his blood, would not concede to their demands. Jobe, in this condition, chose not to betray his friends or to divulge his secret but preferred death. The captors beat him over the head with their guns, knocked out his upper front teeth, and dragged him by the leather strap that they had placed about his neck until he was strangled to death.

These fifteen men who had the courage to murder one man who was tied and disarmed, went back to the pike and told some acquaintances of Jobe's what they had done and said he was the bravest boy they had ever seen.

Word was sent to Jobe's home, six miles away, that he was killed; and the old negro servant, Frank, who had nursed him when a child, volunteered to take the wagon and go for him. He was carried to his childhood home by the faithful old servant and buried in the family burial ground, in the presence of his mother, father, and others. "No braver soldier, no greater patriot, no truer comrade gave up his life in this great struggle of ours for the right against the wrong, Sam Davis not excepted."

It is said that the bloody and cruel act prayed on Sergeant Temple's mind and eventually he went insane.

Dee Smith was a cousin of Dewitt Jobe. Between the two there existed a close friendship. When Smith learned of the bloody deed at Triune that was perpetrated against his cousin, Dewitt Jobe, he became enraged. B. L. Ridley, in his *Journal*, tells the story as follows: "There is a sequel to Jobe's tragic death that in sentiment and devotion is as beautiful as that of Damon and Pythias or of Jonathan and David. Jobe had a kinsman and brother scout, Dee Smith, a neighbor and friend. When he was told of Jobe's torture and persecution he grew desperate and his mind became unhinged. He left the Forty-fifth Tennessee Regiment near Chattanooga, raised the black flag and declared that henceforth he would never take a prisoner. It is asserted that he slew not less than fifty of his enemies. At last they surrounded and captured him twenty miles from Nolensville and took him severely wounded to Murfreesboro. Although in excruciating pain when the doctors probed his wounds, he said that he would die before his enemies should see him flinch. Fortunately, he died before noon the next day, at which time he was to be hanged."

John Bowman, a member of Colonel Paul Anderson's cavalry, was cut off in Hood's retreat and took shelter near Murfreesboro, his home. The Federals caught him near Drennon, a town midway between Murfreesboro and Lebanon, tied him to a tree, and threatened to kill him. Instead of begging for his life, Bowman defied his captors and heaped epithets upon them until they in frenzied rage, riddled him with bullets. The following is one of Bowman's exploits as a soldier as given in B. L. Ridley's *Journal*: "I had an experience with Bowman in 1864 that showed his recklessness and want of fear. While Hood was environing Nashville and Forrest was dashing upon Murfreesboro, seventy-five "Yanks" had been in a blockhouse near Smyrna depot, guarding the railroad between Nashville and Murfreesboro. Things were getting so 'squeally' that they left their fortress at Murfreesboro. Four 'Rebs' had slipped through Hood's army to see homefolks, John Bowman among them. They looked up the pike and saw it black with blue coats. The idea was that naturally they were so badly frightened a shot or two would stampede them, and that we would get at least their wagons and teams. Knowing every pig path, the four Rebs rushed through the cedars and ensconced themselves in a thicket on Searcy's farm alongside the old road. As the seventy-five marched along each 'Reb' on his horse drew his Navy and fired. Did they run; well never in the wide world. I can hear that Yankee officer now cry, 'Halt! Right wheel! Fire!' They peeled the saplings, made shot holes through our clothes and saddles; it looked like demons had turned loose upon us, and seemed that they would kill us in spite of fate. We got over the hill after a time; they did not pursue us nor did we pursue them.   Bowman wanted to go back and attack again, but the rest of us demurred.   We dubbed that battle 'Hardup', for if ever there was a hard time getting out of a thicket that was one. Capture 'Yanks'?   No, we were glad to save our scalps.   It was John Bowman's recklessness that induced four of us to attack seventy-five.   One of the young men, only fourteen at that time, (Dr. C. W. Crosthwait, of Florence, Tennessee, and who received only this baptism of fire during the great war) often now speaks of the battle of 'Hardup' as one which might be recorded.''

There is hardly a school child in Rutherford County who does not know the story of Sam Davis.   It is a story in history books, in magazines and in newspaper columns.   A familiar story and yet one too important to be omitted from any discussion on Rutherford County's military history.

The life and story of the execution at Pulaski, Giles County, Tennessee, November 27, 1863, is well known.   Davis was born October 6, 1842 near Smyrna, Rutherford County, Tennessee.   He spent his early boyhood working on his father's farm.   At the outbreak of the war, Davis was a student at the Western Military Institute (now Montgomery Bell Academy) at Nashville, Tennessee. His instructors were Bushrod R. Johnson and Edmond Kirby Smith, later to distinguish themselves in the Confederate Army.   Davis enlisted in the First Regiment of Infantry.   His work proved so good that when Bragg organized a company of scouts in 1863 Davis was recommended as a member.   This company, distinguished as "Coleman's Scouts" from a nomenclature of Captain W. B. Shaw, came under the personal direction of General B. F. Cheatham.

These scouts, especially active in middle Tennessee, worked in and around the Federal lines securing information from friends and observation of the general status of the enemy.   It was sometimes necessary for them to sleep in thickets and caves and secure food from loyal friends in the territory that they traversed.

The latter part of 1863 General G. W. Dodge, with a large command, was stationed at Pulaski in Giles County Tennessee.   This was an expedition by the Federal authorities to keep open the Louisville and Nashville Railroad.   General Bragg became anxious to ascertain the movements of his enemy; therefore he dispatched Captain Shaw and some of his scouts to this vicinity.   It is said that Shaw entered the town of Pulaski in the guise of a herb doctor, and was able to secure first hand information as to numbers, supplies and the like.   It is said that Dodge had recently received a very important dispatch from headquarters that contained very vital statistics relative to his position and orders for further occupation. How Shaw managed to secure this valuable information has never been told. It has been said that a negro servant employed by the camp found the papers on the General's desk and carried them away to Shaw. There is another version of the incident which involved a young woman. This young woman inveigled a soldier about the camp into bringing the papers to her. Since she was a friend of the chief of the scouts, it was an easy matter to convey the papers to him. At any rate, Shaw, by some ruse, secured the papers and with some other information, including a letter to General Bragg, succeeded in getting the reports in the hands of Davis on November 19, 1863. It was Davis' task to carry these through the Federal lines to the Confederates encamped at Chattanooga. He secreted the dangerous papers in his shoes and saddle. It was a difficult undertaking as the countryside was thick with patrolling cavalrymen. He had traveled only a short distance when he circled a dense thicket of woods and came almost face to face with a small unit of cavalrymen. This unit proved to be part of the Kansas Jayhawkers (Seventh Kansas Cavalry) which was scouring the country in search of scouts. Davis was searched and the papers found. One of the letters found in his boot was a communication to Colonel A. McKintry, Provost Marshall General, Army of the Tennessee at Chattanooga.

Sam Davis was immediately arraigned before General Dodge, who realizing that this information came from close to headquarters, questioned him as to the source. Davis naturally refused to divulge the secret.

After Dodge's efforts to extricate the information proved futile, a commission was chosen for a court martial to try the captive. It is an extraordinary fact that Captain H. B. Shaw was captured at the same time as a person of suspicious character and was in the same cell with Davis. No evidence of recognition passed between the two men. Joshua Brown, who was also in the cell with Davis, gives an account as it was related to him by Dodge some months later.

"The next morning Davis was again taken to General Dodge's headquarters, and this is what took place between them which General Dodge told me occurred:

'I took him into my private office, and told him that it was a very serious charge brought against him; that he was a spy, and from what I found upon his person he had accurate information in regard to my army, and I must know where he obtained it. I told him that he was a young man, and did not seem to realize the danger he was in. Up to that time he had said nothing, but then he replied in the most respectful and dignified manner: 'General Dodge I know the danger of my situation, and I am willing to take the consequences.' I asked him to give me the name of the person from whom he got the information; that I knew it must be some one near my headquarters or who had the confidence of the officers of my staff, and repeated that I must know the source from which it came. I insisted that he should tell me, but he firmly declined to do so. I told him that I should have to call a court martial and have him tried for his life, and from the proof we had, they would be compelled to condemn him; that there was no chance for him unless he gave the source of his information. He replied, 'I know that I will have to die, but I will not tell where I got the information, and there is no power on earth that can make me tell. You are doing your duty as a soldier, and I am doing mine. If I have to die, I do so feeling that I am doing my duty to God and my country.' I pleaded with him and urged him with all the power I possessed to give him some chance to save his life, for I discovered that he was a most admirable young fellow, with the highest character and strictest integrity. He then said, 'It is useless for you to talk to me. I do not intend to do it. You can court-martial me, or do anything else you like, but I will not betray the trust reposed in me.' He thanked me for the interest I had taken in him, and I sent him back to prison. I immediately called a court-martial to try him.'"

The action of the court-martial, November 26, 1863, was to sentence Davis to be hanged the following morning. It is said that Davis evidenced no fear when informed of his fate. He sat down that night and wrote a letter to his mother. It reveals a calmness that is remarkable for a man as young as Davis. It was the same remarkable calmness manifested by young Davis when he looked squarely into the face of the provost martial in charge of the execution and said: "I am ready." And that remarkable calmness remained with him as he ascended the scaffold and stepped upon the trap. After his body was cut down and placed in a coffin it was interred in a grave close to the scene of the execution. Communication was slow in those days due to the absence of regular mail service and it was some days before the Davis family learned of the fate of their son. When letters finally reached them, Sam's father sent John C. Kennedy and Oscar M. Davis, Sam's younger brother, to Pulaski to bring the body home for burial. They went into Pulaski and opened the grave; and after removing the top of the old box coffin, they lifted the body out and placed it in a casket they had brought with them. On their return home they were forced to cross Duck River on a flat boat since all of the bridges were burned. Having crossed the river they proceeded on their difficult journey until they reached the Davis home on Stewart's Creek. Davis was buried in the graveyard in the rear of the home. A number of years ago the state purchased the site and improved the grounds. Today it is a historic spot visited by thousands of tourists each year. A fine memorial highway branches off from the Nashville Highway and passes the home. Davis' final resting place is marked by a shaft of white marble about twelve feet high which is on a granite pedestal. This marker was made possible by contributions from Confederate veterans and friends of Davis. The inscription on the marker reads:

In
Memory of Samuel Davis
A member of the 1st
Tennessee Regiment of Volunteers
Born October 6th, 1842
Died November 27, 1863
Age
21 years 1 month and 21 days
He laid down his life for his country
A truer soldier, a purer patriot, a
braver man never lived who
suffered death on the gibbet rather
than betray his friends and country.

The women of Rutherford County in the early years of its existence present no account comparable to the story of Molly Pitcher. It is safe to assume, however, that those modest but courageous souls played no indifferent roles when war came to their doors or called their men from their homes. But it was not until the Civil War that Rutherford County women received special mention in connection with military affairs. When a husband answered the call of his Southland he frequently left to his wife the management of his plantation and the supervision of his slaves. Many of these proud, aristocratic women were reduced to harder and plainer living than they ever imagined. They brought out the old spinning wheels and handlooms to make clothing for the soldiers as well as for the family. During the war years the women of Murfreesboro and Rutherford County were really diligent aids to the Confederacy. Whenever circumstances permitted they prepared and served food to officers and soldiers, they gave them shelter, they repaired their uniforms, they cared for the sick and wounded The story of the Brick House Hospital has been told and retold and needs only to be mentioned here as one of the avenues through which women served. The memorial, *To Women of the Confederacy* at Baltimore, Maryland, is a typical picture of one aspect of the service of Rutherford County women. But bronze and marble cannot tell the full story of the quick witted and strong hearted women who stood so staunchly by their heroes in gray. At least two Murfreesboro girls were among those wounded by bullets from Federal guns. Molly Nelson was badly wounded as she played in front of her home during one of the skirmishes at Murfreesboro. And Mary Dean Arnold, daughter of Captain Arnold, received a dangerous wound in the side when a group of Federal soldiers fired into the kitchen of her home. The soldiers were searching for her father whom they believed to be hiding there.

If we checked the social history of the county from its beginning to the present time we would doubtless find that many Rutherford County women had become the wives of high ranking military men. One such outstanding event was the wedding of Miss Mattie Ready to General John Morgan. The wedding took place in December shortly before the Battle of Stone's River. In more recent years there has been the marriage of Donna Angelin Smith to Major Jack McCarthy who served in the British Army in World War I, and that of Jean Marie Faircloth to General Douglas MacArthur. Mrs. MacArthur was with her famous husband when he left the Phillipines saying, "I will come back." He went back and Mrs. MacArthur went with him; and she is now with him in Japan. Miss Jean Marie Faircloth volunteered as a nurse in World War I, but the end of the war came before she was called overseas.

The gaiety of the Gay Nineties was somewhat subdued by the sinking of the battleship Maine in the harbor of Havana on February 15, 1898. In about two months there was a formal declaration of War with Spain. About 200,000 men responded to the call for volunteers, and as always Rutherford County was ready with her share. A complete platoon seems to have been raised in the county. A full list of the Volunteers follows: Tom Ferrell, John Malone, Joe Fox, Gerry Jenkins, Tom Darrow, John Gunmen, Charles Tompkins, George Bass, Frank Ledbetter, Roy Battle, George K. Fletcher, William Lytle, John McKinley, John B. Patterson, Harry Bruger, J. F. Duffer, W. S. Manus, D. T. Crockett, W. E. Maynor, H. Y. Crockett, Thomas Smith, and James B. Murfree. Service in the Spanish American War amounted to little more than a brief period of training and a trip across the Pacific.

When President Woodrow Wilson issued the proclamation of war on the night of April 2, 1917, Rutherford County like every county in every state in the Union was entirely unprepared for war. The plan for enlisting and induction went forward speedily. Three men were appointed on the Selective Service Board, namely; Dr. B. N. White, Chairman; J. T. Wrather, Secretary, and E. E. Loughry. By enlistment and induction Rutherford County sent some 1177 men, eighty-three sailors, twenty-two marines, and one thousand seventy-two in the army.

The records show that of that number forty-four were killed or died while in the service and thirty-nine were wounded in action. A roster of commissioned officers show the following men from this county: Lieutenants William S. Anderson; V. S. Campbell; D. A. Bowling; Lyon W. Brandon; Charles W. Burton; Calvin D. Bush; Charles R. Byrn; Simeon B. Christy; Claude W. Covington; Stephen B. Duggin; Edward C. Faircloth; Lee Gilmore; William Eugene Henderson; Robert Edward Lowe; Robert T. McHenry; Leroy Brown Ordway; George L. Osborn; John K. Osborn; R. D. Park; Al Lytle Partee; Grandville S. Ridley, Jr.; James A. Ridley; Thomas Oscar Ridley; Walter Ford Rogers; Asa D. Sharpe; John Gilliam Sharpe; Henry Grady Smith; Isaac Brown Taylor; Charles O. Thomas; Scott Trammel; Aaron Louis Weise; Albert Mason White; Barton Newton White; Captains Macey L. Dill and Matthias Brickell Murfree; Majors James Baird Jones and Joseph Eggelston Johnson King; Colonel John E. Green.

Mrs. G. S. Ridley, Sr., was Rutherford County's Five-Star Mother, having four sons and a daughter in the service. Her son Lt. T. O. Ridley is believed to have been the first Rutherfordian to enlist. Miss Pauline Ridley volunteered as a nurse and completed her training as such, but did not go overseas for service. The Distinguished Service Cross was won by Lt. James A. Ridley for his service in the Battle of Verdun. In a report from the Commanding Officer to the Commanding General written October 28, 1918, special mention was made of the gallantry of Lt. James A. Ridley in the efficient handling of Company A of the 113th Machine Gun Battalion in the absence of its Captain. The work which called forth this special mention was done on September 30, 1918 at St. Quentin Canal.

Murfreesboro was the rendezvous point for the 113th Machine Gun Battalion when the President's call to Federal Service was issued July 25, 1917. The Battalion remained in Murfreesboro while arrangements were being made for the concentration of the Thirtieth Division at Camp Sevier.

The men who returned from World War I have through a very active American Legion served the county in many valuable ways. And many of the Veterans went into the service in World War II. Some of them are still serving nine months after V. J. Day.

When the U. S. Senate refused to ratify the covenant of the League of Nations, many Rutherford Countians knew that the desired results of World War I would not be achieved. No one could foresee, however, that another war was so near at hand.

When the first general registration of military training was called just twenty years later, everyone more than half feared that war was not far away.

The date of the first registration was October 16, 1940. On that day four thousand and seven men registered in Rutherford County.

Joe Frank Herrod was the first man from that number to go into training. He volunteered for the first call and left Murfreesboro on December 6, 1940, just one year and one day before the attack on Pearl Harbor.

The Headquarters Battery of the 115th Field Artillery which had been organized in Murfreesboro left for Camp Jackson on September 16, 1940. After training at Camp Jackson for some months they trained for a while in one of the northeast shore line camps, and were then ordered to Iceland where they spent many weary months before they went to Europe to combat duty. Officers for the battery were: Lt. Col. Hubert McCullough; Major J. A. Sanders; Major Robert Braswell; Captain William Wood; Captain W. B. Carlton, Jr.; and Captain James D. Parks.

The total number of men and women from the county who have served in World War II is not yet available. It is clear that there have been more than twice as many men as were in the first World War. There have been women in every branch of women's service from the Red Cross to the Spars. Many of these women served overseas. Miss Alice Brown was one of the first three women to go from Tennessee. She has attained the rank of Major. She received the Legion of Merit award for outstanding service.

It is a regrettable fact that at the present time no accurate list of officers can be obtained. The length of the list and the ranks shown on the list would give Rutherford County reason for much boasting. We have only a local newspaper's count, and the paper does not claim accuracy, on the number of men who gave their lives in World War II. That number is ninety-six—more than twice the number in the other World War.

Rutherford County has never been a laggard at war. From the days of fighting the Indians with flintlock rifles down to this Atomic Age, whenever there has been a necessity for warriors Rutherford County has furnished her share.

CHAPTER VI

Newspapers and Writers

Although Rutherford County's writers far surpass its newspapers in importance, the press will be treated first because of the chronological setting. The county's papers achieved prominence, for the most part, before the Civil War while most of its important writers came after the war.

THE PRESS OF RUTHERFORD COUNTY

Murfreesboro has during its history had almost twenty newspapers. Although two rivals, sometimes bitter rivals, have been the customary number at any given time, in its early history only one was published, while for a few years after the Civil War the city boasted four.

In 1810 there were only six newspapers in the state of Tennessee. On June 16, 1814, four years later, and hardly three years after the beginning of Murfreesboro, its first newspaper, the *Courier*, was established by the noted publisher brothers, G. A. and A. C. Sublett. It was printed on a Franklin style press similar to the type used for printing the Declaration of Independence. It was issued from an office on the corner of Vine and South Maple Street, then called South Lebanon. The paper ordinarily consisted of four pages, the first devoted almost exclusively to advertisement. All kinds of merchandise were offered to the public, considerable space being devoted to whiskey and medicines. Many merchants merely listed numerous commodities with their prices. Lawyers and doctors were usually content to give their names and places of business. Schools announced their openings and courses of study. Inns, even those in Nashville, often advertised in the *Courier* and later Murfreesboro papers.

Editorials were usually on the second page where also appeared the names of the editors. The remainder of the paper was devoted to news items, local, state, national and international, articles copied from other papers, numerous letters from readers, legal notices, and an occasional article on the advances being made in medicine, science and other fields.

The *Courier* was a weekly paper and its circulation beyond Rutherford County was very limited. This statement is verified by the large number of advertisements from Murfreesboro to be found in the Nashville papers of the early decades of the nineteenth century. But according to Mr. C. C. Henderson in *The Story of Murfreesboro*, the number of subscribers in the county was good. Mail service to Nashville was limited to "once a week", but private carriers facilitated exchanges between the *Courier* and Nashville papers. Mr. Henderson says that "the purpose of the *Courier* was to print the news rather than to mold public opinion."

The Subletts were not averse, however, to molding public opinion; for in 1828 they founded the short-lived *National Vidette*, whose sole aim was to help elect Andrew Jackson president of the United States. It was decidedly anti-administration and opposed the reelection of John Quincy Adams. The Subletts did their share in introducing the opinions of the rugged west into Jeffersonian Democracy.

The length of life of the *Courier* is uncertain. The latest original copies of this paper found today in various libraries throughout the country are dated 1827, while quotations from the *Courier* appear in Nashville papers as late as 1831. Whether the Subletts were editors all that time is uncertain, but there are indications that they were as long as Murfreesboro was the capital of the state. The Subletts also appear to have done considerable printing for the state while the legislature was meeting in Murfreesboro.

The *Courier* naturally acquired great prestige among the papers of the state while Murfreesboro was the capital. As a result of this its news items were frequently copied by other papers.

In the issue of the Nashville *Whig* of November 14, 1825, there appeared an article from the Murfreesboro *Courier* written by Newton Cannon to Messrs. Subletts announcing his willingness to be placed before the state as a candidate for chief magistrate of the state. His letter was in "answer to the suggestion of 'a visitor' in your paper of the 3rd inst . . . ."

The following item also can be found copied in the issue of the *Whig* of November 28, 1825: "Messrs. Subletts: It is requested that you announce in your paper that it is the wish of a good portion of the people of Tennessee that Robert C. Foster, Esq., Speaker of the Senate, would permit his name to be run for the Chief Magistrate of the State. It would be gratifying to the writer of this note if Mr. Foster could in answer consent to place his name before the public."

(Signed)   MANY VOTERS
Rutherford County.

In the Nashville *Whig*, December 13, 1820, is found this article:

Murfreesborough, Dec. 8.

"The Presidential Election"

"Wednesday last at 12 o'clock the college of electors of the President and of the Vice-president met at the office of the Secretary of State and gave the unanimous vote for James Monroe for President and Daniel B. Tompkins for Vice-President."

A list of seven of the eight electors followed, the fourth district not being represented. Then came this interesting comment: "The junior Editor of this paper was elected messenger to carry the statement of the vote to Washington city and he will set out on the execution of his trust in a day or two."

A number of times the Governor's message was published in the *Courier* and reprinted later by the Nashville *Whig*. Some Legislative Acts found in the Murfreesboro *Courier* and used again in the *Whig*, dated September 4, 1822, were:

"The annual salary of the President of the State Bank shall be $1,000; that the cashier's $1500, and that the clerks shall be $750."

"Tax on hawkers and pedlers shall be reduced from $50.00 to $25.00 per annum."

In a summary of the Legislative Acts published October 10, 1822, are found the following titles: a law making imprisonment for debt illegal; and a law for the relief of wives whose husbands have left them, or have driven them from home.

In the Nashville *Whig* of July 24, 1822, there appeared an exciting story. Though there was no big type to make headlines, there was a row of exclamation points following the title.

"Fire!!!!!"

"The courthouse was consumed by fire on Thursday morning last. It was discovered about daylight when the fire had made such progress as to render any attempt to extinguish it useless. It was evidently the act of some base incendiary. The citizens of Murfreesborough promptly united in fitting up the Presbyterian Church for the use of the General Assembly, which it said will more conveniently accommodate them than the Courthouse."

An interesting item can be found in the April 30, 1830, issue of the Nashville *Whig* titled: "Judiciary." "The last Murfreesboro paper contained a complimental notice of the judge who had closed his first circuit court in town today." A lengthy essay on courtroom discipline followed, ending with an appreciation of Judge Mitchell's ability to keep a quiet, dignified order, in which justice is administered, and with this remark: "We would say to some of our State Judges, 'Go thou, and do likewise.'"

In the *Republican and Gazette* of Nashville, dated November 26, 1831, can be found this last item of the *Courier* quoted by a Nashville paper.

"From the Murfreesborough *Courier*", subtitled

"Dinner to Major Eaton"

"On Friday 18th inst., a public dinner was given at Reeve's Tavern in this town as a mark of respect for his personal worth and public services by the citizens of Murfreesborough, and the County of Rutherford, to the Hon. John H. Eaton, late Secretary of War."

Another paper, the Murfreesboro *Monitor* was being published in the 1830's. Though C. C. Henderson, Hale and Merritt, Goodspeed, and John Trotwood Moore, all, fail to mention it in their histories, extracts from it can be found in the Nashville *Union*. One of these in the issue of September 7, 1835, is a copy of a lengthy editorial scoring the enemies of Andrew Jackson who have accused him of fraudulent use of his franking privilege. The second is headed:

"From the Murfreesboro' *Monitor* to the Public."

Then follows an extract of a letter from Charles Ready, Esq., member of the House of Representatives to Mr. Edmund Rucker which relates an analysis of the contents of "Mrs. Cheek's stomach" to determine whether she had been poisoned. Six different experiments had been made in the presence of witnesses. Dr. Troost, Professor of Chemistry, Nashville University, made a lengthy report, the conclusion of which was that there was no trace of arsenic.

Who the editors of the *Monitor* were and how long it lived has not been determined. *Wilson's Union list of serials in libraries of the United States and Canada* lists the *Central Monitor* founded in 1833 and *The Monitor* founded in 1835. Whether they were the same is not known.

In 1837 the *Weekly Times* was established "by the same editors". John Trotwood Moore said, referring to the Subletts, "All of which goes to show something of the way in which the irrepressible editors brought forth papers, undismayed by the brevity of their lives."

But Goodspeed states that the *Weekly Times* was established in Murfreesboro in 1837 as an organ of the Democratic Party, and was edited by Thomas Hegan. C. C. Henderson agrees with the latter and adds that it was the "first partisan paper ever established and published in favor of the Democratic Party" anywhere in the United States.

Dr. Philip Hamer, formerly of the History Department, University of Tennessee, in *Tennessee-a History* says that in 1837 at a convention of Tennessee Editors the *Western Times* (probably the *Weekly Times*) of Murfreesboro was represented by Stephen B. Jones. He, with other assembled editors, agreed upon a statement of principles and approved practices for their profession. "The press is justly considered the palladium of popular freedom", they asserted. In noble, elevated language they declared their responsibility to man, and in that high sense of obligation they adopted a code of ethics by which they would be governed as newspapermen.

According to C. C. Henderson, the Tennessee *Telegraph* was founded a little later and was conducted as a Whig organ under the editorship of E. J. King. Its motto was "The Union of the Whigs for the Sake of the Union." Goodspeed said, "Its motto signified its politics. This editor, like the modern editor, saw the salvation of the country depending upon the support of his paper and his party."

It was the *Telegraph* that made such a valiant fight for the permanent capital of Tennessee to be located in Murfreesboro. In 1843 it asserted, "If the members (of the Legislative Assembly) cannot accede to our wishes, then we go for McMinnville, for Knoxville, for any place before Nashville."

The Murfreesboro *News*, one of the ancestors of the present *News-Journal*, was established in 1848 or 1849 by A. Watkins, and was edited by the Reverend Green T. Henderson. It was neutral in politics until 1852, when it was changed into a Democratic organ. C. C. Henderson says of it, "It was one of the best and most vigorously edited of all the papers in the state and it wielded a powerful influence on the public mind." Goodspeed says of it, "The paper was ably conducted by Mr. Henderson till it was suspended on account of the war, the type and press having been destroyed by the Federal Army."

In opposition to the Murfreesboro *News*, the *Telegraph*, a different publication from the Tennessee *Telegraph*, but following the same policies, was established as a Whig organ. It was first edited by Dan W. Taylor, who sold it to David Maney. Maney sold it later to R. S. Northcott. Northcott was a staunch Unionist, and after the suspension of the paper at the beginning of the war, went north and became a brigadier in the Union Army.

A strange coincidence has just brought to light two rare copies of these rival papers. The older copy, the Rutherford *Telegraph*, is dated January 29, 1853, and its editor at that time was David Maney. There is little difference in the appearance of the two. Both are four-page papers, printed on soft rag paper that feels silky compared with the rough pulp of today. The *Telegraph* is a 7-column paper; the *News* is 6. Murfreesboro was still spelled with "ugh" in 1853. In 1858 the "ugh" was replaced by an apostrophe. Both papers used the first pages for serious and humorous articles rather than for news stories. While the *Telegraph* adhered to the custom of placing some of its advertisements on the front page, the *News* had pushed them to the inner and back pages. Both papers had more advertisements than news. And yet the advertisements read like news, telling of consignments of rich and beautiful imported dress goods, fine perfumes, lately arrived, of whiskies, brandies and wines by the hundreds of barrels and bottles. They told of hand-made shoes, carriages, harness, and other leather goods; of glass, paints, salt, oils, groceries and patent medicines. There were carpets, rugs, bonnets and Negroes, Negroes, Negroes! Compared to papers of our day, there was very much more advertising then; and it was worded differently. It all indicated the prosperity Murfreesboro enjoyed before the Civil War. And although the papers were rivals politically, neither mentioned the other in these particular issues.

The motto of the Rutherford *Telegraph* was "Liberty and Union, now and forever, one and inseparable;" that of the Murfreesboro *News* "We claim the right of thought, and what we think, assert."

One article of interest in the *Telegraph* that indicated partisanship told the story of a Negro's having been found packed so tightly in a bale of cotton that the space occupied by his body was scarcely three inches thick. A long paragraph followed presenting the difference of opinions between northern and southern men and saying that "every debate in Congress has a Negro in it . . . Every knotty question that agitates the States, if split open has a Negro in it . . . . The Negro is in all our policy and his dark shadow is upon all our plans."

An editorial in the Murfreesboro *News* deplored the fact that many Tennessee Democrats had left the party to follow a dark lantern of Knownothingness. In this same issue of the *News* it is stated that Aaron Burr required forty-five days in the beginning of the century to come by horseback from New Orleans to Richmond for his trial, but that the distance could now be made in five days by railway car.

Another item said: "The examination of the students in Soule Female College has been progressing since last Monday and will continue until Thursday night. We doubt not the exercise will continue to increase in interest to the close. We understand the examination thus far is highly creditable to the teachers and pupils." It was learned also from the *News* that the commencement exercises at Union University would last two weeks.

The *Union list* refers to the *Dollar Weekly*, published in Murfreesboro in 1857 and 1858, but nothing further is known of this publication. During the Civil War a paper referred to in the *Union list* as *Daily Rebel* and also referred to by some as the *Rebel Banner* was published for a time in Murfreesboro. A copy of this paper is said to be in Murfreesboro but diligent search has failed to bring it to light.

In 1866, the Reverend Green T. Henderson resumed the publication of the Murfreesboro *News*. Assisted by his son, Reese K. Henderson, he continued to edit and publish it until 1878, when it was sold to "other parties." One of these "parties" was Gid. H. Baskette, who later became editor of the Nashville *Banner*.

During the fall of 1869 and the years of 1870-1871 Captain Richard Beard, born near Canton, Mississippi, and grandfather of Jean Faircloth MacArthur, owned and edited the Murfreesboro *Monitor*, a weekly paper probably organized in 1865 and devoted to the interests of the Democratic party. It was a worthy paper and well edited by Captain Beard, who was a lawyer with a colorful and eventful career in both peace and war.

Following Captain Beard, B. F. Alexander edited the *Monitor*. He was a well educated lawyer, having graduated in 1870 from Union University and in 1871 having received a degree from the school of law of Cumberland University. He had served in the state General Assembly "in faithful and highly efficient manner. He was a Democrat of the old Jefferson type. He always advocated the rights of the laborer and producer."

Like the *Monitor* of the 1830's this *Monitor* passed into oblivion after a life of about ten years.

In 1878 G. T. and Reese K. Henderson founded the *Free Press*, which like the *News* was Democratic in politics but conservative in opinion. Goodspeed says, "The pages of the *Free Press* show that the Messrs. Henderson knew how to edit a paper." Copies of the January and August 1880 issues in the possession of Mr. Chip Henderson attest the truth of this comment. They are neat in appearance, clean and dignified. The advertisements have been moved to the inner and back pages. The front page was used for articles of opinion and of events of state and national interest. The tone of the paper is edifying, emphasis being placed on education, statesmanship and non-sensational news.

The Hendersons conducted the paper until 1888, when it was sold to a young Englishman, William H. Douglas, who published it for two or three years before its suspension.

A copy of Friday, May 12, 1889, shows that W. D. Fox, founder of the Ovoca Orphanage, was the editor, and that its motto was "The Greatest Good to the Greatest Number." It is an "illustrated number to acquaint others with what we are pleased to term a city, representing one of the most precious jewels of the South."

A paragraph headed "Newspapers" states: "Four weekly newspapers find sustenance here. The *Weekly Press* is the oldest, consequently has the pleasurable distinction of visiting more homes than any other journal published in our county." This particular copy is attractively edited, is printed on sleek paper, and contains pictures of famous buildings and leading citizens of Murfreesboro. Its chief boast is that Murfreesboro is "The Home of Cedar, Being the Greatest Red Cedar Shipping Point in the World."

An attractive picture of particular interest is one four columns wide, titled "Murfreesboro Society Bouquet," of nineteen belles of the day, who are matrons and sweet old ladies today.

In 1885, W. C. Frost, a young lawyer of Fayetteville and Columbia, son of a "reputable practicing physician of Bedford County" came to Murfreesboro, and bought the Murfreesboro *News*, "which he conducted in a faithful and efficient manner." Quoting Goodspeed, "He was an unswerving Democrat in politics and his paper which is devoted to the interests of his party is free and fearless in proclaiming the sentiments and principles of Democracy in Rutherford County." He was twenty-six at this time and was recognized in Murfreesboro as an "enterprising and successful young citizen . . . an efficient newspaperman."

Mr. Chip Henderson possesses two copies of the *News* dated March 1, 1888, and December 12, 1889. Both issues show that placing classified advertisements on the front page was still a common practice. Interspersed with the advertisements were jokes, tidbits of gossip, classic references and scientific observations. Instead of news stories on the front page there are serious or humorous articles, some old, others new. The editorials on page two are well written, worthy of any dignified journal. The tribute paid to Jefferson Davis on his death is a gem worthy to be kept along with other American classics. There was no column or page set aside for society notes. Stories of dances, strolling parties and so forth occur any and everywhere. Murfreesboro had a Dancing Academy conducted by Professor Pierri, who taught "fashionable dancing and deportment" in two sessions daily, one for misses and boys in the afternoon and the other for ladies and gentlemen in the evening.

The paper supported prohibition. It spoke with pride of Soule College, Union University, and the Opera House. Bank statements showed that Murfreesboro had outgrown "the burnt scorched desert midway between Memphis and Bristol", as one reporter called it after Lee's surrender.

In "Town Topics" of December, 1889, it is announced that: "Mr. Chip Henderson, son of Mr. Reese K. Henderson, who is well known in the newspaper business in Murfreesboro and Rutherford County, will soon begin the publication of a new paper in Murfreesboro. We have not seen the prospectus of the new paper but suppose that it will soon be out. Murfreesboro is not crowded with newspapers now. It is a thriving young town and we trust the new journalistic venture will do well. Mr. Henderson is not without experience in newspaper work and we have no doubt will pilot his enterprise to ultimate success."

The reference was to the establishment in 1890 by Mr. Henderson of the *Home Journal*, the other ancestor of the present-day *News-Journal*. He conducted it until 1894-95, when he leased it to James S. Baird. In 1896-97 he leased it to Louis J. Burgdorf and Ed. I. McKinley. In 1898 he sold it to Mr. Burgdorf.

In 1894 Reese K. Henderson established the *Independent Banner* and published it until 1898, when C. C. Henderson, his nephew, bought it and also the Murfreesboro *News* which he consolidated under the name of the *News-Banner*.

In 1899, or thereabouts, Mr. Reese Henderson established *Our Country*, which he published about a year. About the same time the Rutherford *Reporter* was founded by John Earthman, but it was short-lived.

In 1911 Mr. J. R. Williams bought the *News-Banner* and published it until 1926, when he sold it to Jesse C. Beesley, Jr., who converted it into a daily paper in 1927. Meanwhile, Mr. Burgdorf continued to publish the *Home Journal* until his death in 1920. The plant was then sold to Andrew L. Todd and W. H. Trevathan. George Burgdorf later came into the firm. It was conducted as a weekly with about 1500 to 1800 subscribers for about six or eight years, when the owners converted it into a semi-weekly. In 1930 a corporation was formed, of which Jesse Beesley, owner and publisher of the *Daily News-Banner*, was a member. In 1931 Mr. Beesley bought an interest in the *Home-Journal*. The *Daily News-Banner* was consolidated with the semi-weekly *Home Journal*. The title *Daily News-Journal* was assumed, and Sid Pigue became editor.

The *Rutherford Courier* was begun in a very modest way by Minor Bragg. With Mr. Bragg as publisher this paper is now an

8-page semi-weekly publication with a circulation of about 3,000. Since 1940 the University of Tennessee has given through the State Press Association awards annually to publications qualifying in community service, editorials, circulation plans, business promotion, local news and make-up. The *Rutherford Courier* has taken six top awards in four years, and has placed second, third and fourth a number of times. After a paper has placed twice successively it is ineligible for the same award the next year.

Mr. Bragg takes pride in the fact that in the fourteen years of the *Courier's* history it has been the training ground for successful newspaper men. Among these are Robert Lasseter, Nieman fellow at Harvard, Fred Travis, later of the Chattanooga *Times*, and Ed Bell, now with the Associated Press.

In 1933 the *Daily News-Journal* was leased by E. W. Carmack. A year later he bought the paper and published it until 1940. In 1940 Mr. Carmack sold the paper to Andrew L. Todd, who in turn sold it to the present owners, Jack McFarland and Major W. E. Rynerson, who constitute the Mid-South Publishing Company. During World War II Mrs. Rynerson became both publisher and editor, since both owners were in the armed services. The paper is a daily except for Saturday, has a circulation of about 4000, and works a staff of twenty besides carriers. It has in Murfreesboro exclusive use of both the Associated Press and the United Press Service. It is independent politically.

A large number of Murfreesboro men and women have achieved distinction in journalism. In the early decades of the nineteenth century many gifted writers contributed to the Nashville papers under *nom de plumes*. "Solon" used to report the meetings of the Legislature and the Governors'· messages. Others writing at that time were "Regulus," "Scerola," "Americus," "Coriolanus," and "Atticus". Others used less classic names, as "A Traveler," "Boxer," "Mercy," "Farmer," and "A Citizen." All of them wrote good, even dignified, prose. One Murfreesboro reporter was very faithful, and his contributions were very much appreciated by the editor of the Nashville *Whig*. Occasionally the editor remarked that he regretted he did not have anything from "our correspondent", or he would say, "Our friend from Murfreesboro reports, . . ."

"Fiat Justitia" was a frequent contributor to Nashville papers in 1821. He assailed corrupt politics and politicians. "Aristides" was his contemporary. He deplored the lack of interest in education and wrote bitterly about the misuse of school funds.

Gid Baskette, of Murfreesboro, was editor of the Nashville *Banner* for forty years, while William E. Beard, dean of Nashville newspaper men, is from Murfreesboro. W. J. Ewing of Murfreesboro was editor of the *American* for many years.

Harrison Robertson of the Louisville *Courier-Journal*, a sketch of whom is given under writers, became almost as famous as "Marse" Henry Watterson, himself, who, by the way, was from Beech Grove, just across the Rutherford County line.

Dr. T. T. Eaton of Union University contributed regularly to religious papers and was a powerful influence in his denomination.

Dixon Merritt, historian and journalist, for a short time worked on the staff of the *News-Journal*. He is famous for his limerick on "The Pelican."

Mary B. Hughes, of local reputation, has done some very fine writing for the *News-Journal* and for Nashville and Chattanooga papers. Her best work is a series of articles describing famous old homes in Rutherford County. These have been collected and published under the title of *Hearthstones*.

Haynes McFadden, owner, publisher, and editor of the *Southern Banker* of Atlanta, Georgia, is one of the Murfreesboro McFaddens. The February 8, 1943, issue of *Finance*, a national magazine published in Chicago, in a 2500 word article about him says, "The versatile Haynes McFadden is one of the most widely known personalities in the Banking world. He is virtually an institution within himself . . ."Other quotations from the article are:

"For versatility, it is doubtful if there is any personality in American Banking who could take the spotlight away from Haynes McFadden.

"Haynes McFadden is a product of newspaper work, having worked on the Louisville Courier-Journal, when the trenchant editorials of the famous 'Old Marse' Henry Watterson were block busters of that day on the journalistic front.

"He is definitely an idealist, who loves nothing better than to discover a literary gem, a beautifully turned phrase, or a forcefully written idea.

"He has set standards for the *Southern Banker* that have placed it in the front rank of the banking journals of the nation.

"The *Southern Banker* is fortunate in having a man of character, ability, brains and a dynamic personality as its publisher and head."

Grantland Rice is America's foremost sports writer. In the September 1944 issue of the *Southern Banker* an article entitled "Murfreesboro . . . The Greatest Little City of its Size" contains a sketch about Grantland Rice.

"In the realm of letters, Murfreesboro's particular star in our time is Grantland Rice, poet and newspaperman. Nothing makes the tedium of time jingle more merrily away than a book of Grantland's verse. It is doubtful if any one has contributed a greater uplift to as many people as Mr. Rice has achieved in his apostleship of good, clean sport . . . Based on normal cleanliness infiltrated through the masses as the chief by-product of his pen, the luster of his life work is an even more important element of American sportmanship and character building."

Rice's career as a writer began in 1901 with the Nashville *Daily News*, whence he journeyed upward with the Atlanta *Journal*, the Cleveland *News*, the Nashville *Tennessean* and the New York *Evening Mail*. For the past dozen years his column "The Spotlight" has been syndicated by the North American Newspaper Alliance and appears in about eighty-five papers throughout the country, including the New York *Sun*.

Mr. Chip Henderson, now retired from the newspaper business, speaks with bright humor of some of his experiences. He tells of having to buy expensive paper from the paper mills in Manchester, Tennessee, of the scarcity of paper after the Civil War, and how, because of this, subscription prices were high and subscription lists were low. He says that publishers and editors lived on wedding cake; that brides gave them cake when their weddings were written up.

Some of his conversation is very grim. He recalls how a Murfreesboro editor was killed on Christmas in Smyrna by a drunken captain. He remembers, too, that many times his own life was threatened by irate readers. Once a friend of his was much concerned because Mr. Henderson went about unarmed and unafraid. Mr. Henderson facetiously remarked, "If they're going to kill you they don't threaten."

RUTHERFORD COUNTY WRITERS

Although Rutherford County has made contributions to the nation in many fields, it is in literature that her sons and daughters have been most highly acclaimed. The county has produced an imposing array of writers headed by Mary Noailles Murfree and Andrew Lytle.

The much quoted statement "Of the making of books, there is no end" might well apply to the most prolific of the several writers which Rutherford County has produced, Charles Egbert Craddock, whose real name was Mary Noailles Murfree.

The background of Mary Noailles Murfree was typical of ante-bellum aristocracy. Her great-grandfather, Colonel Hardy Murfree, came to Tennessee from North Carolina, where he had been noted as a statesman and a military leader of marked ability. His wife was Sally Brickell, the daughter of Colonel Matthias Brickell and Rachel Noailles Brickell, both of whose names are common as given names in Murfreesboro families. Colonel Hardy Murfree, after acquiring numerous tracts of land in Tennessee several of which were in Rutherford County, moved to Williamson County, where he died in 1809. Mary's grandfather, William Hardy Murfree, re-mained in North Carolina to study and practice law and served with distinction as a Jeffersonian Congressman. In 1823 he moved to Williamson County, Tennessee.

In the meantime, David Dickinson, who later married a daughter of Colonel Hardy Murfree, was living on his well-known estate, "Grantland", on Stone's River northwest of Murfreesboro. William Law Murfree, father of Mary, and son of William Hardy Murfree married his cousin, Priscilla Dickinson, daughter of David Dickinson, and became master of "Grantland." It was from this union that Mary Noailles Murfree was born.

William Law Murfree was a scholarly man, a graduate of the University of Nashville, and proficient in four languages. He practiced law in an office on the square in Murfreesboro.

"Grantland" was a large, dark red brick house situated on a hill overlooking Stone's River. The high-ceilinged halls and rooms were spacious and furnished with heavy substantial furniture. There was plenty of room for gracious living, money for every need and slaves to do all the work.

Here, Mary Noailles Murfree was born January 24, 1850.

Her childhood was normal and happy. There was an older sister to play with, a baby brother, a Negro mammy to sing songs, toys and dolls, and a fond father to tell stories and play games in the evenings. When she was five she became a victim of slow fever, which left her a cripple for life. This fact, however, was fruitful in her experience. For her sake the father took the family to Beer-sheba Springs every summer to spend three months in their cottage, "Cragwilde." Here in the midst of scenic beauty, on a shadowed rock, Mary continued her school lessons which she had previously recited to a governess in a brick office in the yard. Here, too, she learned the mountains and the mountaineers whom she immortalized later in her novels.

Mary was never morbid about her handicap. She took pride rather in the fact that she knew more than other children with whom in later childhood she attended school in Nashville Female Academy. She turned her mind to scholarly pursuits rather than to society.

During two years of the war the family lived in Nashville, where they had moved some years before so that her father would be able to practice in a thriving city of 15,000. The other war years were spent in Murfreesboro. These were valuable years, for a great deal of her materials came direct from these experiences.

After the war had devastated southern colleges, Mary and her older sister, Fanny D., were sent to Chegary Institute in Philadelphia. For two years the girls studied French, Italian, German, voice and music. Mary wrote poetry at this time and composed music for her verses. Music was more than a polite accomplishment to her, her sister and their mother. Mary's father had placed intelligence as high as charm in his training of his daughters.

Financial stress, because of the war, came to the Murfrees. "Grantland" was destroyed, and income from their Mississippi plantations fell off, and Beersheba became shabby. But Mary seemed unaffected by these misfortunes. She continued to sing and play for the mountaineers and to learn their ways, and their dialect, not realizing how she would use them later.

People lived languidly in Murfreesboro, discussing the war more than contemporary news. A new "Grantland" was built. But the Murfree family were sufficient unto themselves. They read Scott and Dickens, Eliot, Bret Harte, and Mark Twain. Mary wrote stories and read them to the family. She sent an essay to Lippincotts, which was published under the name of R. Emmett Dembry. Other little pieces followed, but she soon assumed the pen name of Charles Egbert Craddock, from the name of one of her own characters.

Edd Winfield Parks, her biographer, classifies Craddock as a local colorist, and says of her: "In four years Mary Murfree had passed from polite and clever tittle-tattle to reality, as she saw it, and to experimentation with a technique that in a few years was to produce short stories unexcelled by other local colorists."

Mary Murfree did not become a local colorist by design, but by accident, a very natural accident. She had read and assimilated Scott and Dickens. Their influence is clearly detected in her writings, though she did not imitate them. She had many contemporaries who were local colorists: Bret Harte, Mark Twin, Sara Orne Jewett, Mary E. Wilkins Freeman, Edward Eggleston, F. Marion Crawford, Joel Chandler Harris, and William Dean Howells. She was a worthy member of that group, and more than one critic has said that she was the finest of them all.

Mary Noailles Murfree
(Charles Egbert Craddock)

Sarah Childress Polk

During Mary Murfree's lifetime twenty-five books by her were published, consisting of novels, novelettes, and collections of short stories. She began publishing in 1884. Regularly and steadily her books were released during a high tide of popularity that lasted for twenty years. One novel was published posthumously as a serial, and there were a large number of unpublished and even unfinished manuscripts found after her death. Besides her books there were many uncollected articles and stories published in various magazines.

In the Stranger People's Country is probably her most artistic work; but *In the Tennessee Mountains*, a collection of short stories, and *The Prophet of the Great Smoky Mountains*, a novel of religious doubt, are best remembered. All three deserve to be classed as real, even powerful, literature. Mr. Parks, though asserting that her novels "moved men mightily over a score of years", does not believe that her ability as a writer was great enough to support the quantity of her output. He said, speaking of their excellence, "Beyond any doubting, if Mary Noailles Murfree had died then, or had never written another line, her reputation as a novelist would be far higher than it is today." That judgment would not have seemed justified during the days of her popularity. The publications of many of her other books were literary sensations. The greatest sensation that she created, however, was the revelation of the fact that she was not a big rawboned man, but was a petite, cultured, reticent little woman.

Miss Murfree has been accused by our frank generation of being unrealistic. She forestalled that criticism herself by saying that goodness is just as real as evil. She was a southern lady in every sense of the word. She was too truly a Victorian to write anything not "polite enough to parade in public across the pages of the Atlantic Monthly."

A fair criticism can be made of her, though. And that is that her characters are not individuals, but are types. When you have read about them in one novel you know all there is to know of her characters. They are the same, only their names are changed. The mountains are her best characters, and her best talent was revealed in her ability to create atmosphere, sublime, beautiful, haunting.

Miss Murfree wrote two historical novels, noted for accuracy and indicative of tedious research. They were *Where the Battle was Fought* celebrating the battle of Stone's River, in which certain of the characters have Dickensesque qualities, and *The Story of Old Fort Loudon*, thorough rather than exciting.

It is said that Miss Murfree's favorite among her own novels was *The Fair Mississippian*.

Charles Egbert Craddock's first works were her best.   Her later works were written because she had to earn her living.   Her father, mother, and brother died leaving her and her sister, "Miss Fanny", to live many years alone in Murfreesboro.   She had the misfortune to outlive her popularity.   The day of local color was past, as was the taste for Victorian romanticism and the historical novel.   These had to give way to the muckraking sociological novel.

When President Theodore Roosevelt stopped a few minutes in Murfreesboro and spoke from the rear platform of the train, he called out jovially, "Where's Craddock?   She's the person I want to see."   He said in his speech that no honor or praise could be expressed that would voice his appreciation of the literary achievement of Miss Murfree.

It is said that "Miss Fannie", Mary's sister, was once the most promising child of the Murfree family, whose home was a hive of literary activity.   Fannie's was a charm that was marred, so young men thought, by a quiet arrogance and too great intellectual capacity. She was the most practical member of an unpractical family.   She did the shopping, ran the household with a few servants, and entertained callers, giving her mother freedom to play the piano and her sister to write.   With all these duties Fannie found time to write a few articles and short stories, and one novel.

She called her novel *Felicia*.   It is a study of the conflict between a well-bred, socially ambitious wife and her singer husband whose connection with the theater could not be countenanced by her family. The characters are well delineated, the suspense is sustained and the climax is highly dramatic.   Contemporary reviewers compared *Felicia* favorably with the works of Henry James.

Recently, John M. Stahl, a critic of the old school, praised her very highly.   She had "much talent for writing", and *Felicia* was "far more than a tale to amuse, to entertain.   It is a deep subtle study of the inevitable results of the marriage of two different backgrounds, different inheritance and different environment, different ideas and ambitions, different evaluations.   It is a pity that *Felicia* cannot be read by all young people before they marry."

Only "Miss Fannie's" loyalty to her sister, and the feeling that she should make a home for her, prevented her from becoming a prolific and successful author.

William Law Murfree, Sr., father of Mary and Fannie Murfree, wrote a number of good stories and articles that appeared in *Scribner's* and *Lippincotts'*, as well as a number of legal volumes which gained a quiet, but firm popularity among lawyers.   He wrote many editorials in a magazine that he published himself, the *Central Law Journal*, in which he so vigorously demanded a sense of justice and ethics in his profession, that he was quoted by British legal journals. He wrote also a biography, *Colonel Hardy Murfree.*

William Law Murfree, Jr., wrote two legal volumes, *Law of Foreign Corporations* and *Statute of Limitations.* Ill health and early death cut short his gifted career. But the works of the father, the sister, and the brother were overshadowed in the eyes of the world by the phenomenal success of Charles Egbert Craddock.

Next to Mary Noailles Murfree, the best known woman writer of Rutherford County is Will Allen Dromgoole, who was born in Murfreesboro, in 1860. She was educated at the Female Academy of Clarksville, Tennessee. She spent most of her life in her native state and "her writings deal largely with the hopes, sorrows, aspirations and tragedies of the common life in Tennessee."

Her first book was a collection of short stories, *Sunny Side of the Cumberlands.* These stories as well as nearly all of her stories were taken from real life. Other books were *The Farrier's Dog and his Fellows, Fortunes of the Fellow, Harum Scarum Joe,* and *The Heart of Old Hickory.*

Her publisher said of her: "She has a certain charm, which is rare among modern writers, being humorous and pathetic by turns, wonderfully true to life, and yet free from the repulsive elements so often present in realistic sketches . . . . . . She constantly reminds the reader of Dickens, although her writings are free from the tendency to caricature and overdraw."

Her characters appeal to the reader whether sadness or humor predominates. The stories are short enough to be used for readings, and they have so often been used that they are familiar to southern audiences. Their life-likeness and artistic treatment linger in the memory of the reader, and of the audience.

For many years and until her death in 1934, she edited a page "Song and Story", in the Nashville *Banner,* which featured short amusing or touching anecdotes and short poems that appealed to a wide reading public. Probably her most famous bit of verse is "Building the Bridge", which was quoted by both British and American papers in their tributes to her at the time of her death.

For scholarly performance, and enduring literary quality, time will probably verify the statement that Andrew Nelson Lytle ranks first of all the writers of fiction who have lived in Rutherford County.

Andrew Lytle was born in Murfreesboro, December 26, 1903. His father was Robert Logan Lytle, a descendant of the Lytle family that came to this section of Tennessee early in its pioneer days. His mother was Lillie Belle Nelson, also from one of the first families. Many members of these two families are still living in Rutherford and surrounding counties.

Andrew graduated from Vanderbilt University in 1925. He was a student in the school of drama, Yale University, in 1927-28. His play, "The Lost Sheep", won for him a prize offered by the Nashville *Tennessean*.

He has written three successful novels. One of them was biographical, *Nathan Bedford Forrest and his Critter Company*, in which he convinces the reader that the reason the South lost the war was because her leaders failed to recognize the genius of Forrest. Not only does the reader feel the presence of greatness in the man, but he is aware as he reads that the book itself is a fitting memorial to Forrest.

His second novel, *The Long Night*, is the story of Cameron McIvor, whose life is devoted to avenging the death of his father in a long-standing feud in north Alabama. The first half of the book is dramatic, and convincing. But the real worth of the book is in the last half, which contains some of the greatest writing that ever came out of the Civil War. It concerns the Battle of Shiloh.

The Long Night came out a few months after *Gone With the Wind*, and only discriminating readers appreciated the comparison between the two. Margaret Mitchell used her knowledge of the war to tell a highly dramatic story, but Lytle used a more highly dramatic story to show how much he knew of the war, so thoroughly steeped was he in the knowledge of his subject. Yet the consciousness of his detailed knowledge did not lessen the sense of satisfaction for the reader, nor the thrilling horror that powerful writing had prepared for him.

His third novel, *At the Moon's Inn*, is based on the life and exploits of Hernando De Soto. In this novel, the author has brought to life the color, the drama, the pageantry, the religious superstition and the cruel realism of 16th Century Spain, and also the wild, rich, but helpless, unexploited regions of the New World. Against this background De Soto and his followers are not shadowy figures, but are living, breathing, masterful personalities. Lytle's "sense-steeped prose" is sustained and equal to his majestic purpose.

Besides his novels he has written contributing chapters to other books by southern writers.

John Madison Fletcher was born and reared in Rutherford County near Murfreesboro. He was nationally known as a psychologist. He was the son of Burrell Dickenson Fletcher and Elizabeth Ann Alexander Fletcher, both from prominent Rutherford families.

Mr. Fletcher was graduated from the Webb School at Bell Buckle, and from Vanderbilt University. Later he received his Master's degree from the University of Colorado and his Doctorate at Clark University.

He joined the faculty of Tulane University in 1912, went later to the University of Colorado, Stanford and Clark Universities before becoming professor of psychology and lecturer in the Vanderbilt Medical School in 1926. In 1928 he returned to Tulane as professor of psychology, which position he held until his retirement in 1938. In 1942 he rejoined the faculty in connection with the Army and Navy training program. For several years he was dean of the graduate school of Tulane and was professor of education.

Dr. Fletcher was the author of several outstanding articles and books. One of them was professional, *Psychology of Education*, in which he put emphasis on the study of creative thinking. It is more than a duplication of general psychology; it deals with the application of psychological principles to the task of educating youth. He regards education as being not merely a mind-stuffing process but a developed control of the creative capacities of the mind.

His most recent book, *Human Nature and World Peace*, was presented in part at the Dumbarton Oaks conference by ex-Secretary of State Stettinius.

He was 71 years old when he died December 12, 1944.

Another brilliant young writer and college professor is William Yandell Elliot, who was born in Murfreesboro, May 12, 1896. He was a student at Webb School, Bell Buckle, received his A. B. Degree at Vanderbilt in 1917, his Master's there in 1920, a certificate from Sorbonne, Paris, France, and his doctorate from Balliol College, Oxford as a Rhodes scholar, in 1923. He served in the A.E.F. in World War I, has been instructor in Vanderbilt and in the University of California and Professor of government at Harvard. His writings are scholarly, and he has received wide recognition among students of government. During World War II, he had a leave of absence from Harvard, and served as vice-chairman of the War Production Board.

One of his best known books is *Pragmatic Revolt in Politics, Syndicalism, Fascism, and the Constitutional State*. Critics acclaim it to be fresh, vivid, interesting, and deserving to be read by all interested in political philosophy. It presents the thesis that communism, syndicalism, and fascism come short of meeting the needs of men in the modern community, because they are too concerned with the mechanics of social organization and have too little regard for questions of "moral personality" which are vital to the durable social economy of human beings.

Great Britain is a book compiled from a series of Lowell lectures. It is delightful and anecdotal in style, as oral lectures usually are. The purpose of the lectures is to show how the British Empire is changing into an Association of Nations and the causes contributing to such a change.

He wrote also *The Need for Constitutional Reform- A Program for National Security* during the Roosevelt recovery era, in which he contended that the Constitution of 1787 is too rigid for the grown-up United States. He suggested a rational program of new procedures that the government might well adopt to promote security.

Rutherford County also has its contributions to the world of science. Henry Helm Clayton, world famous meteorologist and astronomer, was born in Murfreesboro, March 12, 1861. He was educated in the common schools in the county.

In time he held various positions in different observatories; was a consultant expert; was dean of aeronautics in a school in Boston. He was also an inventor, and an experimenter in the use of kites and balloons. He wrote a number of books and articles on world weather and numerous articles on meteorological subjects.

Lorene Livingstone Pruette is a member of the family known as "The Millers of Millersburg." She was born in a community of Rutherford County known as Millersburg, from which many noted people have come. Of these Lorene Pruette is one of the most important. She is a writer, a lecturer, and a psychologist. She was a student in Agnes Scott College, the University of Chattanooga, Clark University, and Columbia University. She was a member of the Graduate Scholar Faculty of Political Science, Columbia University, 1920-22, and in 1922 became Instructor in the Department of Economics and Sociology, Smith College. Since then she has been visiting teacher and lecturer in a number of other schools and colleges. She began publishing her books in 1924. A list follows: *Women and Leisure*, 1924; *G. Stanley Hall, a Biography of a Mind*, 1926; *Saint in Ivory*, a novel, 1927; *The Parent and the Happy Child*, 1932; *Women With Words*, 1940. She has written contributing chapters for several books on psychology and numerous articles for newspapers and periodicals.

Still another college professor worthy of mention is James Welch Patton, who was born near Walter Hill. He is professor of history at North Carolina State College. His best known work is *Unionism and Reconstruction in Tennessee*, 1860-1869."

Henderson Yoakum, who before the Civil War was prominent in Rutherford County politics, moved to Texas and wrote the most authentic book in print on the early history of Texas.

Harrison Robertson, journalist, was born in Murfreesboro, January 6, 1856. His parents were Thomas Robertson and Elizabeth Elliot Robertson. He was educated at Union University and the University of Virginia. He was with the *Louisville Courier-Journal* from 1879 until his death. He was columnist, dramatic and literary critic, chief editorial writer, and manager of the editorial page from from 1885 until he became Editor-in-Chief in 1929. The list of his books includes *If I Were a Man, Inlander, Opponents, Pink Typhoon,* and *Red Blood and Blue.*

Emmett Gowen was born in Nashville in 1902. He was brought to LaVergne, in Rutherford County, in 1908, along with his father's family to live on a farm in Rutherford County. He and three brothers helped chop, plow and haul. He went to a small county school, often worked as a laborer for twenty-five cents a day, became a sharecropper and made only a scanty living. He enlisted in the marines and after two years returned to Charleston, South Carolina, where he with a group of other marines became involved in an armed sortie against the Charleston police, for which he was sentenced to five years in the Naval Prison at Paris Island. He served two years, during which time he educated himself in the prison library. After discharge he worked as newspaperman for various papers in Memphis, New Orleans, Nashville and New York. At one time he taught creative writing in Commonwealth College, Mena, Arkansas.

His novels are about mountain people and have some of the flavor of *Tobacco Road.* There are three of these, *Old Hell, Mountain Born,* and *The Dark Moon of March.* They would be classed as sociological novels.

His various newspaper articles reveal him to be a labor union man, and he often works voluntarily as a labor organizer. He has always been an ardent admirer of Russia, and he wrote in 1937, "I have a yearning to go to the Soviet Union and see with my own eyes the tremendous advance of civilization that is taking place there."

At present he divides his time between New York and LaVergne.

Two other writers of the sociological novel who have lived in Murfreesboro are Harry Harrison Kroll and Ed Bell.

Mr. Kroll was born in West Tennessee, of sharecropper parentage, lived as a young man as an itinerant photographer, met and fell in love with an Alabama school teacher and decided to get an education in order to persuade her to marry him. He continued his studies until he obtained a Master's degree from Peabody.

For prolific writing he might well be compared to Charles Egbert Craddock, whom he admired very much and whose influence can be detected in the mountainy atmosphere of some of his novels.   His first novel was *Cabin in the Cotton*, the movie of which was the first American film to be shown in Soviet Russia.   Other books have been *The Mountainy Singer*, which celebrates Dave Macon, the "Dixie Dewdrop" of Rutherford County; *Three Brothers and Seven Daddies*, a mountainfolk novel; *I Was A Sharecropper*, an autobiographical novel; *The Ghosts of Slave Driver's Bend*, a mystery; *The Man on an Iron Horse*; and a number of others.   His publishers continue to release his books and magazine articles with clock-like regularity.

His wife, Annette Heard, writes delightful juvenile verse and she wrote one novel, *Return Not Again*, while living in Murfreesboro.

Ed Bell now lives in Murfreesboro.   He has written for many different papers and magazines.   He has two novels to his credit, *Fish on the Steeple*, and *Tommye Lee Feathers*.   He is now working on a third.

Another Tennessee novelist who made her home in Murfreesboro for a while was Maristan Chapman, whose father was a minister here.

Murfreesboro has long been the home of a number of prominent colleges.   It is therefore natural that professors and administrators in these schools should have written books and scholarly articles too numerous to mention.   A few of these, however, deserve a word. R. L. Jones, the first President of Middle Tennessee State College, was author of a widely used textbook in arithmetic.   J. W. Fertig, dean of the same institution, was the author of a book on reconstruction in Tennessee.   Charles D. Lewis, Professor of Education, is the author of *The Rural School and its Problems*, while T. B. Woodmore, Business Manager, recently published a book entitled *College Business*.   This institution has not been without its poets.   Neal D. Frazier and Annie C. M. Frazier published several years ago a volume of intimate and tenderly beautiful verse, *These Bring Peace*, while more recently *Seraphic Dust* by Philip Macon Cheek has come off of the press.

Murfreesboro has also claimed several ministers who were writers of more than local renown.

The Reverend Samuel Davies Baldwin, D. D., pastor of the Methodist church in the 1850's, and President of Soule College from 1853 to 1856, was a scholarly man and an author of note.   His first book was *The Seventh Trumpet*.   It was followed by *Armageddon, The Life of Mrs. Norton, Dominion*, and *The Millennial Empire*. *Armageddon*, published in 1854, was famous throughout the United States.   Its title page read:

"Armageddon: or The Overthrow of Romanism and Monarchy; The Existence of the United States Foretold in the Bible; Its Future Greatness; Invasion by Allied Europe; Annihilation of Monarchy; Expansion into the Millenial Republic, and Its Domination Over the Whole World." It attracted great attention and not a little controversy as to the correctness of the theory presented. Mr. Baldwin and other ministers made extensive lecture tours to present its tenets to the principal cities of the United States.

The Reverend J. B. McFerrin, D.D., was born in Rutherford County June 15, 1807. He entered the ministry when he was eighteen. For many years he was head of the Methodist Publishing House. He wrote an important work, *History of Methodism in Tennessee.*

Dr. Carter Helm Jones, a leading minister of the Baptist Church, lived a few of his brilliant years in Murfreesboro. His one book was a collection of sermons, *Prophetic Patriotism.* He was well known as a master of noble and beautiful diction as well as of stirring and inspirational thought.

Although not a literary figure, mention should be made somewhere in this work of "Uncle" Dave Macon, the "Dixie Dewdrop." "Uncle" Dave lives near Kittrell in the eastern part of the county. For years the big man, with a ten gallon hat, goatee and banjo, entertained small groups in middle Tennessee till the coming of radio enhanced his fame. Today he is one of the favorites on WSM's Grand Old Opry and is no doubt the county's best known citizen. He also spent several months in the west making moving pictures.

CHAPTER VII

Medical Practitioners, Their Professional Organizations and the Development of Public Health and Hospitals

When the early settlers came to Rutherford County, they brought with them, no doubt, similar superstitions and practices, relative to the treatment of diseases, as were familiar to the American pioneers of that day. For some years there were practically no regular physicians in the early settlements. The so-called "doctors" were frequently keepers of inns or horse doctors. When the pioneers became sick they were largely dependent for treatment upon the household remedies they brought with them. Prescriptions for various ailments were exchanged among the neighbors. Fetiches were carried religiously to prevent rheumatism, and other afflictions. Even today, in Rutherford County, there are a few descendants of the pioneers addicted to the practice of carrying "buckeyes" in their pockets to ward off diseases. As late as September 3, 1813, a Negro was hanged in Murfreesboro for "house breaking" and the rope used in the execution was cut up and the small pieces passed out to the spectators as talismans against human ills.

The best trained physicians that located in the frontier communities received their medical education by means of study in the offices of practitioners, and usually supplemented this local tutoring with two courses of lectures in a medical school.

To get anything like a complete record of the early practitioners of medicine in any section of Tennessee is very difficult, if not impossible. This is largely due to the lack of any legal requirement for registration or licensing of physicians until many years after its admittance as a state. Although an attempt was made as early as 1817 to enact a law to regulate medical practice, the effort failed, as did many succeeding ones sponsored by the Tennessee State Medical Association in the years which followed its organization in 1830; and it was not until 1889 that the general assembly passed a law creating a board of medical examiners to examine and to license physicians to practice within the state.

Therefore, from 1803, when Rutherford County was created, to 1830, when the Tennessee State Medical Society was formed, there is comparatively meager information concerning the physicians who practiced within the county. Nevertheless, there are enough data available in certain historical sources, if presented properly, to give one a fair idea of the methods of practice used by the doctors and something of the problems that they encountered during the pioneer period. One of the earliest records of a physician locating in Rutherford County was that of James Loudon Armstrong. He began to practice here in 1809. After being born in Greenbrier County, Virginia, he came with his parents into Kentucky. At the age of sixteen years he commenced the study of medicine with a celebrated physician of that day, Dr. Dudley, in Lexington, Kentucky. When the War of 1812 broke out, he volunteered and served as surgeon during the period of the conflict. He returned to Rutherford County and continued his practice until 1852. When cholera invaded this section of the State, he took an active part in caring for the victims. The latter years of his life were spent in temperance and religious work. He died on April 5, 1868.

The next earliest record of a physician locating in Rutherford County was that of Dr. Swepson Sims. Dr. Sims located near the communities of Salem and Barfield in 1811. He was born in Granville County, North Carolina, on May 16, 1775. After marrying Jane Meriweather Lewis he moved to Tennessee. Apparently he was very active in religious work. On the organization of the Salem Methodist Church in 1812 he was appointed as one of the trustees of that church. He carried on a very active practice in the rural sections of Rutherford County for many years. Since he studied medicine in Philadelphia, it is presumed that he attended the University of Pennsylvania. He died on September 22, 1850, and was buried in a cemetery near the village of Salem.

Probably the most remarkable of the earliest practitioners to come to this area was Dr. Wilson Yandell. He was born December 17, 1774, in Mecklenburg County, North Carolina, and died October 1, 1827, near Murfreesboro. No definite record indicating when he came to this county was found. However, he left North Carolina at the age of nineteen years and came to the eastern part of Tennessee to attend a literary school conducted by a Dr. Doak. After spending some time on classical subjects, he studied medicine by himself for nine years, with probably some supervision from other physicians, before undertaking to practice. As the University of Maryland conferred an honorary medical degree on him without his having taken any lectures there, or in any other medical college, he must have been a man of unusual personality and intellectual ability. Several physicians who practiced in Rutherford County, or other parts of Tennessee, were trained by him. Three of his sons, Lunsford P., William M. and David, studied medicine under his guidance. One of his biographers stated that he was "neither a calomel, lancet, nor opium doctor." This characterization sets him apart as a broad minded individual and one capable of thinking for himself.

About 1800 Dr. William R. Rucker came to Tennessee as a small boy from Virginia. He studied medicine with Dr. Wilson Yandell soon after 1812 in Sumner County, then he spent some time as assistant surgeon under General Andrew Jackson in the war with the Indians. In 1815, he went to the University of Pennsylvania, from which he received his medical degree in 1817. When the First Methodist Church was organized in Murfreesboro in 1821, he was listed as a charter member. He was also a trustee of Soule Female College. Therefore, he must have settled in Murfreesboro immediately after receiving his medical diploma. He died in August, 1861.

Frederick Edward Becton located in Rutherford County soon after graduating from the University of Maryland in 1823. He was born in Craven County, North Carolina, on October 7, 1801. In 1819 he began the study of medicine in Transylvania University and later transferred to the University of Maryland. Apparently he was a very intelligent man and quite skilled in his profession. After marrying Eliza Yandell, the daughter of Dr. Wilson Yandell, he moved to Murfreesboro where he practiced until he went to Mississippi. His health began to fail and he returned to Murfreesboro after a few months and died with pulmonary tuberculosis on June 30, 1837.

Another early physician to settle in Murfreesboro was Dr. James Maney. He was born on February 9, 1790, in Hertford County, North Carolina. After finishing his medical studies in the University of Pennsylvania about 1825, he migrated to Rutherford County and began the practice of medicine. Evidently, he was a progressive and public spirited man, because he was selected as one of the trustees of Soule Female College. He acquired large tracts of land in Mississippi and West Tennessee, and spent considerable time in the management of those interests.

Another very interesting early physician was John Robertson Wilson, who was born in South Carolina, April 4, 1799, and came to Rutherford County with his father, William Wilson, and settled near Milton. He was a good student and attended, in Sumner County, a classical school taught by Samuel P. Black, whose daughter, Eliza

Pitts, he later married. While in Sumner County he studied medicine with Dr. Wilson Yandell, and afterwards attended medical lectures at Transylvania University. He began the practice of medicine in McMinnville, where he was very successful financially, and was able soon to resume his study in Transylvania, and to receive his diploma in medicine in 1824. On his return immediately after, he located at Murfreesboro and formed a partnership with Dr. James Maney. Later he moved to Jefferson at the forks of Stone's River, bought a farm on Stewarts Creek, and practiced medicine in that vicinity until he moved to Mississippi. He returned after a short time from Mississippi and located near Nashville, Davidson County, where he died August 8, 1854.

To give a glimpse of the methods of practice of the time by the early physicians in Rutherford County, a transcript from the "Day Book" of this versatile man is quoted:

"Nov. 15, 1831. Chas. Dement, Dr. (1)

Nocturnal visit, venesection and medicine for negro boy, and staying all night_____$4.00
16th visit, day and night venesection various medicines, etc. Levi_____$4.00
17th, Chas. Dement, Dr.—To visits various medicines, costly-attendance day and night and medical services— Levi_____$5.00
18th, Chas. Dement, Dr.—To visit—attendance day and night and various medicines—Levi_____$4.00
To *puke* for Emeline_____ .25
19th, Chas. Dement Dr.—Visiting Levi day and night_____$4.00
20th, Chas. Dement Dr.—Visit and staying all night_____$3.00
21st, Chas. Dement Dr.—Visit and staying all night and medicines_____$2.00
22nd, Chas. Dement Dr.—To visit and pills for Levi_____$2.00
23rd, Chas. Dement Dr.—To visit and morphia_____$2.00
24th, Chas. Dement Dr.—To visit and operation of Gastrotomy on negro boy, Levi in case of Ileus_____$5.00."

In an excerpt from a letter written by Dr. Thos. C. Black, January 5, 1853, to his brother-in-law, Dr. Wilson, the operation mentioned in the "Day Book" is reported in some detail. "My recollection is that it was a case of Ileus attended with Intussusception, in which all remedies usually tried, embracing bleeding general and local, blistering, and all the purgatives followed by the anodyne treatment failed to relieve, and an operation of Gastrotomy was performed, the intussuscepted portion of the bowel found and pulled

1. I am indebted to Dr. Owen H. Wilson, a leading pediatrician of Nashville, Tennessee, and a grandson of John R. Wilson, for this transcript.

out, breaking up pretty firm Peritoneal adhesions which had taken place between the upper and lower portions of the bowel. The Alvine evacuations immediately followed and the patient recovered speedily." At the same time, Dr. Black, who practiced for a short time with Dr. Wilson, reported several operations of an emergency nature that had been performed by this pioneer surgeon in Rutherford County with very favorable results.

A very prominent early physician to locate in Rutherford County was Dr. Lunsford Pitts Yandell. He was born in Sumner County, on July 4, 1805. When a child he came to Rutherford County with his father, Dr. Wilson Yandell, and received his fundamental literary education at Bradley Academy in Murfreesboro. After studying medicine in the office of his father, he attended the medical school of Transylvania University, and later transferred to the University of Maryland, where he received his medical degree in 1825. In 1826 he opened an office in Murfreesboro, and practiced there until 1831 when he moved to Nashville. Soon thereafter he went as Professor of Medicine to Transylvania University. In 1837 he left Transylvania and went to Louisville, Kentucky, where he helped to organize the Louisville Medical Institute. This organization later merged with the University of Louisville and he went with the combined institution as Professor of Materia Medica. In 1859 he accepted a professorship in a medical school organized in Memphis. When the War Between the States broke out he joined the Medical Corps of the Confederacy. He married Susan Juliet Wendel, of Murfreesboro. This man contributed much to the development of medical teaching and organization. He was a prolific writer on medical and scientific subjects. He died on February 4, 1878, in Louisville, Kentucky.

Doubtless, Rutherford County, as every section of the state, was subjected in its early years to a great deal of quackery by various uneducated, irregular, and unprincipled individuals, who masked their ignorance under such titles as 'Herb Doctors', 'Indian Doctors', 'Cancer Doctors', 'Doctors by Nature', and the like. Anyway, according to Professor Philip M. Hamer, there is evidence that there was a meeting of leaders of the regular medical profession in Murfreesboro a few months prior to 1830 to consider a course of action to get some relief from the undersirable state of medical practice, and that it was decided to seek an act of incorporation of a medical organization from the state legislature. On January 5, 1830, a bill, under the title "An Act to incorporate a medical society in the state of Tennessee" became a law. This act made the following provisions:

(1) That "a sufficient number of learned and intelligent practicing physicians" who with their successors were to constitute until

1860 the Medical Society of Tennessee was to be appointed; (2) that this organization was empowered to elect officers and determine their duties, to have a common seal, to sue and be sued, to elect other practitioners to membership and expel members for misconduct, to enact laws and regulations for its own government, to levy fines and penalties, to fix the time and place of meeting, to elect a board of censors with power to examine applicants and issue licenses to practice medicine and surgery in Tennessee.

Therefore, pursuant to the provisions of the act of incorporation, a meeting was held in Nashville on May 3-4, 1830, and the organization of the Medical Society of Tennessee was completed. The charter members appointed from Rutherford County were James Maney, William R. Rucker, Lunsford P. Yandell, Frederick E. Becton, and Samuel Watkins. Lunsford P. Yandell was elected corresponding secretary.

The records of the state society indicate that the following members from Rutherford County were elected during 1830: L. Ezell, John C. Gooch, William D. Gowen, Alfred Hartwell, Henry Holmes, P. H. Mitchell, Thomas R. Read, George Thompson, William S. Thompson, H. H. Tredway, John R. Wilson and William M. Yandell.

At the meeting in 1831 Dr. Frederick E. Becton read an essay on the "Medical Topography of Rutherford County." In this paper he emphasized the importance of the influence of climate and locality on the incidence and course of diseases. This belief seems to have been quite general with physicians of that period. However, Lunsford P. Yandell, who was a brother-in-law of Becton, disagreed rather pointedly with ideas expressed in the paper in his discussion. A heated argument ensued between the two brothers-in-law, and some unpleasantness was manifested. Geo. D. Crosthwait and J. C. Welborn from Rutherford County, were admitted to membership during that year.

In the History of Tennessee published by Goodspeed Publishing Company in 1886 the names of J. King and Patrick D. Neilson are given as distinguished early practitioners in Murfreesboro, along with those of William R. Rucker, James Maney, Henry Holmes, and Lunsford P. Yandell. No record of their having been members of the state medical society was found. Dr. Thos. C. Black, who practiced many years near the communities of Jefferson and Walter Hill, joined the state organization in 1831 from McMinnville, Warren County, and moved to Rutherford County in 1833.

In 1832 John W. Richardson, who became a very prominent doctor in the county, was granted membership in the state organization. He was born in Charlotte County, Virginia, on November 23,

1809, and came to Old Jefferson with his parents while a child. It seems that he received his medical degree from Transylvania University in 1833. For many years he took an active part in political affairs in the county and served two terms in the senate and four terms in the house of representatives of the state legislature. At one time he was offered the nomination to represent this district in the U. S. House of Representatives, but he declined to accept the honor. Later his son, James D. Richardson, was elected to Congress from the Murfreesboro district and served for twenty years. While in the state legislature Dr. Richardson was very active, although unsuccessfully, in his efforts to suppress quackery by legislation. He died on November 23, 1872, after a life of service to his people and the profession of medicine.

About 1835, along with John S. Taylor, Benjamin W. Avent, joined the Medical Society of Tennessee. He was born in Petersburg, Virginia, on September 12, 1813, and came to Rutherford County with his father's family in 1830. He studied medicine at the University of Pennsylvania and later at Transylvania University from which he graduated in 1834. Immediately after his graduation he opened an office in Murfreesboro, where he practiced until the outbreak of the War Between the States. For sometime he served as a member of the board of censors from middle Tennessee, and was elected vice president in 1851 and in 1857. At the meeting in 1861 he was elected president, but because of the War Between the States he did not preside over the society the following year. During the war he was a surgeon in the Confederate Army. In 1866 he moved to Memphis, where he was appointed Professor of Surgery in the Memphis Medical College. In 1878 he died there from yellow fever.

The records of the state society show that S. R. Gooch, J. M. Watson, and James E. Wendel, were registered in 1840 as members from Rutherford County. Dr. Watson was admitted to membership in 1830 while he was practicing in Williamson County. Apparently he moved to Murfreesboro some time between 1830 and 1840, and opened an office with Jas. E. Wendel. He was born in Rockingham County, North Carolina, on November 20, 1796, and came with his mother to Williamson County. After studying medicine with a private tutor, Dr. Hausack, of New York, he attended the College of Physicians and Surgeons of that city, and received his medical degree therefrom probably before he was twenty-one years of age. He entered immediately upon a very successful practice. However, he formed the habit of drinking to excess and reached the depths of drunkenness. After a time he suddenly announced that he was going to preach the gospel. Thereafter, he became a prominent minister in the Primitive Baptist denomination and helped to organize several churches of that faith in Murfreesboro and Rutherford County. In the meantime, he had not neglected his profession of medicine. His skill as a physician and surgeon became widely known. Finally, when the University of Nashville was organized in 1850, he was elected Professor of Obstetrics and the Diseases of Women and Children. He died in Nashville on September 19, 1866.

After a time interest in the state society began definitely to wane. The few faithful members were thrashing about to create more interest in organized medicine. Lunsford P. Yandell, who had been elected an honorary member in 1832, came frequently from his work in Kentucky to help in the cause. At the meeting in 1841 he, when he delivered the annual oration, said that one of the objects of the constitution of the Medical Society of Tennessee when it was organized in 1830, "was the suppression of quackery" and that "of those assembled on that occasion" many had "long since withdrawn from the Society, in despair of its ever being able, with its present powers, to accomplish this great work." The act of incorporation did not require, unfortunately, that no one could practice in the state without a license from one of the society's boards of censors. Therefore, this omission left a large hole through which charlatans could enter to practice unmolested. Nevertheless, the doctors in Rutherford County apparently lined up well. In 1843, J. H. Charlton, A. W. Nelson and R. S. Wendel joined. Then John W. Richardson was elected president in 1849, and, likely through his influence, the succeeding three annual meetings were held in Murfreesboro. Probably, as a result of his stimulating leadership, a large number of the local practitioners became members, as follows: 1850, J. J. Abernathy, G. M. Alsup, J. B. Armstrong, G. W. Burton, D. H. Johnson, S. W. Knight, P. D. McCulloch, W. A. Smith, D. V. Young and D. H. Woods; 1851, Samuel D. Robison and E. D. Wheeler; 1852, Medicus Ransom; 1857, S. M. Watson; 1869, John Baird and Jas. B. Murfree; and 1861, H. H. Clayton.

When war was declared several of the physicians from this area enlisted and served in the capacities as follows: B. W. Avent, surgeon; H. H. Clayton, captain and surgeon; John Y. Dykes, surgeon and lieutenant; Thomas J. Elam, surgeon; J. W. Gowen, surgeon Robert B. Harris, surgeon; William H. McCord, surgeon; Robert S. Wendel, surgeon; William Whitson, surgeon; Jas. B. Murfree, surgeon; John Patterson, surgeon; Samuel P. Black, asst. surgeon; H. Joseph Warmuth, asst. surgeon; Bartley N. White, and Robert N. Knox served as sergeant and private, respectively, and studied medicine after the war.

The state society in its despairing efforts to regulate the practice of medicine began to encourage the organization of local societies. In Rutherford there was apparently an attempt made to organize a county society as early as 1848. This is indicated by Professor Philip M. Hamer in a biographical sketch of J. J. Abernathy when he says: "He was an active supporter of organized medicine. He was elected president of the Rutherford County Medical Society in 1848, of Franklin County Medical Society in 1876, and of the Medical Society of the State of Tennessee in 1876."[1] Abernathy came to this county about 1842, and moved to Franklin County in 1856. Anyway, this effort likely did not stick. The preponderance of evidence is that this society, as it is known today, was organized on June 1, 1852, with John W. Richardson, president; James E. Wendel, vice president; E. D. Wheeler,[2] recording secretary; S. B. Robison, corresponding secretary; B. W. Avent, treasurer. Other charter members were: J. J. Abernathy, W. T. Baskette, B. H. Bilbro, Thomas C. Black, G. W. Burk, H. H. Clayton, S. W. Knight, W. C. Martin, R. J. Powell. It seems to have had rather regular annual meetings except during the space from 1859 to 1867.

In addition to the early physicians mentioned in different connections previously, the following men, who lived and took active parts in the practice and organization of the profession within the county, are recorded from other biographical sources: J. S. Allen, T. J. Bennett, W. C. Bilbro, R. C. Bogle, M. H. Bonner, J. N. Bridges, J. F. Byrn, J. W. Cartwright, J. H. Chadwick, W. C. Chadwick, W. C. Cook, S. M. Crosthwait, Geo. W. Crosthwait, James W. Davis, J. H. Dickson, J. F. Dismukes, S. S. Duggan, S. B. Duggan, V. K. Earthman, W. J. Engles, J. A. Ewing, E. C. Freas, William Freeman, John J. Garrett, A. N. Gordon, B. B. Gracey, Tid Gray, S. C. Grigg, Joseph D. Hall, J. T. Harris, R. B. Haynes, J. B. Hicks, E. M. Holmes, W. Hoover, D. C. Huff, E. O. Jenkins, E. H. Jones, J. C. Kelton, Robt. F. Keys, L. M. Knight, J. S. Lowry, J. P. Lyon, William H. Lytle, J. E. Manson, J. R. Moon, A. P. McCullough, H. L. McGhee, A. E. McKnight, Joe McLean, S. D. Miller, James B. Murfree, Jr., M. B. Murfree, Sr., M. E. Neeley, W. M. Orr, Geo. W. Overall, J. C. Overall, B. L. Owsley, Rufus Pitts, J. J. Poplin, R. W. Read, W. D. Robison, W. T. Robison, J. F. Rucker, J. J. Rucker, R. Elwood Sanders, T. Sedgewick,[3] E. A. Spear, James A. Spear, J. T. Summers, Robt. Turner, B. N. White, Jr., J. F. White, H. Yeargin, and W. E. Youree. Some of this group were much later

---

1. The Centennial History of the Tennessee State Medical Association, 1830–1930, 136.

2. This physician also had a degree in dentistry. After a time he forsook the practice of medicine and devoted his full time to the practice of dentistry. He was noted for his skill in the use of gold in the restoration of teeth.

3. There is considerable doubt about the given name of this physician who practiced in the community of Midland many years ago.

than others. Naturally, some of the physicians participated in general political affairs. As already stated, John W. Richardson, served terms in both houses of the general assembly. George D. Crosthwait served as state representative and as chancery clerk for several years. J. J. Rucker and M. E. Neeley represented the county in the state house of representatives.

Until 1902 the local medical societies were not connected officially with the state society. During that year the constitution and the name of the Medical Society of the State of Tennessee were changed. The new constitution set up a plan whereby local societies would become components of the state organization and charters granted to them. Therefore, the Rutherford County Medical Society, along with the other local societies in existence at that time, received its charter from the new Tennessee Medical Association in 1902, and from then on its members automatically became members of the state association. After a few years physicians from adjoining counties, where there were no medical organizations, began to apply for membership and were admitted. Several doctors from Cannon County, especially, became very active members.

After 1920 a disturbance arose in the society over the alleged unethical conduct of certain of its members. The controversy which ensued raged for some time without any apparent hope of settlement. Finally, on June 21, 1926, a group of the members from Rutherford and Cannon counties met and organized The Stone's River Academy of Medicine "for the purpose of organizing a society for the presentation and discussion of matters of scientific interest and of affairs relating to the medical profession." This organization was not affiliated with the state association. However, it met once each month, gave scientific programs, and carried on the regular business of the profession. In the by-laws barriers were set up to prevent the induction of undesirable members.

In the meantime the Rutherford County Medical Society was meeting only once a year to elect officers. On the ground that the county society was operating in conflict with the letter and spirit of the constitution and by-laws of the Tennessee Medical Association, a majority of the members asked the house of delegates, through the councilor having jurisdiction, time after time to revoke the existing charter and grant one to the group known as the Stone's River Academy of Medicine. Finally, after the house of delegates was convinced that the controversy with the local members of the profession could not be satisfactorily adjusted, it revoked the old charter and granted one on August 7, 1932, to the Rutherford County and Stone's River Academy of Medicine.

As of July 1, 1946, the Rutherford County and Stone's River Academy of Medicine was composed of the following members, with their addresses:

J. F. Adams, M. D., Woodbury, Tennessee
Carl Adams, M. D., Woodbury, Tennessee
W. Stanley Barham, M. D., Murfreesboro, Tennessee
J. B. Black, M. D., Murfreesboro, Tennessee
James T. Boykin, M. D., Murfreesboro, Tennessee
V. S. Campbell, M. D., Murfreesboro, Tennessee
John Cason, M. D., Murfreesboro, Tennessee
Howard A. Farrar, M. D., Manchester, Tennessee
Gilbert Gordon, M. D., Murfreesboro, Tennessee
J. R. Gott, M. D., Murfreesboro, Tennessee
H. E. Handley, M. D., White Plains, New York
M. D. Ingram, M. D., Woodbury, Tennessee
A. J. Jamison, M. D., Murfreesboro, Tennessee
J. K. Kaufman, M. D., Murfreesboro, Tennessee
Lois M. Kennedy, M. D., Murfreesboro, Tennessee
B. W. Rawlins, M. D., Murfreesboro, Tennessee
J. A. Scott, M. D., Murfreesboro, Tennessee
William White Shacklett, M. D., Palmer, Tennessee
J. M. Shipp, M. D., Smyrna, Tennessee
S. B. Smith, M. D., Overall, Tennessee
R. E. Strain, M. D., Murfreesboro, Tennessee
R. C. Van Hook, M. D., Auburntown, Tennessee
Bart N. White III, M. D., Murfreesboro, Tennessee
S. L. Wiles, M. D., Murfreesboro, Tennessee

When the state legislature in 1889 passed a law establishing a state board of medical examiners, Gov. Robert L. Taylor appointed Dr. Jas. B. Murfree of Murfreesboro as president of the board. He served in that capacity until 1893. This physician, who was a leader in his profession and in civic and religious affairs, was born in Murfreesboro on Sept. 16, 1835. In March, 1859, he received his degree of Doctor of Medicine from Jefferson Medical College in Philadelphia and immediately began to practice his profession in Murfreesboro. At the close of the War Between the States, during most of which he served as surgeon in the Confederate Army, he returned to resume his practice. For more than one term he was mayor of Murfreesboro and was president of the Medical Society of the State of Tennessee during 1875.

After his resignation from the State Board of Medical Examiners, Dr. Murfree studied surgery in New York and was appointed Professor of Surgery in the Department of Medicine of the University of the South at Sewanee, Tennessee. He died on April 24, 1912.

Two of his sons, Jas. B. Jr., and Matt B. studied medicine and practiced in Murfreesboro for many years.

Around 1897 much excitement in and near Eagleville was provoked by Dr. C. B. Heimark. This physician began to practice in that community and, after a few months, was accused of poisoning some of his patients and grave robbing. He was arrested and brought into court in the early part of 1898 and was prosecuted on four charges. "Poisoning," "Unlawful removal of bodies," "Removal of dead body from grave," and "Grave robbing." He submitted to the "Unlawful removal of bodies" and "Removal of a dead body from grave", was fined one hundred and fifty dollars, and was sentenced to six months in the county jail in each instance. After paying the fines and serving the sentences he left the county.

When World War I was declared the following physicians from Rutherford County were accepted for duty and served as medical officers: S. B. Duggan, V. K. Earthman, A. E. Goodloe, Matt B. Murfree, Sr., W. T. Robison, A. D. Sharp, and Bart N. White, Jr.

Also, in World War II several young men from this county were selected as medical officers in the armed forces as follows: Robt. Miles, Matt B. Murfree, Jr., Gilbert Gordon, E. P. Odom, W. W. Shacklett, Howard Smith, Jesse Waller, and Bart N. White, III. In addition to these, J. K. Kaufman and James T. Boykin were medical officers in World War II and moved into the county after their discharge from military service.

In time several men from Rutherford County studied medicine and located in other sections of the country to practice, such as Dr. J. M. King in Nashville, Dr. Joe E. King in New York, Dr. E. M. Sanders in Nashville, and Dr. Will Spain in New York.

This section of the state, as well as other parts, was visited by epidemic diseases early in its history. Cholera struck Tennessee in 1833. Murfreesboro suffered a severe epidemic of this disease from which Dr. Alfred Hartwell died in 1835. Yellow fever caused much alarm at intervals in west Tennessee. When one of the big epidemics of the "yellow jack" devastated Memphis during 1878, Dr. Geo. W. Overall, Dr. J. B. Hicks, and probably other physicians from this area, volunteered for duty to help the victims. Dr. Hicks died there from the disease. Although the Medical Society of the State of Tennessee as early as 1874 recommended to the state legislature that a state board of health be established in an effort to control communicable diseases this step was not taken until 1877. An act was passed by the general assembly in the early part of that year but no appropriation was made to pay the expenses of setting up a board of health. However, the five doctors provided for by the act organized the State Board of Health and undertook to do something about controlling the epidemic diseases. They set about to get boards of health established in the towns and cities within the state. Therefore, the Murfreesboro Board of Health was organized during 1877 with a membership as follows: Jas. B. Murfree, M. D., president; C. B. Huggins, Sr., secretary; H. H. Clayton, M. D., health officer; Medicus Ransom, M. D., Robt. S. Wendel, M. D., and J. B. Palmer.

In 1885 the general assembly passed a law creating county boards of health. The act provided that the county board of health was to be composed of the county judge, or chairman, the county court clerk, and the county health officer, or jail physician. Soon thereafter the Rutherford County Board of Health was formed with Jas. B. Murfree, M. D. jail physician, president; John Woods, chairman of the county court; and W. D. Robison, clerk of the county court.

The first report on the health conditions of the county was made by Dr. Jas. B. Murfree, president of the county board, to Dr. J. B. Lindsley, secretary of the State Board of Health in October, 1885. It was about an epidemic of typhoid fever in the family of John Majors, living in the fifth civil district on Fall Creek near the Wilson County line. In the report Dr. Murfree revealed that a rather neat epidemiological investigation was made of the epidemic. The nine members of the Majors household developed the disease during that summer and four of them died. Excerpts from the report are interesting in that they give an insight into the thoroughness of the investigation of the epidemic, the facilities available to the investigators, insanitary habits and methods with reference to excreta disposal at a rural home and the trend of medical thinking at that time. In discussing the premises of the home Dr. Murfree said: "The privy had not been used for months and was clean. The family had used the garden in place of the privy, and, as after a heavy rain, there might be some drainage from the garden towards the house, this might be considered unfavorable." Further he wrote: "The disease, I think, is attributed to an epidemic influence prevailing in the neighborhood at that time, coupled with a bad sanitary condition of the dwelling and its surroundings. The house in which the family resided is situated in a low flat place, destitute of any drainage, nearly encircled by a large grove of dense forest growth, while the yard thickly set with shrubbery, was covered with tall weeds and grass. At one corner of the house a barrel, half full of dirty water, had sat all the summer. Poultry in large numbers and great varieties, with pigs and dogs, infested the yard, sporting and feeding around and under the house." With reference to the possible source of the disease he added: "The drinking water was from a bored well, one hundred and thirty feet deep, which had been used

Rutherford County Health Department

Doctor James Brickell Murfree

by the family for the past thirteen years. A large family of colored people lived on the farm and used the same water with impunity. I do not think the water was the principal, or sole, cause of the disease. I would like very much for the water to have been analyzed." In a note commenting on the report Dr. J. B. Lindsley said: "A partial analysis of the water was made by Prof. Day, Chemical Laboratory, State Normal College, and found to be quite impure."

In answer to an inquiry from Dr. Murfree, Dr. J. B. Richmond, Baird's Mill, Wilson County, stated that he had treated about twenty-five cases of fever, suspicious of typhoid, with one death, along Fall Creek above the Majors home, during that summer and added: "As regards the Majors family, I am unable to say what could have been the origin of the disease. I presume it was impure water that was the exciting cause, filled with bacteria or microbes."

In order to diagnose definitely the disease involving the Majors family, Dr. B. B. Gracey, assisted by Drs. Geo. W. Crosthwait and Nat Gooch, performed an autopsy on John Majors and reported the findings to Dr. Murfree as follows: "As to the pathology of the disease, we found as I told you, in the post mortem on Mr. Majors, an inflammation of the mucous membrane lining the whole alimentary canal. The inflammation was of a higher grade, I think, in the lower part of the small intestine than in the large intestine, gradually diminishing as it extended upward. The stomach had patches of congestion but not so much as the bowels. We found one or two small ulcers in the lower part of the ilium." This report on the gross pathology of this case indicates very clearly that the man died from typhoid fever. Dr. Murfree gave as his diagnosis of the disease in the epidemic as "typhoid dysentery."

Since the state weather service was going to be discontinued, the State Board of Health, feeling that meteorological data were very valuable in elucidating questions affecting the public health, took over that service in 1885 and appointed voluntary observers in various counties. C. F. Vanderford served in that capacity for a number of years at Florence Station, Rutherford County. He gave reports on the prevalence of diseases in the locality as well as those containing meteorological data.

The first school health work in Rutherford County was apparently started by Miss Jeannette King, Director of Physical Education at the Middle Tennessee Normal College, in Murfreesboro. About 1912 she began, with the assistance of local physicians and dentists, a program of physical examinations with follow-up efforts for the correction of defects in the eight elementary grades of the Demonstration School of the College. Later, through her efforts, the

State Board of Health sent a representative to examine the pupils for intestinal parasites.

Shortly after the close of World War I Miss Maud Cloverdale came, as a public health nurse with the Murfreesboro Chapter of the American Red Cross, and, with the cooperation of the physicians and dentists on a voluntary basis, extended the school health program to many of the rural schools of the county.

Sometime after the beginning of 1920 Miss Maud Ferguson reported for duty to the local chapter as Red Cross public health nurse. She took an active part in promoting further the school health program. After she had been in the county for several months, she learned that the Commonwealth Fund of New York was looking for suitable counties in which to establish child health demonstrations and called the attention of S. B. Christy, Sr., chairman of the local Red Cross Chapter, to that fact. Mr. Christy made an application to the Commonwealth Fund for a demonstration in Rutherford County. After the surveys and other investigations, in which Mr. Christy and Miss Ferguson had important parts, the Commonwealth Fund, with the cooperation of the State Department of Public Health, opened the Child Health Demonstration of Rutherford County on January 1, 1924, with Dr. Harry S. Mustard as director. Under the authority of an act passed in 1921 by the general assembly of the state, enabling counties to establish health departments with full-time personnel and permitting towns and cities to form joint health departments with counties, Dr. Mustard was soon elected health officer of Rutherford and of Murfreesboro. Up to that time all health officers of the county and the city were physicians employed on a part-time basis.

The Child Health Demonstration operated for five years. During that time a program emphasizing child health was developed and its rough outline was as follows:

1. Collection of vital statistics,
2. Prenatal health service,
3. Infant and preschool health service,
4. School health service,
5. Communicable disease control,
6. Sanitation,
7. Laboratory service,
8. Health education.

On January 1, 1929, the Child Health Demonstration officially closed. In the meantime, it had metamorphosed into a county health department, supported largely by funds from the county, the city, and the state, with a full-time personnel consisting of a health officer, an assistant health officer, a supervisor of nurses, seven field public health nurses, two sanitation officers, and two clerks.

Since the health department had assumed obligations to provide field training to students in public health from Vanderbilt Schools of Medicine and Nursing, and the State Department of Public Health, the Commonwealth Fund, in order to facilitate those teaching activities, contributed a beautiful building for housing the Rutherford County Health Department. This building was opened on October 1, 1931.

In 1935 the state legislature passed an act re-organizing the county boards of health. This act provided that county boards of health would be composed of the county judge or chairman of the county court, the county superintendent of education, the county court clerk, the county health officer, two physicians selected from four nominees named by the local medical society, and one dentist selected from two nominees from the local dental organization. At the April term of the county court of that year the new county board of health was organized with the county judge, John D. Wiseman; the county court clerk, J. P. Leathers; the county health officer, J. B. Black, M. D.; the county superintendent of education, W. S. Donnell; W. T. Robison, M. D.; A. N. Gordon, M. D.; and C. C. Harris, D. D. S. This act also provided that counties might have a county physician, in addition to the health officer, who had previously performed the functions of a county physician. Therefore, S. B. Smith, M. D., was elected by the county court as county physician.

During the War Between the States hospitals were established in all of the churches, college buildings, and in some of the larger residences in Murfreesboro by the confederate and federal armies. Too, large homes, like the Hord residence on the Nashville turnpike, were used as bases for treating the wounded particularly during, and after, the Battle of Stone's River. Outside of these temporary hospitals and a few beds set up by individual physicians in connection with their offices, no record of an effort to establish a hospital in the county was noted until 1912. During the early part of that year a small hospital of eight or ten beds was opened in the Dixie Hotel building on College Street in Murfreesboro. Something like a stock company was organized. The doctors connected with the enterprise bought five shares of stock at ten dollars each and interested citizens subscribed enough to make an amount of one thousand dollars. However, it was an abortive effort as the institution was closed on Feb. 17, 1913.

It was not until the early part of 1925 that a movement to establish a hospital in Murfreesboro took definite form. Through the efforts of S. B. Christy, Sr., and other interested citizens, the Commonwealth Fund of New York agreed to erect one of its community hospitals in the city. On June 10, 1925, the board of directors for the proposed institution was organized, executive and building committees appointed, and arrangements made to purchase a lot for the building and to secure a charter. Plans went forward rather rapidly and the Rutherford Hospital with a capacity of fifty beds was opened in June, 1927.

The members of the board of directors named in the charter were Andrew L. Todd, John B. Randolph, J. P. Gordon, George A. Youree, T. R. Whitus, Mrs. Mary E. Marshall, Al D. McKnight, Hans Gebers, Mrs. Margaret B. Haynes, S. F. Houston, John E. Richardson, John M. Butler, R. L. McCulloch, Howard D. Henderson, and S. B. Christy, Sr. The executive committee elected from the board of directors was composed of S. B. Christy, Sr., chairman, J. M. Butler, Andrew L. Todd, Al D. McKnight, and S. F. Houston. The first superintendent was Miss Mary F. Petitte.

During 1938 a Veterans Hospital was located near Murfreesboro and its construction was completed in 1939. On January 1, 1940, this hospital was opened for occupancy with a capacity of 785 beds. Sam Jared, Jr., was the manager and Richard L. Harris, M. D., was chief medical officer. The regional office of the Veterans Administration of Tennessee was also domiciled in this plant. On January 15, 1946, the regional office of the Veterans Administration was moved to Nashville. The institution is now known as the Veterans Administration Hospital. Its capacity is now 1006 beds, with buildings under construction for further expansion.

CHAPTER VIII

Education in Rutherford County

THE PRE-CIVIL WAR PERIOD 1803-1860

The development of education in Tennessee during this period was relatively slow. Dr. Robert H. White in his book "Development of the Tennessee State Educational Organization, 1796-1929," says this condition was due to several causes; the Constitution of 1796 provided nothing for education of the people of Tennessee; lack of interest in education due in part to trouble with Indians; no interest on part of people or Legislature in laying taxes for support of education, for the idea of mass education at public expense was not yet developed; and because of an Act of 1815 providing that orphaned children be educated at public expense, there actually developed a feeling of hostility toward public education.

The early history of education in Tennessee is the story of the early colleges and academies, the latter being in the main private schools taught usually by ministers. Up to 1860 academies and seminaries flourished in Tennessee. These schools bore the brunt of the battle against illiteracy.

Rutherford County was typical of the state. An Act of Congress, April 18, 1806, resulted in the legislature of Tennessee passing an act establishing academies in all counties of the state. In this same year an act was passed providing " . . . that Joseph Dixon, John R. Bedford, John Thompson, Sr., William P. Anderson, and Robert Smith shall be and they are hereby constituted a body politic and corporate, to be known by the name of the Trustees of the Bradley Academy." This act also set up rules and regulations governing boards in operating the school.

PRIVATE SCHOOLS

Thus, we have in Bradley Academy the beginning of organized education in Rutherford County. This academy was supported in the main from tuition charges. Funds received from this source were augmented by gifts and donations, from authorized lotteries, and from the proceeds arising from the Congressional land grant of 1806. During the 1820's the legislature granted special permission to many schools, colleges and academies to raise money by lottery. In 1827 the Commissioners of Bradley Academy were authorized to plan a lottery to raise $5,000 for "erecting buildings or purchasing a library and philosophical apparatus for Bradley Academy." Apparently lotteries were greatly abused because an act in 1835 prohibited them.

Subsequent acts of the Legislature added members to the Board of Trustees and the names of the men added attest to the quality of Bradley Academy. Following are some of the names listed: Thomas Rucker, Joseph Herndon, Robert Bedford, Mark Mitchell, Frederick Barfield, Benjamin McCulloch, William E. Butler, James Maney, William Lytle, William Dickinson, Edmond Jones, David Dickson, William Yandell and Samuel Anderson.

Bradley Academy was well known throughout middle Tennessee. Samuel P. Black appears to have been an early headmaster. Dr. Robert Henderson, first pastor of the Presbyterian church, was also connected with the school for a time. Henderson came to Murfreesboro from Maury County where he had taught James K. Polk. Because of Dr. Henderson and because Bradley Academy was so highly esteemed, Polk entered the school. According to an unverified report John Bell also attended Bradley Academy.

On October 18, 1834, the Trustees of Bradley selected Benjamin Barlow as Superintendent and advertised as follows "Board near Bradley Academy from $18 to $24 per session. Parents must furnish school with wood."

In 1848 the Trustees of Union University were made Trustees of Bradley Academy and given permission to use the building and lot as long as the University remained in Murfreesboro.

In 1815 Jefferson Seminary of Learning was established. It was housed in the old courthouse. The following were named to the Board of Trustees and given permission to use the old court house for school purposes: John Coffee, Peter Legrand, Shelton Crosthwait, George Simpson, and Walter Kibble.

There are those who claim that Soule College was organized in 1825, but the school organized in this year was known as the "Female Academy." The first trustees of the Female Academy were F. N. W. Burton, Dr. W. R. Rucker, M. B. Murfree, and Dr. James Maney. This school was for girls exclusively, "these heretofore being mixed schools." Besides the ordinary branches taught there were in addition Rhetoric, Philosophy, Belles-lettres, Painting,

Needle-work, and Music. The teaching was done by the Misses Mary and Nancy Banks.

The Female County Academy was founded in 1829. One acre of ground was purchased in the north part of town for $100 and a two-story brick building of four rooms was erected. A suitable course of study was prepared, and the services of Miss Keyser were obtained. The school was soon in successful operation. The Reverend Baker, who became the husband of Miss Keyser, was employed as one of the teachers. After Mr. and Mrs. Baker retired from the institution Mr. and Mrs. G. T. Henderson conducted the school successfully, after whom Mr. and Mrs. Blackington took charge. In 1850 the school had grown to such proportion that an enlargement was found necessary, and one acre of land was purchased of William Lytle and added to the grounds on which additional buildings were erected. The first teachers in the Academy after the enlargement were Mr. and Mrs. Fellows.

Salem Male Academy was founded in 1837. John S. Russwurm, James M. King, Elias King, Benjamin Johnson, Benjamin C. Ransom, John Rawson, and William Ledbetter were named trustees.

Typical of the schools of this era was the "Murfreesborough" Female Seminary described in the *Central Monitor* for January 18, 1834 as follows:

"Mr. and Mrs. S. B. Bowles will open on the first Monday of January next in Murfreesborough a school for the instruction of young ladies in Reading, Writing, English Grammar, Arithmetic, Geography, with the use of maps and globes, History, Rhetoric, Logic Composition, Natural Philosophy, etc. To the above branches will be added Plain and Ornamental Sewing, Lace Work, Embroidery, Rug Work, Beadwork, Drawing, Painting on paper and velvet, with every other branch of education usually taught in Female Academies . . . a philosophical apparatus will be procured as soon as practicable and experimental philosophic lectures will be delivered on mechanics, hydrostatics, pneumatics, etc . . . the new brick building of David Wendell will be commodiously fitted up for the purpose. Trustees of the school are Charles Ready, Jonathan Currin, Charles Wiles, Henry D. Jamison, William F. Lytle, V. C. Cowan, and William Ledbetter."

Other schools operating during this period were: Midsylvania Female Academy, incorporated in 1834 and located five miles southwest of Murfreesboro, Stone's River Academy, incorporated in 1852; Tennessee Baptist Female Institute, with 83 students in 1854; Eaton's College for Women opened in 1853 in building later known as the Perkins' Home; Union Hill Academy, incorporated in 1856; Milton Male and Female Seminary, incorporated in 1858.

An interesting school advertised in the Murfreesboro *Weekly Times* on September 19, 1840:

> "Madame Blaique will open a dancing school if enough pupils can be procured. Hornpipe, Highland Fling, Gahotte, Minuet, Gallopode, etc. will be taught. Twenty lessons $10, payable at end of session. Subscription lists open at Major Bostrick's Hotel."

In 1850, Census reports showed 629 enrolled in colleges, academies, and private schools of the county. The annual income from these schools was reported as $7,896.

PUBLIC SCHOOLS

During this period public education had hardly made a beginning but the people of Rutherford County were making an effort to educate the children. Common schools were without adequate funds and many attempts were being made to support the state and its business without resorting to taxation.

The scholastic population of Rutherford County in 1839 was 4440 and the total amount of money apportioned to the twenty-five districts was $2,766.79. In 1858 the scholastic population was 5195, while the amount of money distributed was $3,896.25, every district receiving funds and operating schools. In 1859 seventy-five cents was received from the state for each scholar in the county.

The United State Census for 1840 gives interesting facts concerning education in Rutherford County. There were no universities or colleges, but five academies and grammar schools, enrolling 244 pupils. There were twenty-four primary and common schools with 633 enrolled, 253 of whom were sent to school at public charge. Illiteracy was high, there being 1805 white people over 20 years of age who could neither read nor write. The U. S. Census for 1850 showed that there were 51 public schools, with 53 teachers and 1673 pupils. A common school district for about ten families was formed in Rutherford and Cannon Counties in 1856. The commissioner elected got pro rata share of all funds from each county.

One of the best friends of education in Rutherford County during this period was not a school man. He was William Ledbetter who proposed to the Constitutional Convention of 1834 that "A select committee be appointed to inquire into the question of the amount of the common school fund belonging to the State, of what said fund consisted, how invested, and to report the best method of insuring same against diminution, and what constitutional provision was necessary to guarantee the perpetuation of this fund for the use of the common schools forever." Mr. Ledbetter was placed on this committee and Section 10 of Article XI of the Constitution of 1835 was the result of the work done by the committee. Mr. Ledbetter further served the cause of education as chairman of the Educational Committee of the Senate and was responsible for the Act of 1836 which provided for the appointment of a State Board of Common School Commissioners.

UNION UNIVERSITY

After several vain attempts to establish a school of high grade in different parts of Tennessee for the advancement of their denomination and the education of their ministry, the Baptists of the state, working through the Baptist General Association of Tennessee and the Tennessee Baptist Educational Society and aided by the Baptists of North Alabama and Mississippi, founded Union University, at Murfreesboro. Rev. Joseph H. Eaton, president of the University from its opening in 1848, until his death in 1859, had the greatest share in its founding and in its subsequent success. Dr. Eaton was one of the most distinguished educators in the history of Tennessee. That the people of Murfreesboro appreciated his character and ability is shown by the fact that they raised for him a special endowment of $10,000. The following characterization of Dr. Eaton is taken from Cathcart's Baptist Encyclopedia:

Dr. Eaton was a man of great earnestness, laboring with an untiring zeal that nothing could thwart. As an educator he had but few equals, being distinguished for his power of imparting instruction, and stimulating a love of knowledge; for a thorough control over students, shown in discipline and in influence upon their characters; and for his ability to win the affection of his pupils. As a preacher Dr. Eaton was earnest and impressive, of impassioned utterance and rapid delivery. His power to fix the attention and impress his thoughts upon his hearers has seldom been equaled. He won the enthusiastic devotion of those who knew him, of all classes and grades of society. His fellow-ministers, professors, the churches to which he preached, his many students, and his servants all loved him as few men are loved. Handsome in person, gracious in presence, genial in manners, and winning in conversation, he was eminent in the qualities which make men beloved in the home circle, as well as by the public.

Union University was chartered in 1842, but did not open its doors until January, 1848. It began operations upon the faith of a pledged endowment fund of $55,000. This fund, or most of it, had been subscribed on the scholarship plan. Accordingly, in 1852 by this means the income from tuition fees was reduced nearly 50 per cent. Nevertheless, the University throve greatly. Beginning with an attendance of 50 or 60, it reached in one year before the war an attendance of 330. It graduated during this anti-bellum period 173 students, about 38 of whom were ministers of the gospel. A number of them went as missionaries to foreign fields. Though not professing to vie with the great theological seminaries, Union University supported a chair of theology. In order to encourage young men to study for the ministry, it charged them no tuition fees, whatever might be their denomination. Among those who were members of the faculty at this time were Professors Paul W. Dodson (Mathematics), J. M. Pendleton (Theology), George W. Jarman and William Shelton.

Union University was brought low by the Civil War. From May, 1861, to January, 1868, operation ceased. Endowment was lost, apparatus and library were scattered or destroyed, and buildings dismantled. In addition to these problems, there were unpaid debts hanging over the University. On the 7th of July, 1868, it owed $24,155.53. However, things soon improved. Funds to pay the greater part of the debt were raised and the school experienced a marvelous revival. In 1869 the property was transferred to the Tennessee Baptist Educational Society, to be held in trust for educational purposes, under and by the direction of the trustees of the University. The first President and faculty after the war were: Rev. Duncan Selph, A.M., President; George W. Jarman, A.M., Professor of Ancient Languages; T. T. Eaton, A.M. (son of the first president), Professor of Mathematics; and J. M. Phillips, Principal of the Preparatory Department. In January, 1871 Dr. Selph resigned and Rev. Charles Manly, D.D., was chosen in his place. For the three years ending 1871-2 the attendance was 150, 181, and 161 respectively. The "school system" prevailed, there being seven schools: Moral Philosophy, English, Latin, Greek, Mathematics, Natural Science, and Modern Languages. The M. A. Degree was granted on completion of seven, B.A. of six, and B.P. of five years in the schools.

On October, 1873, Union University closed its doors, the immediate occasion being the prevalence of cholera in Murfreesboro and the great financial panic of 1873. Deeper down, the reason was to be found in the hope of the Baptists of Tennessee that a change of location might be utilized to secure an endowment.

In October, 1873, the General Association of Middle Tennessee and North Alabama decided to establish a central university for the Baptists of the Southwest. The institution was located at Jackson, Tennessee, and has operated there continuously since its establishment.

SOULE COLLEGE

The earliest college to be established in Rutherford County was Soule College. It was not only a college in name, but also in reality, as from one to two years of college work was given at the institution throughout its existence. Recent evaluations of the work of Soule graduates have allowed two years college credit after the satisfactory completion of one year in residence.

Soule College had its inception in a meeting of "male members of the Methodist Church in Murfreesboro on July 14, 1851" which meeting was called by the Reverend Thomas Madden, pastor of the Methodist church. The college was named for Joshua Soule. He was born in Maine and became a bishop in the Methodist church. He took part in the disruption of the M.E. church and retained his post in its Southern branch, living in Nashville.

The Board of Trustees, composed of T. W. Randle, L. H. Carney, B. W. Avent, W. F. Lytle, Joseph Watkins, William Spence, Simeon B. Christy, John Leiper and D. D. Wendel, met on August 9, 1851, and elected the Reverend J. R. Finley, D.D., as President for a two year term with the understanding that, "if he had not realized for himself one thousand dollars a year, after paying his assistants a reasonable price for their services, the committee pledged themselves to make up the deficiency." Dr. Finley agreed to these terms and the opening was set for the first Monday in September, 1851, in the old Female Academy.

The corner stone of the "new and commodious college edifice will be laid by the Fraternity of Masons on Saturday, the 3rd of July" so stated the minutes of the Board of Trustees. The building was occupied in November, 1853.

In the meantime Dr. Finley had resigned the presidency and had been succeeded by S. D. Baldwin, pastor of the Methodist Church of Murfreesboro. Dr. Baldwin became quite a noted lecturer and writer, being the author of "Armageddon: or the Overthrow of Romanism and Monarchy."

Dr. Baldwin took over the school during its second year, and according to the report of the visiting committee, appointed by the

Annual Conference, the year was highly successful. The following statement is from the report of the committee:

The great desire and effort of the Trustees and friends of this institution have been, from the beginning, to build up an institution where a thorough education of the mind and heart might be obtained, without that superficial, gaudy show, to the neglect of the impartation of sound and useful knowledge, and the training of the mind to a proper mode of thinking and reasoning, which is but too characteristic of female schools; and thus far, we are happy to say, they have succeeded well; and we are persuaded that under the vigilant supervision of the present able and efficient faculty 'Soule Female College' will do honor to its name. And we hereby notify those who wish their daughters to obtain simply the art of talking nonsense, and showing off in superficial tinsel, they had better not send them to Murfreesboro; for here they will be compelled to study, or be exposed at the critical moment.

In October, 1856, Mr. C. W. Callender was elected president of the college. He was the first school man to fill the position. He served the school for two years. Following Mr. Callender as presidents were George E. Naff, 1858-1862; J. R. Plummer, 1866-1868; D. D. Moore, 1868-1874; J. B. West, 1874-1878; John R. Thompson, 1879-1889; Virginia O. Wardlaw, 1892-1905; Martha Hopkins, 1906-1917.

The administration of Miss Wardlaw was the most interesting, the most profitable in many respects, but the strangest in the history of the school. This was a period of mysterious happenings, of queer incidents, and of gossip. It is reported that, immediately after the arrival of Mrs. C. B. W. Martin (Miss Wardlaw's sister) at the school, things became unsettled. The girls were changed from room to room without reason. The sisters were continually roaming about the building. One former student remembers waking one night and seeing all three sisters in her room, mumbling around the stove. Next morning it was explained by one of the teachers that they had smelled something burning. This same person was invited to spend the night with Miss Warlaw on one occasion. All night Miss Wardlaw would sigh and say, "My God! My God! My Sister!"

Another story has it that the sisters, dressed in black and heavily veiled, would call a carriage, always at night, and drive to the cemetery where they would hover around a grave and talk. No colored driver would ever answer these calls for a carriage.

Whether all the stories told about the Wardlaws were fact or fiction, it is true that most people in Murfreesboro looked upon them as being very queer, but very brilliant and interesting.

In the beginning of her administration, Miss Wardlaw was looked upon as an educated, cultured woman and impressed all those who knew her with her progressive ideas of education. The following advertisement is typical:

Higher Education for Women. Full College Course. Frequent stereopticon illustrations on subjects studied. French, German, and Italian spoken and taught. Education, Art, Dress Making, Bookkeeping, Typewriting, Commercial Law. Lectures by Vanderbilt Professors.

In 1905, the following report was made to the U. S. Commissioner of Education: instructors 14; students, primary 20, preparatory 45, and college 160; value of library $900; value of science laboratory $500; value of buildings and grounds $15,000.

The first graduating class finished the course in 1854. The exact date of the organization of an alumni association is not know, but reference is made to such an organization as early as 1873. The association was kept intact until the closing of the school in 1916.

Throughout the history of the school, the pupils were supervised closely in regard to dress and in regard to all matters of moral or religious nature. During the administration of Miss Hopkins, the girls were required to wear the school uniform. The college requested parents to keep their daughters' expensive jewelry at home, to supply dresses of pretty but not costly material, and to have their underwear made with neat plainness. On no occasion were low necks and short sleeves permitted. Every pupil had to be provided with overshoes and an umbrella.

Mrs. Hyde and Miss Hopkins took over Soule College when it was at the point of being closed and the property sold for business lots. They made a fine effort to restore the school to its former prominence and for a time succeeded. However, the competition of other private schools, and the rapid growth of public schools proved too great for them to cope with. In February, 1917, they sold the property to the City of Murfreesboro. A public high school was built on the property the following year.

EDUCATION IN RUTHERFORD COUNTY
1861-1909

In 1867 a progressive educational measure was enacted, providing for a State Superintendent of Common Schools, for County Superintendents, for a tax levy upon both property and polls for the support of the Common School System. This law was passed by the "Carpetbag" legislature, and was the first educational measure in Tennessee to provide for the office of County Superintendent of Schools.

In 1873 another important school law was passed. It was substantially a reenactment of the Act of 1867, charging state and county officials with the administration and the supervision of the Public School System, and making a direct levy upon the property of the state for the support of the public schools.

PUBLIC SCHOOLS

Following the passage of these two acts, public schools began to take form. However, private schools continued to operate and were often combined with public schools, teaching public school pupils upon agreement made with public officials.

The early public schools were beset by many difficulties. Superintendent W. H. Wallace sized up the situation in Rutherford County in these words:

> Mountains of prejudice have been overcome, and the way in a great measure prepared for a hearty cooperation of all the districts with the friends of public schools. Great difficulty has been experienced in getting active working directors to take hold of the school interests. Nearly all of the teachers of this county have received a part of their salary from the people. The total amount paid in this manner is not stated. The enrollment and attendance, as usual, is much larger in the colored than in the white schools. The want of schoolhouses for the colored schools has delayed their opening, although three or four new houses were built during the year. Schools of some kind have been established in every district in the county. An average of three schools to the district was expected to be in operation this fall.

In 1869 there were 76 white schools and 36 colored schools employing a total of 112 teachers. Thirty-six hundred pupils were enrolled and the average attendance was 3100. Total appropriation for these schools was $28,624.13. The following subjects were taught: Alphabet, Reading, Spelling, Writing, Arithmetic, Grammar, and Geography.

Scholastic population, enrollment, and average daily attendance gradually increased during this period. In 1874 the scholastic population was 5,904 white and 5,058 colored, or a total of 10,962. In 1896 the total was 14,271. The enrollment during this period ranged from a low of 5,835 in 1875 to a high of 9,608 in 1905.

In 1874 there were 85 white schools and 44 colored schools in the county. The number of schools varied from a high of 191 in 1885 to a low of 118 in 1907. In 1874 there were 96 white teachers and 43 colored teachers. The lowest number of teachers employed during the period was 131 in 1901. The average salary per month for teachers changed little during the period, being $30 in 1894 and $36.31 in 1907. The average length of term did not show a steady increase. In 1874 the term was 110 days, dropped to 71 days in 1883, but rose to 145 days in 1907.

One important measure of the progress of a school system is the amount of money appropriated for education. In 1872 the school tax was fifteen cents on each $100 worth of property, but in 1875 the tax rate was cut to five cents. Superintendent A. J. Brandon, Sr. had this to say about the cut in rate: "The lowering of the school tax in January from 15 cents to five cents on the $100 worth of property was very unfortunate for the public schools in this county."

The tax rate ranged from a low of five cents in 1875 to thirty cents in 1907. There was also a thirty cent privilege tax for schools in 1907. The per capita cost of tuition per month was eighty-two cents in 1874. It dropped to a low of 42 cents in 1894 but was $1.16 in 1899.

The state superintendents were very proud of the low tuition cost in the public schools. Thomas H. Paine said in 1884: "The average cost of tuition per pupil per month in our private schools is $1.70, while that of the public schools is 59 cents, thus making a difference of $1.11 per pupil per month in favor of public schools."

There was little increase in the amount of school funds during this period. In 1874 Rutherford County received $5,031.33 from the state, $31,268.69 from the county, and $2,360.30 from other sources, making a total of $38,660.32. In this same year expenditures were as follows: $30,066.08 paid teachers, $7,050.47 for buildings and furnishings, $500 superintendent's salary, and $1,282.43 for other expenses, making a total of $38,898.98. In 1907 the receipts were: $8,503.28 from the state, $23,966.82 from county property tax, $6,100 from poll tax, $3,374.97 from privilege tax, $245.00 from other sources, or a total of $42,190.07. These funds were spent as follows: $40,262 salaries of teachers, $4,889.09 new buildings, etc., $1,282.96 for furniture and fixtures, $310.85 for county board of education, $187.40 for census, $800 superintendent's salary, $2,208.42 other expenses, making a total of $49,941.02.

The problems of the period as well as the progress are summed up in the following statements from county superintendents:

In 1874 Superintendent E. C. Cox said: "Many of our teachers are young and inexperienced, while others are rather farmers than teachers . . . "

A. J. Brandon, Sr., in 1876: "The schools are better than in the previous year.   Teachers are better qualified and more practical."

In 1878, he said: "The people, I think, are getting to take more interest in public schools, and if we can succeed in raising them to the right standard, they will not only be the most popular, but the best supported.   The people will be willing to be taxed for their support when they afford the best educational facilities."

G. H. Baskette in 1880: "The public school system has a strong and lasting hold upon the public mind."

Reese K. Henderson in 1883: " . . . The teachers have been prompt in attending school."   And in 1864: "The teachers throughout the county are discharging their duties acceptably . . ."

James D. Nelson in 1887: " . . . while others are dragging along in small log houses, furnished with slab benches, etc., employing favorite teachers who only want a few dollars to pay for some particular contract in regard to some real estate.   This class of teachers is an injury to the progress of our schools."

He said in 1889: "The schools are improving slowly but steadily, and the improvements have come to stay.   The directors are building central houses, employing the best of teachers, paying them to work, and seeing that they do it to advantage."

In 1890, Mr. Nelson said: "We also have some of the best schools of the state in our county, viz: Eagleville High School, Hermitage High School, Fosterville High School, Rutherford College, Cedar Hill High School, Oakland High School, Porterfield High School, Milton Seminary, Rucker Seminary, Lascassas Seminary, Walter Hill High School, Stewart's Creek Seminary, Seventh District Central High School, Salem Seminary, King's Wood High School, Eleventh District Central High School, Rockvale High School, Murfreesboro High School for boys, and Murfreesboro Seminary for girls."

N. D. Overall in 1896: "We are proud of the number and excellence of our secondary schools."

J. D. Jacobs in 1909: "I think the sentiment among the people of the county is strongly in favor of the establishment of high schools for the county, and for an appropriation by the state of the funds to encourage the establishment of the county high schools."

PRIVATE SCHOOLS

Public education showed considerable growth during this period. However, private schools still played an important part in education in the county, although declining in number and importance. The following were chartered during this period:

Sweet Briar Academy 1883; Fosterville Educational Institute 1883; Milton Female Academy 1880; Smyrna High School 1894; Portersville High School 1889; Rucker Seminary 1890; Murfreesboro Seminary for young ladies and children 1886.

State reports for 1877 showed that there were 33 private schools in the county, 46 teachers, 1,127 enrolled, an average daily attendance of 896, and an average cost per pupil per month of $1.87. In 1882 there were reported 16 private schools, 17 teachers and 308 pupils.

In 1889 the following were reported: Murfreesboro High School, R. D. Robertson, Principal, three teachers, enrollment 75; Eagleville High School, G. M. Savage, Principal, enrollment 187; Milton High School, N. D. Overall, Principal, 75 enrolled; Christiana Seminary, A. J. Brandon, Principal; 90 enrolled.

In 1891, reports showed that the Murfreesboro Seminary was operated by Miss Anna McFadden and three other teachers. There were 90 pupils enrolled and an M.E.L. degree was granted.

In 1892 reports showed twelve private schools with thirty teachers and an enrollment of 920 pupils. Readyville High School, S. W. Alexander, Principal, had an enrollment of 120 pupils.

Reports for the year 1901 showed the following: Milton Seminary, R. A. Raylor, Principal; Murfreesboro Academy, S. C. Parrish, Principal; Rucker Seminary, E. H. Childress, Principal; and Smyrna Fitting School.

The report for 1907 showed that Miss Ransom's School was operating with two teachers and 20 pupils.

Of especial interest is the Mooney School which was founded in Franklin, Tennessee. Mr. W. D. Mooney and a Mr. Wall had operated a school in Culleoka, having taken over when the Webb School was moved from Culleoka to Bell Buckle. In 1889, Mr. Mooney received a charter for Battle Ground Academy. He operated this school for several years, and when the building burned, he was persuaded to move to Murfreesboro. The school was opened in Murfreesboro about 1902 and operated here for seven years.

The building occupied by the school was on East Main Street and was taken over by the County and operated as East End School for a number of years after Mr. Mooney left Murfreesboro. He went to Harriman, Tennessee, after leaving Murfreesboro. From there he went to Danville, Virginia, and concluded his teaching career at Riverside Academy, Gainesville, Georgia.

The building now occupied by the Bristol Nelson Physiological School was the home of the Mooneys during their stay in Murfreesboro. Two frame buildings were erected on these grounds and were used as dormitories.

The Mooney School was noted for its scholarship as well as its athletics. Mr. Mooney is said to have had the first preparatory school football team in the South. He was a great lover of sports and did most of the coaching himself. Mrs. Mooney, who now lives in Nashville, says that she made the first suits for the football team.

Mr. Mooney believed in solid scholarship. He always deplored the passing of Greek and Latin from the curriculum. Vanderbilt University valued the school very highly and many of the "Mooney boys" made excellent records at Vanderbilt, both in scholarship and athletics.

Reports for 1904 showed a total of 135 pupils and four teachers.

This school was followed by the Anderson School for Boys.

TENNESSEE COLLEGE

The third school to be established by the Baptists of Tennessee was Tennessee College for Women. It was authorized in 1905 and opened in 1907 in Murfreesboro in response to what was felt to be a need for a school for women, under Christian control, of high grade and honest standards. The ideal of the founders was to offer the very best educational advantages under positive Christian influences. The original property of Union University was used, and a large donation was made by the citizens of Murfreesboro and Rutherford County.

By-laws adopted provided for twenty-seven directors to be known as trustees. The first officers of the board were C. R. Byrn, President, C. S. Smith, Vice-President, Leland Jordan, Secretary, and R. W. Hale, Treasurer. All trustees selected were to be members of Missionary Baptist Churches. An executive committee was to attend to immediate business during the year. Between the time of the selection of this first board and the laying of the corner-stone on September 6, 1906, titles to property were cleared up and a charter was drawn up. The property on which Tennessee College was placed had been purchased from M. B. Murfree by the Board of Trustees of Union University in 1845. At the removal of Union University the property had, after some uncertainty, remained in the hands of the Union University trustees in Murfreesboro.

In the fall of 1906, George J. Burnett and J. Henry Burnett signed a contract as President and Business Manager, respectively, of Tennessee College. These two men came from Liberty College in Kentucky where they had been held in high esteem.

The school officially opened on September 11, 1907, "as one of the greatest events of the year in the state of education." President Burnett described the occasion in these words: "The Lord smiled approvingly on this day." The faculty for the first year consisted of seventeen persons. "These brothers have spared no pains and expense to gather around them teachers of rare culture and splendid training in the best schools of this country and abroad."

Admittance to the college for the first year was on the basis of completion of two years in a high school or academy of high grade. Examination on entrance or a certificate from the principal of the school was required. The curriculum of the college department included fifteen courses, listed under the following heads: Philosophy, Psychology, Political Science, Natural Science, Classical Languages, Modern Languages, Music, and Art.

The enrollment for the first year was one hundred ninety-nine, one hundred and thirty-one of whom were boarding students. The first five years saw not only a maintenance of standards, but an increase in enrollment, facilities, and courses in instruction. In 1908 an addition was made to the building. In March, 1909, the Board of Trustees passed a resolution that "the object or ideal of Tennessee College is the establishment and development of a college for higher education of women." A campaign for $150,000 was launched to raise an endowment.

At the close of the year 1909-10, a definite change in the work offered by the college was recommended to the Board of Trustees. There was discussion of dropping the elementary department. More important, however, was the decision to offer an additional year of college work and thereby complete the A.B. course. President

Burnett felt this step to be urgent since high school principals preferred recommending a four year, accredited college to their graduates. As a result of this revised curriculum, the Bulletin of 1910-11 carried the announcement that "Tennessee College will confer the degree of Bachelor of Arts upon any student who satisfactorily completes the course of study outlined below." The first ambition of the college, the right to confer Bachelor's degrees on young ladies, had been reached.

The period 1912-1917 was one of progress at the school. The enrollment during this period was around two hundred forty. In 1914 the elementary department of the school was closed and the preparatory department established as a separate department.

The period 1917 to 1923 was impeded by the World War. The enrollment during this period was approximately 125, the primary department having been discontinued. Enthusiasm ran high in 1919 because of the "75 million campaign." Tennessee College under the plan of expenditure was to receive $400,000 and the *Tennessee College Magazine* for December, 1919, spoke enthusiastically of "No debts, a new heating plant, a new library and a new dormitory."

In 1920 property known as the "Thomas Property" was purchased. In 1921 the Board took action to strengthen the college department by stating that "it be the sense of this Board that our President project the work of the college on a basis looking to the making of Tennessee College a standard college."

In 1922 President Burnett offered his resignation. It was accepted, effective June 1, 1923, and Dr. Harry Clark had this to say in the *Baptist and Reflector:*

This is another case where the denomination loses the services of one of its strong men because burdens grew too heavy for him to bear . . . For years there have been positions for President Burnett to go into business at twice the salary he is now receiving, but he has held on out of loyalty to the Baptist cause. It is therefore fitting that we should express our appreciation for his heroic efforts.

Dr. E. L. Atwood, then Vice-President of the school, was made acting President and on March 4, 1924 he was named President.

Dr. Edward Leland Atwood was born in Clinton, Kentucky, October 30, 1872. He received the A.B. degree from Georgetown in 1901. He attended the Croyer Theological Seminary and received the B.D. degree in 1909. In 1916 he was awarded the D.D. degree from Union University. He came to Tennessee College as professor of Bible and religious education in 1921.

Dr. Atwood laid great stress on standardization, but he met the same problems which had been met previously. In his annual report for 1927 he openly faced the issue with the Board.

In 1928 Dr. W. H. Woods was selected as field representative in an endeavor to raise $350,000 for endowment. In 1929 the school was admitted to the Association of Colleges of Tennessee. In 1930 the school was conferring the Bachelor of Arts and the Bachelor of Science degrees and the work was approved by the Southern Association of Colleges.

Dr. James A. Kirtley was dean of the college for many years and was acting president for one year.

During the depression of the early thirties, the college underwent severe financial difficulties. Members of the faculty and administration received only a small per cent of their stipulated salary. The Board of Trustees issued $100,000 in bonds on February 8, 1933.

Due to high-powered student solicitation the enrollment for 1935-1937 was one hundred seventy, the highest in the school's history. In 1937-38 the enrollment had dropped to only seventy-eight and was very low during the last year of operation of the college.

In July, 1940, Dr. Atwood was retired by the Board of Trustees and Reverend Merrill D. Moore, pastor of the Baptist Church, Newport, Tennessee, was named as his successor. Mr. Moore resigned the presidency in March, 1942, and relinquished his work with the commencement exercises June 9, 1942. The enrollment for the last year of his administration was ninety-four. The bonded debt was reduced by some eight or nine thousand dollars during the two years tenure of Mr. Moore.

On June 9, 1942, Dr. John B. Clark, former dean of Mercer University, became president and head of the social science department. He served in this capacity for four years, until the college closed on July 1, 1946.

Dr. John Bunyan Clark was born in Hamilton, Alabama, June 6, 1887. He was educated in the public schools of Alabama, and in 1907 received the B.S. degree from Alabama Polytechnic Institute. He was awarded the A.M. degree by Vanderbilt University in 1910. He attended Harvard in 1911 and received the Ph.D. degree from New York University in 1926. He was principal of high schools in Alabama for a number of years. From 1917-1920, he was a member of the State Department of Education of Alabama. He was professor of history and economics at Alabama Polytechnic Institute from 1920-1927, going from there to Judson College where he served as Dean. In 1929, he went to Mercer as professor of history and dean of the college of arts and sciences.

There was an indebtedness of $24,000 on the college when Dr. Clark took charge. Through the efforts of Dr. Clark, the Women's Missionary Union, and the Baptist Cooperative Program, by November, 1945, the college was not only free from debt, but had on hand a cash balance of approximately $135,000.

Dr. Clark offered his resignation on October 19, 1945. It was accepted by the Board of Trustees November 6, 1945. On November 14, 1945 at the Baptist Convention in Nashville, a committee was appointed to investigate and report back to the 1946 convention on the advisability of making Tennessee College co-educational. On December 11, 1945 the state executive board voted to merge Tennessee College and all its assets with Cumberland University at Lebanon. On January 10, 1946, this merger was approved by a majority of the Board of Trustees.

Following this action, the minority group of trustees filed suit to enjoin the Baptist Executive Board and the majority of trustees from transferring the property. The injunction was dissolved and the city and county purchased the property for a high school.

On June 20, 1946, by order of attorneys of both factions, Dr. Clark turned over to representatives of Cumberland University approximately $115,000 in cash and U. S. bonds, and $8,000 of student notes receivable.

During the last years of Tennessee College, a great many improvements were made in the physical plant; additions were made to the library and equipment; the curriculum was revised; plans were approved for new buildings; but the action of the Baptist Executive Board and the Board of Trustees brought to an end Tennessee College in Murfreesboro after an existence of over forty years.

EDUCATION IN RUTHERFORD COUNTY
1909-1946

In 1909, the so-called "General Education Bill" was passed. This law unified the public school system and provided for the growth and the expansion of the state education system. A considerable increase in funds was provided by this act, more than a million dollars increase being provided in 1910.

DEVELOPMENT OF PUBLIC SCHOOLS

Rutherford County profited by this act, as shown by a steady increase in school funds. In 1907 the total receipts for education in the county had been $42,190.07. In 1913, receipts for elementary schools alone amounted to $62,118.72, part of the increase coming from county funds, the tax rate being 25 cents during this year. In 1925, the county received $41,090.77 from the state for elementary schools and $110,549.19 was raised in the county from a 42 cent tax rate.

In 1925, another significant change was made in the state school law. One important provision of this act was that any county which would levy a 50 cent elementary tax could share in a state equalization fund to provide an eight months term for elementary schools. Under the provisions of this act, Rutherford County continued to show an increase in school funds. In 1930, there was received from the state $37,254.34 for elementary schools. The 50 cent county levy brought $5,630.00 and $9,754.80 came from county offices, making a total of $163,139.75 for county elementary schools. The city received $48,173.48 for elementary schools.

Reports for 1944 showed the total assessed valuation of the county to be $16,481,709. The tax rate for schools was .08 state elementary, .62 county elementary, .38 county high school, or a total of $1.00 for the county. This was 58 per cent of the total tax rate of $1.72. In this year, the county received $95,149.37 from the state for elementary schools, and $139,609.80 from all sources in the county, making a total of $234,759.17.

Reports for the school year ending June 30, 1946, give the picture of the public school system in the county. There were a total of 52 elementary schools; 4 white one-teacher schools and 18 colored one-teacher schools; 9 white two-teacher schools and 4 colored two-teacher schools; 15 white three-or-more-teacher schools and 2 colored three-or-more teacher schools. The enrollment in these schools was 4,519- 3,637 white pupils and 882 colored pupils. The average daily attendance was 3,893 - 3,141 white pupils and 752 colored pupils. A total of 330 finished the eighth grade course - 275 white pupils and 55 colored pupils.

A total of 149 elementary teachers were employed in 1945-1946 -5 white men, 111 white women, 7 colored men, and 26 colored women. The average annual salary paid these teachers was $1,216.80 for white men, $1,084 for white women, $1,135.45 for colored men, and $1,105.-60 for colored women. Of the 149 teachers employed, all except eight held permanent professional certificates, the eight holding permits.

The census report for Rutherford County, completed in June, 1946, shows a total of 7,876 boys and girls of the ages of 17 and under. Of this number, 2,835 were of pre-school age and 869 were over school age. There were 1,407 colored boys and girls and 6,469 white boys and girls. Of the number of school age, 636 were not enrolled in school.

An interesting phase of development in the school system has been the growth of consolidation and transportation. As early as 1877, there was some effort at consolidation. Reports for this year showed three graded schools and four consolidated schools in the county. In 1887 there were 4 consolidated and 4 graded schools. In 1899 there were five consolidated schools. As early as 1916, transportation was used, there being seven schools using a total of 14 wagons. The average cost per pupil hauled was $1.16 per month. In 1921, the number of consolidated schools was fourteen; 14 wagons and trucks hauling 490 pupils daily at a cost of $2.00 per month. By 1930 the number of consolidated schools had grown to 19. There were 50 wagons and trucks hauling 1,629 pupils daily at a cost of $2.10 per month.

The latest printed report (1944) showed that pupils were being transported to 19 elementary schools and nine high schools. A total of 52 vehicles was used, 23 all steel buses, 28 other buses, and one wagon. 2,491 elementary pupils and 709 high school pupils were transported daily. The total spent for transportation was $46,247.42, $8,816.00 of which came from state funds. The per capita cost was $18.13 for the year.

Another important development has been the growth of school libraries. As early as 1892 Superintendent Overall reported a circulating library of 75 volumes for teachers. In 1907 there were 1,080 volumes in all libraries. In 1913 there were 14 libraries for teachers and two public school libraries. In 1925, there were 49 libraries, containing 6,320 books, valued at $4,194.00. In this year, city libraries contained 672 books.

One provision of the School Act of 1909 was that one per cent of the General Education Fund was to be used to assist in the establishment and the maintenance of public school libraries, one-fifth of said library fund to be used for maintaining circulating libraries for the public schools.

This gave impetus to the growth of libraries and there was a steady development. A circulating library was started in 1936. There are now about 3,000 volumes in this library. There are also libraries in every school of the county, and there are approximately 15,000 volumes in these libraries.

HIGH SCHOOLS

The development of public high schools has come within the last thirty years. As early as 1877 the Peabody Fund granted $150.00 to the Murfreesboro High School, but this was a private school.

In 1889, Eagleville, Milton, and Christiana were referred to as high schools, but these were private schools. Superintendent Overall said in 1896, "We are proud of the number and excellence of our secondary schools". In 1907, Smyrna Fitting School was changed to a secondary public school. However, these schools were not public high schools as we know them today.

Superintendent Jacobs said in 1908, "I think the sentiment among the people of the county is strongly in favor of the establishment of high schools for the county and for an appropriation by the state of the funds to encourage the establishment of county high schools.

In 1909, the "General Education Bill" provided that 8 per cent of the General Education Fund was to be used for the maintenance of high schools, said high schools to be graded by the State Board of Education.

Following the passage of this Act, seven high schools were established in 1909. There were 299 pupils enrolled, taught by sixteen teachers, at a cost of $6.49 per month per pupil. In 1913, there was one first class high school, six third class schools, with 396 enrolled. There was spent for operation in this year, $10,693.93.

In 1916, high schools were operating at Murfreesboro, Christiana, Eagleville, Kittrell, Lascassas, Rockvale, and Smyrna. In 1919, there were thirteen high schools, including two-year schools.

In 1921, an act was passed requiring each county to establish and maintain one or more first-class, or four-year high schools. In this same year, there were 14 white high schools in the county and one colored high school in Murfreesboro. There were 37 teachers employed, 705 pupils enrolled, and $35,946.49 was spent for high school education.

In 1921, there was a total of 59 graduates from the high schools. In 1930, there were 118 graduates, with an average daily attendance of 1,017. The average salary for 56 high school teachers in this year was $1,189.33.

In 1944, the total receipts from state and county funds for high schools was approximately $107,000 and the expenditures amounted to $105,000.

In 1946, the following four-year high schools were operated: Central at Murfreesboro, enrollment 446; Christiana, enrollment 86; Eagleville, enrollment 74; Kittrell, enrollment 98; Lascassas, enrollment 64; Rockvale, enrollment 63; Smyrna enrollment 137; Walter Hill, enrollment 62; Holloway (colored) enrollment 159. A two-year school was operated at the Training School with an enrollment of 83. There was a total average daily attendance of

1,183. Sixty-seven teachers were employed in the high schools all of them having four years or more of college training.

BOARDS OF EDUCATION

For many years public schools were administered by district boards. There were as many as 52 district directors in Rutherford County. In 1877, Superintendent Baskett said that one of the obstacles to success was the indifference of directors. An Act of 1907 created a County Board of Education and made the unit of school administration the county as a whole instead of the school districts. This act provided for a board of five members. The first board under this act was composed of B. M. Rucker, Chairman, W. H. Gregory, W. J. Owen, R. M. White, Jr., and T. A. Richardson.

Rutherford County did not remain under this general Act very long as there were 26 members of the Board in 1911, plus the chairman, who was the County Superintendent. In 1914 there were 25 members of the Board, W. L. Johnson being the chairman. In this same year there were seven members of the High School Board, J. P. Leathers being chairman.

In 1921 an act was passed providing that County Boards of Education be composed of seven members elected for seven years each. Rutherford County complied with this act until 1945. B. B. Kerr served as chairman of the Board for most of this period.

In 1945 a special act was passed providing for new school districts and a board of eleven members. This new board is made up of the following: W. H. Westbrooks, Chairman, Elmus Alexander, Ben Brown, T. P. Burns, J. M. Coleman, Wrather Coleman, Will O'Brien, Hoyte Parsons, Hollis Short, E. L. Williams, and John Wood.

MURFREESBORO CITY SCHOOLS

Murfreesboro has operated an independent school system for elementary pupils for a number of years. In 1891 an act of the Legislature gave the city authority to levy a school tax. The report of the State Superintendent for 1895 showed the city to have a population of 5,000, with 2,571 school population. In this year there were 407 white pupils and 356 colored pupils enrolled. There was one white school and one colored school, each taught by six teachers. Mr. E. C. Cox was city superintendent.

Mr. Cox was born at Saulsbury, Tennessee, October 11, 1836. He came to Murfreesboro in 1856 to enter Union University, graduating in 1860 as valedictorian of the class. He taught mathematics

Main Building, Middle Tennessee State College

Murfreesboro Central High School. This building formerly
housed Tennessee College for Women.

and history at Murfreesboro Female Institute. He later held a similar post at Old Ward Seminary. He served as county superintendent, city superintendent, and for many years was identified with the educational development of the county.

P. A. Lyon was superintendent of the Murfreesboro schools from 1905-1911.

In 1918, J. C. Mitchell came from Winchester to take charge of Central High School and the city schools. He retired in 1945, and was succeeded by B. E. Hobgood, a member of the faculty of State College.

In addition to Central High School and Holloway High (colored), which are operated jointly by the city and county, the city operates Crichlow and Bradley Schools. Crichlow school for white pupils has eighteen teachers and an enrollment of 726. Bradley school for negro pupils has 10 teachers and an enrollment of 385.

There are two other schools in Murfreesboro, but they are not operated by the city. The Training School is run jointly by the State College and Rutherford County, while McFadden is a county school.

MIDDLE TENNESSEE STATE COLLEGE

The General Education Law of 1909 created the Middle Tennessee State Normal School and defined the purpose of its establishment—"for the education and professional training of teachers for the public schools of the state." The law also set up conditions for admittance. The school "shall be open and free alike to white males and females, resident of the state of Tennessee, but no person shall be admitted who is under sixteen years of age and who has not finished at least the elementary school courses prescribed for the public schools of the state; nor shall any person be admitted who does not first sign a pledge to teach in the public or private schools of the state of Tennessee, within the next six years after leaving the school, at least as long as he or she has attended said school."

There was much competition among the Middle Tennessee towns for the location of the college, but through the efforts of A. L. Todd, who was a member of the State Board of Education at the time, and other citizens of Murfreesboro and Rutherford County, the school was located at Murfreesboro. The city of Murfreesboro gave $80,000 toward the establishment of the school; the county gave $100,000 and the state $70,000. The original plant cost approximately $237,000.

The original plant consisted of an administration building, a dining hall, the President's home, a central heating plant, and a girls' dormitory. The first tract of land purchased consisted of fifty acres, but soon 134 acres were added. The board of Education rented two cottages for use of girls and the boys used Forest and Craddock Halls, located near the building formerly used by the Mooney School for Boys.

The school opened on September 11, 1911, with R. L. Jones as president, assisted by a faculty of 14 teachers.

Mr. Jones was born in White County in 1867. He attended district schools and at the age of 17 he began his career as a teacher. He later attended Onward Seminary in White County, and Burritt College at Spencer. After graduating at Burritt, he attended the University of Chicago.

In 1891, he was elected superintendent of the schools of White County. He became president of Doyle College in 1895. In 1897, he went to Chattanooga, teaching in the high schools of Hamilton County until 1903. In 1901, he was appointed a member of the State Board of Education. From 1903 until 1907, he was superintendent of the schools of Hamilton County. He resigned this position in 1907 to accept the State Superintendency of Tennessee, being appointed by Governor M. R. Patterson.

He left the presidency of the Normal in 1919 to accept the superintendency of the Chattanooga schools, where he remained for two years. He returned to the presidency of the Normal in 1921 and remained until 1922. In this year he left the Normal to accept the position as superintendent of Memphis City Schools, where he served until his death in 1938.

The opening enrollment of the school was 175 students. Two regular courses were offered, (1) the Academic course to prepare teachers for the elementary schools; (2) the Normal Course to prepare teachers for the public schools of the state—the completion of this course entitled the student to a diploma which is a life certificate of qualification to teach in any of the public schools of the State. Local cash receipts from July 18, 1913, to October 8, 1914, amounted to $35,730.12. The amount of money paid by the state from the beginning to September 14, 1914, was $126,175.92. There were seven graduates for the normal diploma in 1912 and two for the academic certificate.

In 1922, the following courses were offered: (1) the three-year certificate course, the completion of this course entitles one to teach in the elementary schools of the state without examination: (2) the one-year certificate course, the completion of which confers the same privileges as the three-year course above; (3) the two-year certificate course-entitling the holder to teach in any public school of Tennessee except county high schools of the first class; (4) the three-year diploma course carrying the right to teach in any public school in Tennessee.

In 1922-23 the total enrollment, including the summer quarter enrollment of 1180, was 1542. Total receipts from the state, including $52,185.40 on hand at beginning of year, was $147,139.99. Local receipts of $84,578.60 made the total for 1922-1923 $231,898.59.

In 1922, thirty-seven two-year diplomas were granted. This was the first year three-year diplomas were granted, eight students receiving them. Beginning in 1923, no diplomas were issued except to those completing three full years of college work. There were 26 members of the faculty in this year. The last two years of high school work were given in 1924-1925.

It was in 1922 that Mr. Jones again left the Presidency of the school. He was succeeded by P. A. Lyon, who had been acting president while Mr. Jones was in Chattanooga.

Pritchett Alfred Lyon was born in Rutherford County on March 20, 1868. He graduated from the Winchester Normal College in 1891, attended Vanderbilt University, and received an honorary L.L.D. from Southwestern University in 1931. He was head of the Auburn Seminary in Kentucky from 1892-1900. He was principal of schools in Nashville from 1900-1905. From 1905-1911 he was Superintendent of Murfreesboro Schools. When the Normal School opened in 1911, he became head of the department of mathematics and served in this capacity until 1920. In this year, he was made dean and also was acting president from 1919-1921. He was elected president in 1923 and was active in this position until 1938. In this year he retired from active service and was made President Emeritus.

Beginning with the school year 1925-26, the Middle Tennessee State Normal School became known as the Middle Tennessee State Teachers College. The General Assembly in 1925, authorized the maintenance of a State Teachers College in each of the Grand Divisions of the State, and the State Board of Education took the necessary action to convert the Normal School into a Teachers' College.

In May and August, 1926, the degree of Bachelor of Science was conferred for the first time. Forty-eight students were awarded degrees.

The law provides that "Each Teacher College or State Normal School shall maintain a training school in which shall be taught all the subjects for elementary schools as prescribed by this act and in which may be taught such other subjects of elementary and high school grades as the State Board of Education may prescribe."

For many years the college was hampered because of the lack of proper facilities for the Training School, but in 1929 a new building was constructed on a fifteen acre site donated to the state by the city of Murfreesboro. The training school is now adequately housed, well equipped and it serves as a laboratory for practice teachers.

In 1935, the report of President Lyon to the State Board showed a total enrollment for the regular year of 1289. A total of 141 degrees was awarded this year. A total of 40 full-time faculty members and officers was employed. The State appropriation for the school for this year was $56,000. All other income totaled $123,232.90, making a total for use of the school of $179,232.90.

In 1938, Q. M. Smith was elected president of the College. Mr. Smith was born at Buffalo, Tennessee, May 11, 1891. He received a B.S. degree in 1917 and an M.A. in 1927, both from Peabody College. He served as principal of Bradley County High School from 1914-1920. In 1920, he was elected President of Tennessee Polytechnic Institute and served in this capacity until he came to the Murfreesboro institution. In 1920, he was President of the State Teachers Association and served as President of the Tennessee Education Association in 1938.

A significant change was made by an act of the Legislature in 1939. Students were no longer required to sign a pledge to teach, and it became possible for a person to graduate from the college without meeting the certification requirements. Prior to this change, the State Board of Education, in February, 1930, changed the name from Middle Tennessee State Teachers College to State Teachers' College, Murfreesboro. In 1941, the State Board of Education approved another change in name and the General Assembly of 1943 legalized the name, Middle Tennessee State College.

Although the training of teachers remains the chief function of the school, the scope and function have been broadened. In addition to the regular courses for teachers, the school now maintains a well-equipped commerce department; offers pre-medical, pre-dental and pre-legal training; operates an airport and an aviation program, and is giving special emphasis to the training of veterans.

There are three programs offered veterans: (1) the regular four-year college program leading to the B.S. degree, (2) an accelerated college program which will enable the veteran to complete a special subject in less than four years or to make up deficiencies in the shortest possible time, (3) a program for those who have not completed high school.

In February 1943, the Army Air Forces College Training Program was started and continued through June 30, 1944. More than one thousand men passed through the program during this time.

In addition to the original buildings, others have been erected during the years. By the fall of 1922, the following additional buildings were ready for use: Jones Hall, a dormitory for men; a gymnasium; a laundry; a dairy barn; and the Moffitt House. In 1925, the State Board of Education authorized the construction of a library. This building was erected without a special appropriation, being built with accumulated local funds.

In 1929, the General Assembly appropriated $200,000 for the construction of needed buildings and the purchase of equipment. The Training School and Lyon Hall, a dormitory for women, were built with these funds. In 1931, an appropriation of $225,000 was made for the erection and equipment of a Science Building. It was occupied in the fall of 1931.

In 1940, the Industrial Arts Building was erected largely as an N.Y.A. project. A second building of the same size and design was erected in 1945. Plans are now under way for the construction of a new gymnasium.

By 1944, the war had cut the enrollment greatly, there being a total enrollment of 397. There were 49 degrees awarded this year and a total of 47 full-time faculty members and officers was employed. The State appropriation received for this year was $115,284.17 and receipts from local sources amounted to $256,220.23, making a total of $371,504.40.

At the present time the enrollment of the college is about normal, with almost eight hundred students in attendance. The faculty is composed of Q. M. Smith, President, N. C. Beasley, who has been Dean of the college since 1927, Clayton James, Dean of Students, Benton Judd, Registrar, and about sixty teachers. Outstanding educators and writers too numerous to mention have been associated with the college.

The College is a member of the Tennessee College Association, of the American Association of Teachers Colleges and of the Southern Association of Colleges and Secondary Schools.

CHAPTER IX

Religion in Rutherford County

INTRODUCTION. The religious history of Rutherford County conforms well to the general pattern for middle Tennessee. Among the first settlers there were some lawless people who were little influenced by religious feeling. The controlling group, however, was composed of men and women of deep religious convictions. It is therefore not surprising that churches were organized within a few years after the first settlers arrived. The very first settlers, however, were in no position to erect buildings or even to organize congregations, so pressing were the problems of making a living. Their religious desires had to be satisfied with family worship or with the meeting of a few friends who were indeed fortunate if a visiting minister from an older settlement happened to be in the locality. It was not long, however, before groups of people of the same faith were meeting regularly in some home, or even in barns, or in good weather, in the open for worship. The next move was a permanent organization with the services at least of a part time preacher. The final step was a church house owned by the congregation.

This chapter is divided into three sections: 1. The Period of Organization and Dissention, 1800-1860; 2. The Period of Post Civil War Expansion; 3. A History of Certain Outstanding Churches.

THE PERIOD OF ORGANIZATION
AND DISSENTION 1800-1860

THE BAPTISTS. Although the Presbyterians are usually credited with being the first denomination to become established in Tennessee, the Baptists were the first to make permanent organizations in Rutherford County and have always been the most numerous. They will therefore be discussed first.

The best sources of information about the Baptists in the county before the Civil War are Bond's *History of the Concord Association*, and the *National Baptist Register*. The Concord Association in its early days included churches from several middle Tennessee counties

174

and even today has a few churches outside of Rutherford County. Furthermore at no time has the Association included all Baptist churches of the county. However, this Association has long been identified with the Stone's River basin and a study of its history is necessary to get a clear picture of the Baptists of Rutherford County.

The first Baptist church organized in middle Tennessee, according to Bond, was in 1783. It was located on the Sulphur Fork of Red River near Clarksville. By 1796 there was a sufficient number of churches in the area to organize the Mero Association. In 1806 the Association boasted thirty-nine churches with a membership of about two thousand. In that year the body was divided because of its size. Three years later another division was found desirable and the Concord Association came into being. It included churches from Rutherford, Williamson, Davidson, Wilson, Sumner, Smith, and perhaps other counties. A year earlier the Elk River Baptist Association to the south had been organized. This association included the Beech Grove Baptist church, which at that time was in Rutherford County, and perhaps other churches in the southern part of the county. In 1810 the Concord Association had twenty-two churches with 873 members. The first regular annual session of the Association was held at the Cummings meeting house in Rutherford County. The Baptist churches known to have been in Rutherford County at this time were the Republican Grove and Mount Pleasant churches organized in 1800, the Rock Spring church organized in 1804, and the Overall Creek church (later the Beesley Primitive church) organized in 1805. The date of the organization of the Cummings church is not known. It was probably located near Jefferson, the county seat. There were no doubt other Baptist churches in the county by 1810.

The following Rutherford churches were admitted into the Association according to its minutes during the next few years: Stewart's Creek, 1813; Bethesada, 1814; Philadelphia, (Bradley's Creek), Bethlehem, Flat Rock, and New Hope, 1819; and Sanders' Fork (now in Cannon County) in 1822. The Association held its annual sessions before the war at the following Rutherford County churches: Overall's Creek, 1815 and 1816; Providence, 1819 and 1833; Rock Springs, 1823 and 1849; Bethel, 1824, 1829, and 1855; Philadelphia, 1834, 1837, and 1842; Bethesda, 1835; Murfreesboro 1847 and 1857; Enon, 1852, and Fellowship, 1856. Other churches referred to in the minutes of the Association before 1850 were Cripple Creek and Cross Roads.

After 1820 the meetings of the Association were none too harmonious. Disputes arose over Calvanism, Campbellism, foot washing, missions, Sunday schools and a state convention. It is not surprising, therefore, that by 1860 there were four or five different Baptists groups in the county, not to mention the rapidly rising Church of Christ.

In 1822 the Association was divided. This division appears to have been for administrative reasons rather than because of a schism. After that time the Association centered more and more in Rutherford County.

In 1824 sharp arguments broke out over Arminianism. This, in the main, was a recession from the rigid Calvanistic doctrine of predestination. This view was held generally by the Methodist. The Methodist camp meeting which reached Rutherford County in 1812 had a profound effect on all religious bodies.

This religious fermentation was for the most part national in scope though in pioneer Tennessee and Kentucky it appears to have experienced more violent expression than in the older parts of the country. Disputes were becoming so violent that in 1826 part of the Concord Association met at the Overall Creek church to discuss a future course. In 1827 eleven churches including the Rutherford churches of Bethel, Bethlehem, Providence, and Flat Rock held a special meeting to discuss the heated issues. During the same year a called meeting was held in Sumner County where a heated discussion arose over Campbellism. Elder Peyton Smith of the Overall Creek church vehemently opposed predestination. During the same year at the regular meeting of the Association in Wilson County the majority "excluded the last vestige of Calvanism" and formed a new Association called the "Separates" or Concord Number Two. Eleven churches remained Calvanistic and were called "Regulars" or Concord Number One.

The following quotation by a Baptist leader of the times quoted by Bond throws some light on these disputes from the Baptist point of view:

"About this time the churches (more or less) of the Concord Association and, indeed of nearly all the associations throughout the length and breadth of the land, were in a perfect ferment by the leaven of Campbellism.

"But though mixed as they were the Separates and the Campbellites, moved together for four or five years, (I do not remember the precise time as I write from memory) when they met at Fellowship M. H., Rutherford County. By this time Campbellism had become so offensive and odious to the Separates, they being in the majority, pushed the Campbellites off into the woods. Smith and Curlee had become quite conspicious, and the principal leaders of the Campbellite host. Hoisting their colors they proclaimed the Reformation in every valley and on every hill top.   Wherever they went entering the churches they scattered firebrands among the members dividing or bursting up the churches, and many went down to rise no more.   The church at Nashville then numbering 131 members was rent, only five continuing faithful.   The majority took the house and the small minority were left without a place to worship, save in the public street or some friendly house.   Thus the Association which numbered forty-nine churches, twenty ordained ministers, four licentiates and a membership of 3399 was reduced to eleven churches and 805 members."

It is not known in all cases what Rutherford churches remained in the old organization.   In the *National Baptist Register* of 1836 only four Rutherford churches are listed in the regular Concord Association.   These were Providence, Overall's Creek, Bethlehem, and Flat Rock.   The majority went over to the Separates, or entered the Church of Christ which was established in the county soon after 1830.   Some Baptist churches no doubt remained independent of any organization.

In 1833 the Tennessee State Baptist Convention was formed. Many Baptist opposed this as a centralization movement that would restrict the liberties of the individual churches.   At the regular meeting of the Concord Association (Number One) in 1834 certain member churches asked for an expression of opinion on the subject of a state convention.   A called session the following year further discussed the subject.   In 1836 the Providence and other churches asked that the Association be dissolved.   Their motion was carried and eleven churches formed the Stone's River Association.   This was the Primitive group.   They were extremely Calvanistic, opposed to a state organization as well as Sunday schools and missionary societies, and generally practiced foot washing.   The remaining churches in the Concord Association became affiliated with the state convention and were commonly called Missionary Baptists.   The Providence and Overall's Creek and possibly other churches in Rutherford County joined the Primitive group.   The Mount Pleasant congregation split, both factions using the same building for a number of years.

Prior to the Civil War, Dr. J. M. Watson, one of the leading surgeons in the state and one time professor of medicine at the University of Nashville, lived in Murfreesboro and was considered the most outstanding Primitive Baptist preacher in the United States.   He is said to have preached to more people than John Wesley.   A book of his sermons was published.

When the primitive group left the organization, the Concord Association (Number One) found that its differences with the Separates (Number Two) over predestination were not so pronounced. In 1842 the two groups reunited though it is possible that a few Separates remained independent or joined the Duck River Separates.

In 1850 the Concord Association made an attempt at reconciliation with the Primitives and sent a letter to the Stone's River Association suggesting a merger of the two bodies. The Primitives, however, "threw the letter under the table."

A few lines should be written about the Duck River Baptists, sometimes called the Baptist Church of Christ. They are Separate Baptists and withdrew from the Elk River Baptist Association about the same time that the Concord Association split over predestination. The Duck River Baptists oppose presdestination but because they practice footwashing they are often confused with the Primitives.

The federal census (which is very inaccurate for religious statistics but is often the only source available) lists sixteen Baptist churches in Rutherford County in 1850 with a seating capacity of 5700 and with property valued at $7775. Ten years later only nine churches with seating space for 3250 persons are listed. Apparently only members of the state convention were reported in 1860.

PRESBYTERIANS. When Rutherford County was established in 1803, a schism in the Presbyterian church was under way. In 1802 the Cumberland Presbytery was established out of the Transylvania Presbytery. The new organization included churches in both Tennessee and Kentucky and was a part of the Synod of Kentucky. The camp-meeting movement sponsored chiefly by the Methodists appealed to many Presbyterians as it did to Baptists and others. The physical manifestations at the revivals caused much agitation in Presbyterian ranks. The revivals with a large number of conversions caused a sudden demand for more Presbyterian ministers. The result was that the Cumberland Presbytery inducted into the ministry some who had not completed the regular course of study prescribed for the profession. In 1805 the Synod of Kentucky condemned this practice and a year later dissolved the Cumberland Presbytery and reunited it with that of Transylvania. In 1809 the General Assembly of the church confirmed the action of the Synod of Kentucky.

In 1810 at Dickson, Tennessee, a group of churches formed an independent organization and called it the Cumberland Presbytery. At first they seemed not to have intended permanently to leave the parent church. However, the organization grew rapidly in middle Tennessee and Kentucky. In 1813 the group decided to become a distinct denomination under the name of the Cumberland Presbyterian Church. The term Presbyterian as used in the rest of this chapter refers to the parent organization and the term Cumberland to the new body though the Cumberlands to this day are Presbyterians.

Both branches of the church figured prominently in the early life of Rutherford County though the Presbyterians were the first to organize.

The first Presbyterians to settle in the area soon to become Rutherford County came to the eastern part of the county and perhaps to Stewart's Creek. They arrived about 1800. Another early group settled in the vicinity of the Murfree Spring, the site soon to become Murfreesboro. There appears to have been no early Presbyterian settlements west of the line later followed by the Nashville, Chattanooga and Saint Louis railroad. In fact there has never been a Presbyterian church west of the railroad except a few weak Cumberlands.

The early Presbyterians like other denominations worshiped in homes. The Methodist camp meeting at Windrow in 1812 probably had something to do with the organization of the first Presbyterian churches in the county. The decision to make Murfreesboro the permanent seat of government for the county probably influenced the establishment at that place of the Murfree Spring church, the first Presbyterian church organized in the county. This church, soon renamed the First Presbyterian Church, Murfreesboro, attained such prominence that it was twice chosen as the meeting place of the Tennessee Synod before 1830. A brief history of the First Presbyterian Church, Murfreesboro, will be given later in this chapter.

The next Presbyterian churches organized in the county were Hopewell and Stone's River. Both are still in existence. The former is located at Milton, while the latter is between Halls Hill and Porterfield. The Cripple Creek church, southwest of Readyville, was organized a few years later.

The Stone's River and Hopewell churches were organized in 1816 by the Reverend Jesse Alexander who at that time was pastor of the Murfreesboro church. The Reverend Alexander for forty-seven years served various churches in Rutherford and adjoining counties. He was born in North Carolina in 1781. In 1802 he came to Tennessee and settled at Milton. He died during the Civil War. The loss of his eyesight did not cause him to give up his labors. The "blind preacher was a familiar figure with his saddle bags and Bible as he rode on Sundays to fill his appointments, his faithful horse often his only guide."

The Smyrna church though not formally organized till about 1820 under the leadership of the Reverend Samuel Hodge appears to have had its beginnings with a group of Presbyterians who met at Jefferson as early as 1810 while that town was the county seat. After Murfreesboro became the seat of government the Jefferson group was instrumental in organizing the Smyrna church. This church has left its mark on the history of the county. Few, if any churches in the county, have had more prominent family names on its roll. They include Weakley, Gooch, Davis, Keeble, Martin, Bradford, Cannon, Aldrich, Patterson, Thompson, Tucker, Wade, Gracey, Edmondson, Chapman, Hibbett, Hight, Hill, Holloway, Lowry, Neely, Nelson, Towns and others.

The next Presbyterian churches in the county were the colonies established by the Murfreesboro church under the leadership of Reverend William Eagleton who was pastor of this church from 1829 to 1866. Unfortunately all of the colonies established by Dr. Eagleton were destroyed by the Civil War or by population changes.

Before discussing the colonies of the First Church a word should be said about the influence of the Methodist camp meeting on the Presbyterians. While most Presbyterians objected to the extreme emotionalism of the early camp meeting, many leaders recognized the value of a toned-down evangelism and advocated the use of the camp meeting as a means of converting sinners. Perhaps another influencing factor was the inroads the Methodist and Cumberlands were making into Presbyterian ranks. Dr. Eagleton and many others were advocates of the camp meeting. Three camp grounds apparently used by Presbyterians are referred to in the early literature of the county. One was the Norman ground about seven miles southeast of Murfreesboro on the west fork of Stone's River; another was the Sulphur Springs ground about four miles northwest of Murfreesboro. The most famous, however, was the McKnight or Center Nursery ground north of the Stone's River church. It was established in 1831 and for years rivalled the Windrow and Overall Methodist grounds. It was said of the McKnight ground that "order was the prevailing characteristic, it seemed that the power of God and His presence were felt and recognized by all." As many as fifteen visiting Presbyterian ministers would assist in these meetings, two to four at a time. Among these were William Eagleton, Matt Marshall, Amzy Bradshaw, William Porter, R. T. Brantly, and A. H. Deshiel. It is said that in eighteen meetings 535 professions of religion were recorded.

In 1851 Dr. Eagleton held a meeting at the Norman camp ground near where the Mt. Tabor Cumberland church now stands. A number of persons united with the Murfreesboro church. Other successful meetings were held and by 1853 there were sufficient

Presbyterians in the area to justify the establishment of the Mt. Tabor church with over fifty members. A building was soon erected on the Manchester pike. This church did not last long and its place was taken by the Cumberlands. It probably was destroyed during the Civil War.

The Sulphur Spring road camp ground also developed into a church under the wing of the Murfreesboro church. After several meetings a church was established in 1854. The building was destroyed by the war and the congregation disbanded, many returning to the Murfreesboro church and others moving to new homes. The vacant lot on which the building stood is now claimed by no one.

In 1848, a mission established at Double Springs, three miles east of Murfreesboro, resulted in many in that section being converted to the Presbyterian faith. No church, however, was established there.

CUMBERLAND PRESBYTERIANS. Little is known of this faith in the county till after 1835. They are known, however, to have had camp meetings and perhaps organizations in the area soon after 1820. The first available reference to this denomination in the county is in the *Western Methodist* of September 12, 1834, which refers to a Cumberland camp meeting ground near Murfreesboro in 1821. Three of the earliest churches organized were the Sugg's Creek church on the Wilson County line north of Jefferson, the Jerusalem church near Jefferson and the Lytle's Creek church about three miles south east of Murfreesboro. Mrs. Seat of the Jefferson community, a descendant of General Coffee who once owned the property on which the Jerusalem church was erected, thinks that the Sugg's Creek church was first, the Jerusalem church second. The official records of the Lytle's Creek church state that 1836 was the date of its formal organization. The Murfreesboro Cumberland church was not organized till 1858, though pastors from the Lytle's Creek church preached to a small group in Murfreesboro as early as 1845. Some time after the establishment of the Murfreesboro church, the Lytle's Creek church moved further out on the Manchester highway to where it now stands and took over the name Mt. Tabor, a title formerly used by the Presbyterian church in the area. The facts relevant to this move are not clear. It has been suggested that the Presbyterian church was destroyed by the Civil War, and that the Lytle's Creek church now being overshadowed by the Murfreesboro Cumberland church decided to move. This is speculation rather than fact, however.

The growth of the Cumberlands after 1840 was very rapid. The federal census of 1850 lists seventeen Presbyterian churches in the

county with seating capacity of 5000 and with property valued at
$9025.00.   It is probable that well over half of these were Cumber-
land churches, though some of them did not have buildings.   In
1860 the two branches are listed separately.   The Presbyterians
reported only three churches with seating capacity of 2000 and valued
at $3500.   It is known, however, that there were at least five and
possibly seven Presbyterian churches in the county at that time.
During the same year the census reported 19 Cumberland churches
with seating space for 3550 and property valued at $3850.   Evidently
the newer branch of the Presbyterians was growing more rapidly
than the older group which was apparently being restricted by its
exclusiveness, as well as by competition from other denominations
who appeared to fall more in line with the tenets of Jacksonian
Democracy notwithstanding the liberalism of Dr. Eagleton and
others.

THE METHODIST.   It is probable that Methodists came into
the area soon to become Rutherford County as early as the Baptists
and the Presbyterians.   Little is known of them, however, before
1812.   The Stone's River circuit makes its appearance in the annual
reports of the Tennessee Conference in 1813.   Since these reports
for years listed only circuits, they give little official information about
the first individual churches.   The best source of information on
the early Methodists in the county is found in McFerrin's *History of
Methodism in Tennessee*, published in 1886.   The following quotation
from that book is attributed by the author to the Reverend Sterling
M. Cherry of the Tennessee Conference.

"I am chiefly indebted to General William H. Smith, J. J. Jarratt,
James E. Stockard, and P. W. Brown for the items contained
in this sketch of the History of Methodism in the Stone's River
Circuit, which once embraced the territory included in the Murfrees-
boro and perhaps Shelbyville stations, Middleton, Unionville, Beech
Grove, and a portion of Nolensville and Shady Grove Circuits.

"Methodism was introduced into Rutherford County at an early
date.   In the year 1812 there was regular preaching at the dwelling
houses of John Windrow, Thomas Jarratt, Charles Locke, James
Rucker, and Nat Overall.   Societies were organized and log church
houses built at those places in a very few years, most of them as early
as 1814.

"The first camp meeting began at Windrow's on the 15th of
August 1812.   The camp ground was located on the western slope of
a large hill, nine miles southwest of the present city of Murfreesboro,
not then built.   The four acres of ground were given by John Windrow.   It was a beautiful grove of dense sugar maple, affording an

ample screen from the sunshine, and partial protection from slight showers. The camps were constructed of cedar rails covered with boards, all sloping the same way. The ground rose in elevation sufficient to give the speaker, standing at the lower edge of the place of worship, a commanding view of a large congregation assembled. Learner Blackman was presiding Elder of the District (Nashville) and was in charge of the meeting. Brother Jarratt says that John Manly and Thomas King were the preachers on the circuit. The following are the first who camped on that consecrated and celebrated ground: John Windrow, Edmund Lawrance, Thomas Key, James Bass, Robert Smith, Abraham Primm, Bolling Fisher, Major Ralston and ———— Arnold. Many others came in wagons and some occupied cloth tents. People came forty miles to attend the meeting, and demonstrations attending the preaching of the Word under these grand old trees, was truly wonderful. From scores to hundreds of conversions were reported annually. But the great camp meeting was in 1820. T. L. Douglas was the Presiding Elder but Sterling Brown is remembered as the chief speaker.

"On Sunday morning the sun shone out and a vast congregation assembled. Brother Douglas announced one hundred conversions already at the tents. The manifestations of convicting and saving power increased daily. Sterling Brown would preach in the morning and men, and women would fall as men go down in battle, until the space alloted for penitents was filled, and the slain of the Lord lay scattered throughout the enclosure. Some would start to leave the ground and fall on the way, others alarmed would rush back to the camp-ground and go to the altar, and in many instances, never get up until they arose praising God . . . The result of that camp-meeting was 350 conversions. From that number several soon entered the ministry. I have the names of Abraham Overall and Martin Clark, for many years members of the Tennessee Conference, and faithful and useful in their Master's service, and Jesse Lamb a prominent member of the Cumberland Presbyterian Church . . .

"I believe Brothers William H. Smith and J. J. Jarratt who are both living on this charge now attended forty nine of the fifty camp-meetings held at Windrow's from 1812 to 1861.

"Overall's camp ground twenty miles east of Windrow's was the appropriate name of the place where for forty years or more, Robert Overall, Rev. Abraham Overall, and Rev. Nance Overall, and their father, children and neighbors held their annual feasts of the tabernacles. James G. Overall thinks the first camp-meeting was held there as early as 1813. A number of Overalls became preachers; Abraham, Nance, Asbury, Lorenzo, Nathaniel, and John Wesley, I believe . . .

"Lytle's Camp Ground was on Stone's River near Murfreesboro from 1827 to about 1843 or 1845 when it was removed to Halls higher up the river . . .

"The society of Thomas Jarratt built a log church house, called Salem, five miles southwest of Murfreesboro, in 1814, which gave place to a brick church in twenty years, which has just been remodeled at a cost of one thousand dollars, and has a flourishing society of eighty five members. The name of Dr. Sims is precious to the memory of the oldest members of that church.

"A society was formed at Rucker's as early as 1812, four miles north of Murfreesboro, which was afterwards removed a mile or two south where Emory was built and there was a good society there for many years . . . At our last Conference Overalls and Emory were attached to the Shady Grove Circuit.

"The Rev. Ebenezer McGowan came from Virginia to Rutherford County, Tennessee in 1816 and held worship at Rucker's for some years. His home, seven miles north of Murfreesboro, became a preaching place. In 1827 he deeded a beautiful grove near his home for a church, a small comfortable house, called Bethel, built of logs . . ."

Reverend Cherry further states that a church was built at Overall's in 1813 while the Asbury Society was organized "perhaps as early as 1815." He also notes that it was reported that "Rev. Lorenzo Dow preached at Halls Hill, near Overall's, on a work bench, from the text 'Turn ye to the stronghold, ye prisoners of hope.'"

When the Stone's River Circuit reported in 1814 it had 540 white and fifty-one colored members. The first pastor of this circuit was Jesse Cunningham. The great camp meeting of 1820 resulted in the organization of a church in Murfreesboro. Thereafter this faith experienced a remarkable growth in the county. The federal census of 1850 listed nineteen Methodist churches in the county with a seating capacity of 5280 and property valued at $9,160. In 1860 thirteen churches, with a seating capacity of 7600 were reported.

THE CHURCH OF CHRIST. Although the Church of Christ is one of the largest denominations in the county today, it had only four small churches in 1860 according to the federal census.

The Christian Church, as an organized body, grew out of the teachings of Alexander Campbell who was originally a Presbyterian minister. He became prominent in Pennsylvania soon after 1800 though he spent the last thirty-five years of his life in Bethany, Virginia where he edited the *Millenial Harbinger*. He and his followers were for a time affiliated with a Baptist group. Differences soon developed and by 1829 his followers had become a distinct group. It might be added, however, that union with the Baptists was discussed by members of both groups till well after the Civil War.

The Church of Christ spread rapidly after 1830, especially in the Ohio Valley where the democratic spirit of the west often condemned the idea of centralization in church organization. This same love of decentralization caused the Primitive Baptists to refuse to join the Baptist State Convention. The decentralization movement, however, caused a lack of emphasis on uniform church records and it is difficult indeed to get much authentic information on the early Church of Christ in Rutherford County as well as later statistics.

The records of the Concord Baptist Association show how the teachings of Campbell split the Baptists in middle Tennessee after 1820. One of the first churches of Christ in middle Tennessee was that at Nashville. Campbell reported in the *Millenial Harbinger* that when he visited Nashville in 1831, the church had 250 members. He also visited Columbia and Franklin. A church was in existence in Maury County by 1835 or perhaps earlier.

The date of the establishment of the first church in Rutherford County is not known. No building was erected in Murfreesboro till 1859 though services were held there in the early thirties. The federal census of 1850 listed only one Church of Christ in Rutherford County with a seating capacity of 250 and property valued at $1200. Miss Mary Hall whose ancestors have long been identified with the Church of Christ thinks that two churches, the Antioch near Porterfield and the Science Hill Church near Readyville, were established before the Murfreesboro Church. The federal census of 1860 lists four Churches of Christ in the county with seating capacity of 2950 and property valued at $7000.00. The fourth church, in addition to the Antioch, Science Hill and Murfreesboro, was probably the Lavergne church which is mentioned in the *Harbinger* in 1857.

When Campbell visited Nashville in 1835 he reported that the church there had grown to 600 members. In 1855 he again came to Tennessee at which time he visited Murfreesboro. The following interesting quotation is from his pen: "On Monday evening accompanied by Brother Fanning of Franklin College and Brother Carnes of Burrit College we made a visit to Murfreesboro, thirty-six miles distant from Nashville. The occasion of which was a very polite and urgent request tendered us from the students and faculty of the Baptist University (Union University), located at that place; to which also was added the request of a portion of the citizens of that place. On our arrival (at seven o'clock) we found in attendance a very crowded house patiently awaiting our appearance. Citizens, faculty and students being convened, and having no time to prepare an address we gave them an extemporaneous speech on all things in general, on some things in particular, and certain other things. All, however, bearing upon man as he was, man as he is, and man as he must hereafter be. We were more suggestive than demonstrative, more rhetorical than logical, more catholic than sectarian, and more liberal than finical. As to the fruit, or the impression, we learned nothing, returning early next morning to Nashville." He makes no mention of a Christian Church at Murfreesboro at this time.

By 1860 the Church of Christ had become well established in Rutherford County which was destined to become one of its strongholds.

SLAVERY AND THE CHURCHES. In addition to schisms over questions of organization and of doctrine, the slavery issue caused a split in certain churches. The National Baptist Association divided on the issue in 1845. In all probability most of the churches in Rutherford County in this organization went with the southern branch. It must be remembered, however, that a majority of the Baptist churches in the county were not members of the State Convention and therefore of the national organization.

The Methodist also split in 1845. Since the Methodist church was highly organized and all churches of that faith belonged to the state conference, it is probable that all churches in the county went with the southern branch. No churches in the county were reported in the annual minutes of the Northern Methodist Church till long after the Civil War.

The Presbyterians did not split till 1859-1861. While information is indeed scarce, it appears that all churches in the county except Hopewell joined the southern group. This church for a time was a member of a synod in north Alabama. After a few years, however, it cast its lot with the southern branch. Since the Cumberlands were, for the most part, found in the south, naturally no schism on the slavery issue took place.

By the outbreak of the Civil War the Baptists, Methodists, and Presbyterians all had strong organizations in Rutherford County, the Cumberlands probably outnumbering the parent body. The Church of Christ, the last to appear on the scene, was making steady progress. There were a few Catholic and Episcopalian families in the county but too few in each case to effect an organization. The Baptists, Methodists, and Presbyterians had split into northern and southern branches over the slavery question.

THE POST CIVIL WAR PERIOD

Religious history in Rutherford County since the Civil War has been characterized by three major developments. 1. The rise of Negro churches; 2. The continued growth of the older denominations, though in some cases this has slowed down in recent years; 3. The coming into the county of certain of the newer denominations that had their beginning in the latter part of the nineteenth century. Each of these will be briefly discussed.

The Civil War played havoc with the churches in Rutherford County. Let it be remembered as is pointed out in another chapter that the fighting in Rutherford County was most severe and that the city was occupied by northern troops for a considerable time. Many church buildings were burned or torn down. The aggregate seating capacity of churches in the county according to the federal census of 1860 was 31,850 while ten years later it was only 17,275. Even if one makes allowances for customary errors in the federal religious censuses, great destruction must have been wrought by the occupying forces. The Presbyterians appear to have lost three buildings including the attractive brick church at Murfreesboro. In addition to the physical side of the picture, the churches of the area had the problem of regaining lost morale as well as what to do with Negro members.

THE RISE OF NEGRO CHURCHES. The negro is by nature very religious. He demonstrated this quality prior to the Civil War in the south where both encouragement and restrictions were common, as well as in the north where he had more freedom for self-expression. When, after the war, he assumed control of his religious destiny in the south, he followed the same general pattern as that of his former master. The strong Negro churches today bear the same names and have substantially the same beliefs as the strong white churches. Radicalism in religion appears to have invaded the ranks of each race to a comparable degree. It is true that the Negro today is somewhat more emotional in the expression of his faith than his white brother, but no more so than the white pioneer of the west in the early part of the nineteenth centry.

In the south before the war, the whites usually looked after the religious life of the slaves. Bishop McTyere of the Methodist church sums up the practice of his church in the following words: "As a general rule slaves received the gospel by the Methodist from the same preachers and in the churches with their masters, the galleries or a portion of the body of the house being assigned to them. If a separate building was provided, the Negro congregation was an appendage to the white, the pastor usually preaching once on Sunday for them, holding separate official meetings with their leaders, exhorters and preachers, and administering discipline, and making return of members for the annual minutes."

The above description would no doubt apply to the churches of Rutherford County generally. The Stone's River Methodist circuit before the war regularly listed Negro members as well as a Negro mission. While no records are available for Presbyterian churches of the county, the church at Murfreesboro had a gallery for colored people. The Shiloh Presbyterian church in Sumner County, the oldest of that faith in middle Tennessee, in 1830 listed 123 white and thirty-eight colored members. The records of the Providence Primitive and of the Murfreesboro Baptist churches show numerous Negro members. Camp meeting grounds regularly had sections for the colored race.

At the close of the war the problem of what to do with Negro members immediately presented itself. The ultimate solution was complete separation though it took some years and a few Negroes remained in the white churches till their death.

The Cumberland church after discussing the matter for a few years held a meeting at Murfreesboro in 1869. Here it was decided to separate the races and the Colored Cumberland church came into existence. For a time this body was fairly numerous in Rutherford County. In 1906 the Federal census listed 242 members. By 1916 the number had dropped to 137. Since that time none has been reported.

There are three large negro Methodist bodies, namely, the African Methodist Episcopal Church, The African Methodist Episcopal Zion Church, and the Colored Methodist Church. There are also a considerable number of Negro churches formerly affiliated with the Northern Methodist Church which are now in the United Methodist group.

The African Methodist Church, the largest of the group, was formed soon after the Revolutionary War. Negro members, in the north, dissatisfied with certain discriminations against them, began to hold separate services as early as 1787 when a group in Philadelphia withdrew, built a church and secured the services of a negro preacher. By 1816 the church had become an independent organization. Before the Civil War little effort was made to spread the organization to the south. After the war, however, the church spread rapidly and is today well organized in all of the former slave states. This church, like most Negro Methodist groups, agrees substantially with the Methodist Episcopal Church in doctrine. This is the largest Negro Methodist Church in Rutherford County with about five hundred members at present.   The most outstanding church of this denomination in the county is Allen's Chapel in Murfreesboro.

The African Zion church was also organized in the north long before the Civil War.   Although it is almost as large as the African church in the nation and in the state it has never reported any members in Rutherford County in the federal census.

After the Civil War about 80,000 Negroes remained in the Southern Methodist church.   In 1866 in New Orleans steps were taken to form two separate bodies.   This was accomplished when in 1870 the colored members held their first general conference at Jackson, Tennessee.   It appears that for a time after the war there were many Colored Methodist in Rutherford County.   Census reports in recent years, however, show less than a hundred members.

The Northern Methodist church came into Rutherford County sometime after the Civil War.   In 1890 the Federal census listed four northern churches with a membership of 670.   By 1916 the number had grown to 1317.   Ten years later it had declined to 632, while in 1936 only forty-two members were reported.   The last number is much too low.   The annual report of the Tennessee Conference of the northern branch for 1908 lists circuits at Christiana with 102 members, at Salem with 70, Smyrna 223, Murfreesboro with 167, a mission at Eagleville with 23 members and a station at Murfreesboro with 325 members, a total of over 900 members.   Most of these evidently were Negro churches, but it is impossible to say just how many since the reports do not list the white and Negro members separately.   It is known, however, that the Murfreesboro station listed was the Key Memorial Church.   This is one of the most outstanding Negro churches in the county.   It was organized February 18, 1866 and their building erected a year later.   In 1938, the year before unification, this church reported 222 active members and 75 inactive.   The rapid decline of this church in the rural sections of the county in recent years is no doubt due in part to migrations and to competition from other groups.

While there are a number of colored Baptist groups in the United States, the most important group, by and large, is the Negro Baptist Church.   It came into existence as a result of the Civil War.   This is the largest Negro denomination in the nation.   Immersion as a means of baptism has always appealed to the Negro; in fact, many colored Methodists practice immersion.   The Federal census for Rutherford County for 1936 reported seventeen churches with 1849 members, while in 1926 the number reported was 1865.   The First Baptist church of Murfreesboro, is the most outstanding church of this faith in the county.   It celebrated its eightieth anniversary in

1946. It has 350 members. The Mount Zion Baptist Church of Murfreesboro is another outstanding church of this faith in the county.

The Colored Primitive Baptist church, like the white Primitive Baptists, has declined in recent years. The Mt. Zion church in Murfreesboro is the only church of this faith that the writer was able to locate in the county.

There are four colored Churches of Christ in the county including the East State Street church located in Murfreesboro. The congregation in Murfreesboro was organized soon after the Civil War and is one of the oldest colored churches in the county. It now has about eighty members. It might be added that the colored branch of this church has not grown as rapidly in the county as the white branch.

There are two colored Churches of God in the county, one in Murfreesboro and the other at Rockvale. Both are very small.

WHITE CHURCHES SINCE THE CIVIL WAR.   When the Civil War was over the white people in Rutherford County not only had the task of rebuilding their economy on a different labor system but had to recover much that had been lost in cultural and spiritual areas of life.   Schools and churches had to be rebuilt and congregations reorganized.   Although comparable statistics on membership changes immediately after the war are incomplete, all major denominations except perhaps the Southern Presbyterians appear to have made considerable gains.   The same trend is true, for the most part, since 1890.   A brief summary of each white denomination will now be given.

THE BAPTISTS.   This is still the largest denomination in the county.   The census for 1890 reported fifteen Southern Baptist (Missionary) churches with a membership of 1549.   Ten Primitive Baptist churches with a membership of 543 were reported for the same year.   The Free Will Baptists reported two churches with forty-five members.   There were also several Duck River Baptist churches which were not reported.   Since 1890 the Southern Church has tended to absorb all other groups except the Duck River churches. The Southern group reported 3302 members in 1926 while the official records of the Concord Association for 1945 reported 4392 members for the county.   The Primitives dropped to 106 members in 1926 and now have only two small churches, the Providence Church near Walter Hill and a church at Eagleville.   The Freewill Baptists have not been reported by the census since 1890 though a few are said still to be in the county.

The Duck River Baptists, though a small denomination found only in a few southern states, have at least held their own in recent years. Today they have four churches in the county with a total membership of 548. Mr. S. F. Shelton, who lives in Rutherford County near Beech Grove, has for years been clerk of this denomination.

THE METHODISTS. For years after the war this church continued its revivals with vigor and made many converts. By 1890 it was the largest denomination in the county though it was exceeded by the combined Baptist groups. In recent years it has become somewhat more conservative, and shouting for the most part has "gone out of style." In 1890 the Southern Church had twenty-four churches with a membership of 2390. In 1926 it had 2792 members. In 1939 the Northern, Southern, and Protestant Methodists united. In 1944 the records of the united church showed 23 churches with a total membership of 3231 in the county. There were a few Protestant Methodists in the county at one time. Most of them appear to have come into the southern branch before unification.

THE PRESBYTERIANS. In 1890 the census reported eighteen Cumberland churches in the county with a membership of 1467. This church experienced great growth both before and after the war and reached its peak about the turn of the century. The Southern Presbyterians reported, in 1890, four churches with 515 members. It is known, however, that there were five churches in the county at that date. In 1906 the Cumberlands had dropped to 1053 while the Southern had risen to 905. This shift was due to the proposed union of the Cumberlands with the Northern Presbyterians which took place in 1906. When the union was approved, the majority in the county refused to abide by the decision of their general assembly, and continued as Cumberlands. Some joined the Methodist while others went into the southern branch. This was especially true in Murfreesboro where the southern church was without the services of a pastor. This church issued a call to the pastor of the local Cumberland church, R. G. Newsome, and he accepted bringing with him the majority of his congregation. Only four Cumberland churches in the county joined the union, those at Lavergne, Christiana, Lascassas and one in the Eagleville vicinity though this church is thought by some to have been just over the county line. The last two named soon expired, the Methodist purchasing the Lascassas building. The other two with a combined membership of about 150 are still functioning as the only northern churches in the county.

The Cumberlands in the county who remained with their church have had a struggle, though, within the last decade, they have made some gains and have reopened a few old churches that for a time were closed. In 1916 they reported 585 members, while in 1926 the number was 530. Their last annual report shows seven active churches with a membership of 604.

The Cumberlands of Rutherford County are justly proud of two outstanding ministers whom they have contributed to the nation. One of these was John Royal Harris, who was reared in the Jefferson community and was a descendant of General Coffee. He preached at one of the largest churches in Pittsburg and was also president of Cumberland University. The other was William Moses Woodfin who also preached for a number of years at Pittsburg and later was pastor of the Edgewater Presbyterian Church of Chicago, one of the largest in the nation.

THE CHURCH OF CHRIST. This church like others suffered from the war. In 1866 a meeting was held in Murfreesboro because of the "present scattered, destitute and distressed condition of the brethern generally in the south . . . " Delegates were present from Tennessee, Alabama, Missouri, Kentucky, Georgia, and Virginia. There were twenty-five delegates from Rutherford County churches. Elders John W. Hall and W. H. Goodloe were prominent in the proceedings. In addition to Murfreesboro, delegates were listed as being present from the Smyrna, Lavergne, and Union churches in Rutherford County. This meeting apparently gave new life to the church and was followed by a great growth, especially in Tennessee. In 1870 thirteen churches with a seating capacity of 1850 were listed in Rutherford County in the census reports. In 1906 there were listed 1965 members.

Prior to the Civil War differences developed among the members of this faith over music in the churches and other issues. Various terms have been used to distinguish the two factions. Those favoring music are often referred to as progressives while the others are called conservatives. About 1900 the arguments between the two groups became more heated and many churches split. The Murfreesboro church divided in 1908. The majority remained with the conservative group. In 1916 the census reported 2157 conservatives and 255 progressives in the county, while ten years later the respective membership was 2275 and 154. The 1936 census which is conceded to be too low for most denominations lists 2008 conservatives and 147 progressives. According to Rev. C. M. Pullias the conservatives have at present thirty-one churches in the county. The number of members is variously estimated at from 2500 to 4000. The first figure is probably closer to the true number. This church has, however, had the most rapid growth of any of the major denominations in the county since the Civil War.

CATHOLICS.   Before the Civil War there were several Catholic families in Rutherford County. Mass was occasionally said at the home of John Stanfield. General Rosecrans is reported to have attended mass at Murfreesboro during the war. Fr. Jaquette appears to have been the first who visited the mission here.

Later, Sunday devotions were conducted in the home of Mrs. S. B. Christy. By 1918 a sufficient number of families were in town to justify the renting of a room in the Masonic building and a Sunday school was organized. On September 15, 1929, the congregation moved into a beautiful little building on Lytle street, constructed through the generosity of Mr. and Mrs. Hoffman of New York. Miss Essie Hancock has long been one of the faithful members. The federal census of 1926 reported 36 members while in 1936 the number had risen to 45.

EPISCOPALIANS. There were no doubt a few Episcopalians in Rutherford County before the Civil War but no information concerning them is available. The present church was organized in the 1880's. The federal census of 1890 reports six members. The first services were held in the Knights of Pythias Hall. The first building was at Shiloh on the Lascassas pike about 1896. The sanctuary window was given by Bishop Quintard. In 1898 a building was erected in Murfreesboro on Spring Street. In 1927 it was moved to its present location on Main Street and was remodeled. In 1936 the federal census reported 51 communicants. Its most famous members have been the Murfree sisters, Mary N. (Charles Egbert Craddock) and Fanny N. Mr. George Darrow was also a member for years.

NEWER DENOMINATIONS. In the latter part of the nineteenth century a number of new denominations began to spring up. This movement is still in progress. Social, economic and perhaps political conditions, in some ways, resembling the conditions that produced the camp meeting and schisms in many Protestant churches in the early part of the 1800's were responsible for these new churches. They appealed especially to the poor and disappointed, to some who were not satisfied with their own church and to others who had never been in any church. While Rutherford County had never been a stronghold for these newer denominations, they have entered it and are apparently here to stay.

Although the Seventh Day Adventist church was organized in Boston in 1844, its growth was slow for a time. In recent years it has increased relatively rapidly. In Tennessee it almost trebled in membership from 1906 to 1936. There is one church in Rutherford County. It was organized east of Murfreesboro on the Woodbury road over fifty years ago. In 1945 it erected a small but adequate building on Fourth Avenue in Murfreesboro. The membership is about 35.

The church of the Nazarene was organized in Providence, Rhode Island, in 1886. It has had a remarkable growth in recent years. In 1916 the federal census reported 48 churches with a membership of 1903 in Tennessee, while in 1936 the number of churches had risen to 74 with a membership of 5416. A church of this faith was organized in Murfreesboro about 1938. Three years ago the congregation moved into a new church located on Vine Street. The membership at present is about 80.

One of the most beautiful structures in the county is the house of worship of the Church of Christ, Scientist, located on East Main street. This building was designed by Will Bell and constructed by Bell Brothers in 1942. This faith reported five churches in Tennessee in 1906 with a membership of 337. In 1936 it numbered ten churches with 1404 members. The Murfreesboro congregation had its beginning in 1917 when meetings were held in a home. In 1926 the Woman's Club was used. During the same year the organization became a Christian Science Society, a branch of the First Church of Christ, Scientist, of Boston.

The Churches of God, of which there are many groups, have increased rapidly in recent years. So much confusion exists between the groups—all called themselves the "Church of God"—that at times it is almost impossible to arrive at accurate conclusions as to their numbers. One branch, sometimes called the "Church of God, Reformation Movement," was organized in 1881. It was two congregations in Rutherford County. One is the Spring Street church in Murfreesboro, which recently erected a building. It has about 35 members. There is another congregation at Rockvale. These churches do not stress talking in "unknown tongues" as do many of this faith.

The Bilbro Street Church of God (Tomlinson branch) has its headquarters in Cleveland, Tennessee. It has grown quite rapidly in recent years. Its meetings are characterized by much shouting. The church at Murfreesboro has about sixty members. It is reported to be trying to buy a site in Murfreesboro for a college.

OUTSTANDING CHURCHES

THE FIRST PRESBYTERIAN CHURCH OF MURFREESBORO.[1] While this is not the largest church in the county, it was the first to be organized in Murfreesboro and for years was one of the

1. Most of the information in the following sketch was obtained from an unpublished history of this church by Miss Anne Eleanor Campbell whose family has long been identified with Presbyterianism in Murfreesboro.

most outstanding in middle Tennessee. It has long been identified with many of the county's leading families. Especially was this true in the pre-Civil War days.

The church was organized in 1812 by Dr. Robert Henderson. The first meeting place of the church was a log schoolhouse on land belonging to Colonel Hardy Murfree near the city spring. The charter members have already been given.

In 1820 a brick building, forty by sixty feet, was erected, the first in the town. It was located in the old cemetery on Vine Street where a marker now commemorates the spot. The church had a gallery for slaves and also a choir loft in the gallery. It was used by the legislature as a meeting place after the county courthouse burned in 1822 while Murfreesboro was the capitol of the state. A floor was laid on a level with the balcony. The House of Representatives used the downstairs while the Senate used the upper floor. By 1827 the church had 128 members. In 1852 an act of the legislature made the pastor and elders of the church the legal representatives of the organization.

The most famous pastor of the church was Doctor William Eagleton. Though born in Blount County he is more identified with Rutherford County where he was pastor of the Murfreesboro church from 1829 to 1866. He encouraged camp meetings of the dignified type where a silent reverence took the place of shouting, and he was partly responsible for the success of the McKnight camp ground in the eastern part of the county. He also organized churches on the Sulphur Spring and Manchester pikes as well as a mission on the Woodbury road. The Civil War, however, seems to have wrecked his dreams to make these churches permanent. By 1853 he had raised the membership of his church over 300. A marble plaque on the wall of the present church auditorium commemorates his services to the community.

The old building was destroyed by the northern army during the Civil War and the brick used for kitchen furnaces. Certain members of the congregation saved the bell by concealing it for the duration of the war. A new structure was erected at the site of the present building in 1867 at a cost of about $18,000. In 1913 this building was destroyed by a tornado. The present building was completed in 1914. The present membership is about 500. Subscriptions are now being taken for a new organ to cost $12,000.

Among the important pastors of recent years are Doctor E. A. Ramsey, Doctor J. Addison Smith, Doctor Edgar W. Williams and Doctor J. H. McCain. The present pastor is Reverend Ralph M. Llewellyn. Clerks of the session have been David Wendall, James F. McFadden, Doctor J. B. Murfree, Sr., William Park, E. J. Reid,

and the incumbent, C. B. Bell.   D. L. Ledbetter is now chairman of
the board of deacons.

Prominent names appearing on the list of Elders and Deacons
other than those already mentioned are Wm. H. McFadden, Gideon
Baskett, Doctor James Maney, Jonathan Currin, D. D. Wendell,
Charles Ready, Dr. J. E. Wendell, J. T. McFadden, Jr., W. Y.
Elliot, J. W. Ewing, William Wendell, Dr. J. B. Murfree, Jr., P. A.
Lyon, Dr. M. B. Murfree, Dr. W. T. Robison, Adam Bock, George
Walter, James Clayton, N. C. Maney, and D. P. Perkins.   The
church is noted for the outstanding work of its women's organization.

THE FIRST METHODIST CHURCH OF MURFREES-
BORO.   This institution which today boasts over one thousand
members is said to have come into being as a result of the famous
camp meetings at Windrow's in 1820.   The church first appears in
the records of the Tennessee Conference in 1822 at which time it
was joined with Shelbyville.   The combined members of the two
churches was 78 white and 62 colored.   In 1827 it was joined with
Lebanon for a short time.   In 1830 it became a station.   Robert
Paine, who later became Bishop Paine, was the first pastor.   The
following nineteen were charter members: Benjamin Blankenship
and wife, William Ledbetter, Martin Clark, G. A. Sublett, Edward
Fisher and wife, Thomas Montague and wife, John D. Nugent,
Doctor H. Holmes, David Haynes, Edmund Jones and wife, John
Lytle and wife, Levi Reeves, Willis Reeves, and William Rucker.
Descendants of many of these are living in the county today.   It is of
interest that "Mother" Wasson, a member of the church in its
early years, boasted of having received the sacrament from the hands
of John Wesley.   In 1823 the congregation decided to erect a building.   It was constructed on the land donated by John Lytle where
the recently burned high school stood.   The building cost about
$1800.   In 1828 the Tennessee Conference met at Murfreesboro.
Since that time about a dozen meetings have been held in this city.

In 1844 a new church was completed.   It was just south of the
present structure.   The building still stands.   It had a gallery for
colored people as well as a basement which was sometimes used for
Negroes.   The church grew rapidly for the next few years and was
instrumental in helping to found Soule College in Murfreesboro.

The following interesting quotation is from the pen of Rev. John
B. McFerrin in 1853.   "By request I visited Murfreesboro, Tennessee, and preached a funeral sermon in memory of Mrs. Sarah Polk
Phillips and Mrs. Joanna Jetton, daughters of W. R. Rucker.   They
were nieces of Mrs. President Polk.   About three years before I had
married both parties under one ceremony and now in one funeral

discourse the last tribute to two excellent Christian women, both members of the Methodist church."

During the war the church was badly damaged and for a time the congregation worshiped in the Cumberland church. The damaged structure was soon repaired. In 1888 the present structure was erected. Mr. Wash Henry was the contractor. N. C. Collier, James Reed, John B. Ransom, Horace Palmer and perhaps others were on the building committee. The pulpit was sent from Texas by R. W. Sanders in memory of his mother. In 1908 T. C. Ragsdale came to the church as pastor with the avowed purpose of building a Sunday school building and a parsonage. He was successful in both undertakings. Recently the old parsonage was changed to a Sunday school annex and a new one purchased on Lytle Street.

Numerous prominent ministers have served the Murfreesboro church including two who later became bishops. The first pastor of the church, Robert Paine, after a successful career as a minister, was elevated to the bishopric, the ambition of every Methodist minister. As bishop he frequently visited Murfreesboro and presided over conferences held there. The other pastor to become bishop was Paul B. Kern who came to the church in 1912. He was responsible for the establishment of the Wesley House and was one of the most highly regarded ministers ever connected with the local church. The Murfreesboro church is justly proud of the association of these two men with the congregation.

Outstanding pastors before the Civil War in addition to Paine were Lorenzo Overall, one of the pulpit orators of middle Tennessee, Edward C. Slater, who later was pastor of the McKendree church, and Samuel Baldwin, author of Armageddon. Baldwin was also president of the Soule College as were several other pastors of the church. John B. McFerrin, outstanding author and preacher both before and after the war, was another distinguished divine who served as pastor for the Murfreesboro congregation.

Just before the turn of the century J. D. Barbee, who was later an agent for the publishing house, and A. G. Dinwiddie were outstanding pastors. In 1904 George A. Morgan, a pulpit orator of considerable reputation, was sent to the church. In 1916 W. W. Alexander, who was later associated with the Commission on Interracial Cooperation, was pastor. Recent pastors have been E. P. Anderson, D. E. Hinkle, J. F. Baggett, J. R. Parsons, B. B. Pennington, and Willard Blue. The present pastor is C. B. Cook.[1]

In 1930 the College Place Methodist church was established in the eastern part of Murfreesboro, across the street from the State

1. Much of the material for this sketch was furnished by Mrs. T. S. McFerrin.

Teachers College. Professor and Mrs. Neal Frazier were leading
spirits in the new church. James Cox was the first pastor. This
church recently sold its Boulevard property and purchased a house
on East Main Street. The membership is near 200.

THE FIRST BAPTIST CHURCH. This church with a mem-
bership today of over one thousand is one of the largest in the county.
It began, however, much later than the Presbyterian and Methodist
churches. It was organized on June 8, 1843, under the name of
United Baptist Church of Christ in Murfreesboro, Tennessee. The
name "The First Baptist Church" of Murfreesboro was taken up
about 1870. There were sixteen charter members all coming from
near-by Baptist churches, as follows: from Nashville, twelve; Overall's
Creek, three; Fall Creek, one; The charter members were as follows:
Burrell Gannaway, John Muller, Nancy Molloy, Charles C. Johns,
George D. Crosthwaith, Eliza Crosthwaith, Thomas H. Maney,
Fanney N. Maney, Fanny Priscilla Dickinson, Mary Louisa Bell,
Rev. Cyrus Smith, Dorinda L. Smith, Rev. Joseph Eaton, William
H. January, James Franklin Fletcher, and Jane Fletcher.

The Rev. C. B. Howell preached the first sermon. The first
meetings were held in Fletcher's schoolhouse which probably was
located on Vine Street. In March, 1860, it was resolved to build
a new church the following year. For obvious reasons the building
was not erected till 1868. It was located on Main Street and was
referred to as the "Red Brick Church." In 1889 a resolution was
passed to repair the church. C. H. Byrn, H. H. Williams, C. O.
Thomas, M. F. Jordan, and J. C. Patey were named as a building
committee. It was decided, however, to build a new church which
was dedicated in 1892.

In 1913 the church was outgrowing its accommodations and
a building committee composed of R. W. Hale, chairman, C. H.
Byrn, A. L. Todd, W. C. Bilbro, E. T. Rion, A. J. Jones, and John
Williams was appointed. The present building, a monument to the
Baptist people of the city and county, was completed in 1920. As a
result of the depression, the church in 1936 was not able to meet its
financial obligations and the building was bought by the bondholders.
For a time the congregation worshiped in the auditorium of Tennessee College. In 1937 a plan was prefected whereby the bondholders resold the building to the congregation. In 1907 a house
for the pastor was purchased while the present pastorium was erected
in 1915. The church has an excellent pipe organ, the gift of Mr. and
Mrs. Andrew Todd in 1923, as a memorial to their son, Aaron.

Outstanding pastors of the church include, T. T. Eaton, Edgar
Estes Folk, I. J. Van Ness, A. C. Davidson, Austin Crouch, F. C.

McConnell, Carter Helm Jones, and Leland Sedberry. The present pastor is Griffin Henderson.[1]

THE MAIN STREET CHURCH OF CHRIST. The following quotation from the directory of the church prepared in 1913 by the Reverend G. Dallas Smith, pastor of the church, is the best source of information available on the early history of the congregation.

"The Church of Christ in Murfreesboro is probably about one hundred years old. It is known that as early as the year 1833 there were a few members of the church who met from place to place— sometimes in the courthouse and sometimes at other places, as they had no regular place of meeting. About the year 1850 the congregation began to meet regularly in a brick school house which was located near what is known as West Vine Street, near Lytle's Creek. Here they continued to meet for worship until the year 1859 when they purchased a lot on the corner of Main and Academy Streets and erected thereon a substantial and commodious brick building. All funds used in building this house were furnished by members of the church . . .

"During the war the house was used, sometimes by the southern soldiers and sometimes by the federal soldiers, as a hospital or as a place to conduct religious services . . .

"In the year 1900 it was decided to build a new and better house as the old one then in use was over forty years old. Accordingly the old house was torn down and the present building erected at a cost of $12,000. All of the funds used in building this house were likewise contributed by members of the church. Brother J. M. Haynes, now deceased, furnished almost half of the amount. While this house was being built the congregation met again at the court house.

"But as the congregation grew in wealth and popularity the spirit of innovation also grew and developed. Some of the members became tired of the simplicity of the New Testament work and worship. Hence dissentions arose and the church for a few years was involved in strife and confusion. This finally terminated in a number of the members withdrawing from the congregation and establishing, in the first Lord's day in August, 1908, a congregation more in harmony with their views. This congregation is just completing a handsome building at a cost of probably $20,000 or $25,000."

Reverend Smith apparently overlooked the fact generally accepted in Murfreesboro that James A. Garfield, who was a member of the Church of Christ, preached for this congregation in Murfreesboro while with the northern army of occupation.

1. Most of the above information on the Baptist Church was furnished by Mr. Frank E. Bass.

In 1913 the Main Street Church had a membership of about 350. At present it boasts over twelve hundred members and is probably the largest church in the county. The present structure was remodelled in 1922.

Pastors of the church have been C. K. Marshall, W. H. Goodloe, C. M. Day, G. W. Able, A. P. Aten, Jas. E. Scoby, A. N. Gilbert, A. M. Growden, Geo. A. Gowen, H. G. Fleming, W. L. Logan, J. Paul Slayden, T. B. Larrimore, G. Dallas Smith, A. B. Barrett, C. E. Woodridge, C. M. Pullias, J. P. Ezell, Joseph Netherland, Tolbert H. Kennedy, and the present pastor, George De Hoff.

The Westview Church of Christ was organized in 1930. It has had a remarkable growth and now has about 300 members. C. M. Pullias is pastor.

During the past year two new Churches of Christ have been organized in Murfreesboro, one on North Boulevard and the other on North Maple Street.

CHAPTER X

Economic History of Rutherford County

Paraphrasing the words of a once popular melody, the girls and boys of Middle Tennessee State College may often be heard singing the praises of the land and area in which their institution has its setting as dormitories ring with,

"M'-B-O-R-O, down where Stone's River flows
The girls are the fairest, the boys are the squarest
Of any old place I know."

The youthful enthusiasm of these young Tennesseans for the community in which they live and learn does not belie the actual conditions which exist in that county which occupies more than six hundred square miles in the exact center of Tennessee.

AGRICULTURE

Favorable climate, a sturdy and industrious population, geographic setting, historical development, and good farm lands combine to make Rutherford County one of the richest and most progressive of all the ninety-five counties of Tennessee. A drive along some of the main highways of the county would not convince a casual observer of the richness of the soils found in the rural areas. In referring to the farm lands between Murfreesboro and Shelbyville, in both Rutherford and Bedford Counties, a book published in 1939 under the Federal Writers Project and entitled, *Tennessee, American Guide Series*, had the following to say, "The country is flat and grown sparsely with cedars. Outcrops of bedrock rising in many places above the shallow topsoil make this poor farming territory. It was once said that 'a man living back in the cedars has got to scratch and sweat mightily if he wants to starve decent.'" The authors responsible for the above statement might view the situation somewhat differently today if they should visit certain farms in the vicinity of the area which they described. Through hard work and vision some of the farms have within a short time become the most productive in the county. Through long range planning, careful

management and scientific practices, which have been encouraged
by various farm organizations, owners have been able to bring apparent waste land back into production and at the same time to
provide a measure of security for themselves and their tenants. A
program of diversification, followed by many of the farmers, assures
a cash income every month of the year and makes it possible for em-
ployees to receive a year-round wage.

The story of the farms in this area is but an example of what can
be done on the farm lands of Rutherford County which are situated
near the bottom of the great bowl known as the Central Basin of
Tennessee. Unfortunately, however, those who have tilled the soil
during the past years of the history of Rutherford County have paid
too little attention to the terrific toll in soil erosion. Since the days
before the Civil War, farmers have thought in terms of raising the
crops which would produce the most ready money. These were
for the most part, cotton, corn, and tobacco.

The entire system of agriculture for the county before the Civil
War depended upon slavery. In 1810, seven years after the formation of the county, there were 1,080 heads of families dwelling within
the boundaries of the county. Four hundred and five of these owned
slaves. The following is a list of those who owned twenty slaves or
more:

Dan Marshall	42	John Lenoir	20
Fred Bickton	20	John Smith	40
Bennett Smith	39	William Mitchell	21
Samuel Bowman	20	John Reed	37
William Moseley	29	Robert Bedford	34
Alex McCulloch	31	William Lytle	23
Henry Marable	31	Robert Smith	22
Thomas Rucker	29	Dan Parker	45
James Burrus	37	William Warren	24
Mark Mitchell	28	Sally Caswell	20
James Rucker	32	Ezek Moore	24
Isaac Shelby	33	Thomas Washington	27

In the same year, according to the United States Census, fifty-one
heads of families owned from 10 to 19 slaves each, two hundred and
nineteen owned from 2 to 10 each and one hundred and eleven owned
only one each. It was therefore not unusual to find upon the minutes
of the court such items as "bill of sale from James S. Conway to
Mary Mitchell for three Negro slaves for life named David, Charity,
and Minerva was this day presented in open Court and the execution
thereof duly proven by the oath of James Boone and Thomas C.
Mitchell, subscribing witnesses thereto and ordered to be registered."
Slaves were frequently offered for sale by advertisements in local

newspapers while a reward was occasionally offered for the return of a run-a-way slave. In 1820 there were 5,227 Negroes in the county out of a total population of 19,552 while in 1850 the Negro population had risen to 11,978 out of a total of 29,122.

One might well wonder what activities engaged the slaves and their owners on the early farms of Rutherford County. In 1803, an act was passed by the State Legislature "To purchase for the State of Tennessee the patent right of Eli Whitney and Phileas Miller of a machine or new invention for cleaning cotton, commonly called the 'saw gin' ". Although four Rutherford County citizens in 1804 were granted the right to use this patent a gin was not erected till 1808 or 1809.

Another insight into the agricultural and industrial history of Rutherford County is found in a letter written by Col. Frank Nash of Murfreesboro to his father in North Carolina, February 26, 1818:

"I will be able to plant about 5,000 tobacco hills, and as much cotton and ground enough, if a tolerable year to make about 500 or 600 barrels of corn and if my tobacco ground turns out like my neighbors, which by the by, I hope it will surpass, I expect a good crop of tobacco. Old Captain Black, here on Stone's River planted the last year 80,000 hills, and from it has passed 38,000 pounds of tobacco besides the officials' tobacco; and besides this killed 33,000 pounds of pork, working 13 or 14 hands. But I cannot do as well this year having to build my house and all outhouses, stables, etc. My house with four rooms will be done in three weeks and then I will have more done than can be done without my being here. We have the finest rock for building I have ever seen."

By 1840 Middle Tennessee was one of the greatest corn producing areas of the nation. During that year Rutherford County, which was near the top for the entire United States, produced over three million bushels of Indian corn. After that date competition with the middle west and perhaps soil exhaustion caused a decline. In 1850 the county produced close to 15,000 bales of cotton of 400 pounds each and 170,000 pounds of tobacco while 490 pounds of rice were harvested in the low river land areas. Wheat, rye, and other grains while produced in some quantity were decidedly secondary to corn and cotton. In 1850, 184,536 pounds of butter were produced for sale along with 1,475 pounds of cheese. Some hemp was also grown before the war. The cash value of the Rutherford County farms of 1850 was fixed by census reports at approximately four and a half million dollars, with live stock valued at close to a million dollars. The value of farm machinery was fixed by the 1850 census at $138,898 and there were found on Rutherford County farms 9,995 horses,

2,227 mules, 7,359 milch cows, 2,010 working oxen, 25,604 sheep and 88,794 swine.

It need not be supposed that hard labor, from sun up to sun down, marked all of the life of the people of early Rutherford County. An old county newspaper reveals that In the 1820's and 1830's in a large number of Tennessee counties, there was a pronounced move-ment for the raising of thoroughbred horses and the construction of race tracks as an incident to the industry. It looked for a time that Rutherford County would take a place in the forefront. On a small scale, attention had been given to the raising of pedigreed horses in the county and many men of high character and note took part, among them Parry W. Humphreys and Charles Ready. In the 1830's Jockey Clubs were organized in every grand division of Tennessee. The local race-course was at Major John Bradley's home, Hurricane Hill, near Murfreesboro, and the 'meets' were held about the first of September. Purses ranged from $50 to $500 and high grade horses were entered. Some of these were Racolet, Stockholder, Sir Archy, Waterloo, Volunteer and others. The last name, Volunteer, was a son of the great English Volunteer, winner of the great derby stake. Cock fighting was also a popular sport and many fine game chickens were raised in the county.

Agriculture in Rutherford County prior to the Civil War was indeed prosperous though signs of a decline were present by 1860. By 1870, however, the war and the dark days of reconstruction had caused the picture to change. There were fewer horses, mules, and oxen to till the soil. These had been taken away for use in both the Union and Confederate armies. The loss of slave labor, although never as important in Tennessee as in near by states, had begun to change the agricultural pattern. Very few Rutherford County farmers again attempted to grow tobacco in any large quantities. Cotton never again reached its early importance in Rutherford County. This despite the fact that in 1925 Tennessee produced 510,000 bales valued at $47,343,000 and Rutherford County was among the leading counties in the average yield per acre. For more than twenty-five years after the war, the farm lands of Rutherford County decreased in value, although this was true of almost all the southern farm communities as well. The hardships in the years following reconstruction days, however, brought to many southern farmers the ability to fall back upon their own resources and to find a kind of self-sufficiency in themselves and in the soil. Thus the farmer began gradually to feed himself and those who engaged in other pursuits. The Rutherford farms in addition to the main money crops began to grow larger quantities of such crops as pota-toes, beans, peas, wheat, rye, oats, barley, and other products needed for both man and beast.

This diversification program was first stimulated by the Federal Government and the University of Tennessee and later by the state college at Murfreesboro which for some years maintained an efficient department of agriculture and an experimental farm. The county agricultural and home demonstration agents have also aided in the program while the Federal Government and the Tennessee Valley Authority have in recent years encouraged a scientific land use plan embracing reforestation, terracing, the use of cover crops, and numerous other desirable practices. The county has a number of progressive farm organizations including a Grange which maintains a market for farm produce. Since the turn of the century the county has had a number of farmers who were able to combine successfully theory and practice in agriculture. All of these and other factors too numerous to mention have in recent years caused Rutherford County again to attain the place in agriculture which it held before the Civil War. The most important outgrowth of this diversification movement has been the rise of the dairy industry. Its history will be briefly traced.

The sale of butter and cheese from the rambling sales cart had become an important source of revenue long before 1840, and has remained an important source of revenue to this date. It has been stated that no section of the country offers greater inducements to those who wish to enter the dairy industry, for blue grass grows readily in all parts of the county, the mild climate permits year-round grazing and the cool pure water of the springs and creeks adds to the health of the cattle and aids in preservation of dairy industry. The first Jersey cattle brought into Rutherford County were owned by Mr. J. H. Crichlow and Dr. J. J. Rucker. Major Jesse Sparks is said to have brought the first Jersey bull to the county from the Isle of Jersey soon after the Civil War. The first "Medal of Merit" cow east of the Mississippi River and second in the United States was raised on a Rutherford County farm. Since the importation of this breed into the county, dairying has become more and more important.

About 1890, the first creamery was organized in Murfreesboro by a group of enterprising men. The creamery ran for about twelve months and was discontinued. Eric Carlson was the first person thereafter to own a cream separator, but soon, there were many in the county and the need for creameries became increasingly greater. The Rutherford County Cooperative Creamery was organized in 1914 and by 1935 was producing 1,345,000 pounds of butter. The Carnation Milk Plant was constructed on the Lytle estate in 1927 and opened for business on October 7 of that year.   In less than a year's time this company was purchasing 200,000 pounds of milk each day from the farms of Rutherford, and adjoining counties.   This entire supply is canned and sold to brokers and jobbers, who in turn sell it to wholesalers in Tennessee and nearby states.   Wilson and Company now manufacture cheese and butter at the plant formerly operated by the Clark Dairy Products Company.   Murfreesboro also is an ice cream center of considerable importance.   The Consumers Supply Company and the Red Rose Dairies supply much of middle Tennessee as well as parts of other states with a variety of frozen delicacies while the Murfreesboro Pure Milk Company has more than a local business.   In dairy products the county is now first in the state and near the top for the entire nation.   There is little wonder then that the dairying industry is today referred to as "Rutherford County's four million dollar industry."

The Jersey Cattle Club of Rutherford County was organized in 1924.   Mr. George King took the lead in getting this club started and twelve charter members helped in the work during the first year. In the second year the club won nearly every medal given at the Tennessee State Fair.   By 1928, there were 241 owners and breeders of registered dairy cattle in Rutherford County.   All but one of these owned Jerseys, the only important breed in the county.   By 1937 the number of owners and breeders had grown to 267 and there has been a steady increase since that date.   The Jersey Cattle Club has grown in importance and maintains a full-time office in Murfreesboro. Shows are held annually and plans are made for increasing the number and quality of the Jersey breed.   The section around Murfreesboro and Nashville has as thickly populated area of registered Jerseys as any section of its size in the world, and these Jerseys average a much higher percentage of butter-fat than do the Jerseys of the country as a whole.

Notwithstanding the rapid development of the dairy industry, beef cattle were not neglected by many farmers of the county.   For a time the Shorthorn and Aberdeen Angus were popular but in recent years the Hereford is far in the lead.

Since the Civil War interest in fine horses has waxed and waned. Immediately after the war the poverty of the area caused emphasis to be placed upon work stock rather than pleasure animals.   By the turn of the century, however, there was wide spread interest in race horses, both pacers and trotters, and many money winners were bred and trained in the county.   Many of the finest horses of the country raced annually at the local fair grounds, one of the most famous in the South. When interest in this type of horse began to wane, Rutherford County like many others in middle Tennessee, was smitten with the Tennessee walking horse craze, and horse shows are held in Murfreesboro once a week during the summer months. The middle Tennessee horse show season is opened in May of each year by the annual Kiwanis Club charity celebration. In preparation for these events and for other shows in middle Tennessee, Rutherford owners spend many months in training magnificent horses for the three-gaited and five-gaited classes which are a part of all good horse shows. The small "walking ring" where riders practice their mounts for the big occasions may be found in all parts of the county. The fair, with horse races, was restored to the county in 1946.

When the first world war broke out in 1914, Rutherford farmers were in a relatively prosperous condition. Europe's demand for farm products soon caused farm prices to rise and this, coupled with inflation at the end of the war, resulted in a fabulous increase in the value of farm land. The average value of farm land had increased from fifteen dollars an acre in 1900 to fifty-seven dollars in 1920. Many farmers and others bought farms at these inflation prices, making a down payment and hoping to discharge the remainder of the obligation with money derived from the sale of high priced farm products. The deflationary years of 1920 and 1921 caused many to become bankrupt. Although the 1920's were once referred to as "Coolidge prosperity" the farmer did not prosper and when the depression of 1929 came not only the marginal farmer but many successful ones were forced into bankruptcy.

When the "New Deal" was inaugurated in 1933 the average farmer in Rutherford County who had survived the crash was in dire need of aid from someone. Naturally under such circumstances, one runs to the government with outstretched hands. The first phases of the government's agricultural program were generally received with favor by the farmers of the county, a few Republicans even lining up behind the President. As time went on the program became less popular and much criticism was heard in some quarters. Notwithstanding these complaints the farmer by 1939 was making some progress. The following table based on federal census reports for 1939 for certain items and 1940 for others, and with comparisons ten years earlier, in most cases, will perhaps give the best short picture available of agriculture conditions in the county in the decade immediately preceding the recent war. The figures in parenthesis represent Rutherford County's rank among the ninety-five counties of the state.

TABLE II. POPULATION, WEALTH, AREA, AND AGRICULTURAL PRODUCTION

Item	Year 1940		Year 1930	
Population	33,604	(14)	32,286	
Area	641	(11)		
Assessed Wealth	15,789,608	(12)		
Value of Farm Lands and Buildings	13,985,951	(8)	15,906,505	
Value of all Animals on Farms	2,669,766	(1)	2,681,139	(2)
Value of Horses on Farms	422,756	(5)	313,352	(3)
Value of Mules on Farms	606,695	(12)	499,504	(14)
Value of Cattle on Farms	1,261,461	(1)	1,364,865	(1)
Value of Swine on Farms	156,992	(4)	229,270	(4)
Value of Sheep on Farms	110,636	(6)	80,591	(8)

	Year 1939		Year 1929	
Value of all Farm Products, Sold, Traded or used by Households	3,002,949	(9)	4,446,789	(9)
Live Stock and Live Stock Products Sold or Traded	1,702,101	(4)	2,297,890	(5)
Dairy Products Sold	801,638	(3)	1,145,105	(2)
Poultry and Eggs Sold	310,540	(4)	624,615	(5)
Value of all Crops Harvested	2,294,120	(11)	3,013,455	(20)
Value of Cereals Harvested	863,369	(11)	1,226,684	(9)
Corn Harvested for Grain	762,807	(8)	1,170,427	(9)
Wheat Thrashed	67,571	(16)	48,826	
Other Grains and Seeds	61,300		19,313	
Hay and Forage	778,714	(1)	707,108	(4)
Cotton	364,166	(18)	757,347	(21)
Tobacco	26,065	(47)	25,250	
Irish and Sweet Potatoes	32,963	(61)	56,213	
Vegetables	121,145	(50)	185,174	
Fruits and Nuts	38,919	(36)	19,315	

If population, in which the county ranks fourteenth and assessed wealth, in which it ranked twelfth, are used as criteria it will be seen that Rutherford County is relatively high in agricultural production. It has consistently for some years stood among the ten most productive counties of the state. In value of all animals on its farm it ranked first. In dairy products sold it ranked third, exceeded only by Davidson and Shelby Counties. It probably produced a greater volume of such products than either of these counties. The large demands of Nashville and Memphis for milk result in higher prices for dairymen in these localities. The county was also first in hay production. In total value of all farm products sold, traded or used by households it ranked ninth. The county is also outstànding in its production of poultry. Since Tennessee is the leading poultry state east of the Mississippi River and south of the Ohio, Rutherford is therefore one of the outstanding counties in the entire South in this respect. The county stands high in swine and sheep. The county though eighteenth in cotton is probably growing as much of that crop as is advisable. The county is relatively low in tobacco, potatoes, vegetables and fruits. Perhaps some increases should be made in these crops in the future. This table also shows that Rutherford County maintains a good balance between livestock and field crops. This along with the fact that much of the ground of the county is level is rapidly checking soil exhaustion. Some terracing is also being done.

The recent war affected agriculture in the county as it did everything else. There was some increase in production as a result of the demands for more and more food. Prices of farm products again rose, but price ceilings were fairly successful in preventing wholesale inflation. The chief problem of the farmer during the war was labor and lack of machinery. The draft cut heavily into the farm population. Many farmers who were "gentlemen" and, to that time had merely supervised their lands, and even their wives and daughters, found it necessary to engage in hard work. Household servants became almost a thing of the past. Old machinery was repaired and much borrowing took place. Notwithstanding these handicaps the farmer prospered and today is in the best financial condition he has been in for years. So are all other groups, however, a fact which still holds many farmers in a relatively low position.

A few developments in agriculture as a result of the war as well as natural growth will be mentioned. The income of the county farmers is today almost eight million dollars, more than twice what it was before the war. According to a survey made in 1945 livestock sales in that year amounted to $2,269,766, crop sales amounted to $2,294,120 while the total received for dairy products exceeded three million dollars. Farm values have increased very rapidly and many farms are changing hands at prices considered generally as inflationary. Fortunately many of these sales have been for cash, and deflation will not be such a burden as where the purchase is made on a time basis.

As a result of the war an increase was noted in the acreage of soy beans. The same is true for winter oats. The increase in oats is in part, the result of a successful experiment of James Haynes, one of the county's leading farmers, whereby three rows of oats are planted between corn rows in late summer or early fall. This not only checks erosion but furnishes pasture during the winter and will often produce as high as seventy-five bushels of grain to the acre. The last ten years has also seen a large increase in the acreage planted to alfalfa. Another new crop is buckwheat, while experiments are being made with burr clover. Much of the corn now raised is hybrid, some of which is cross bred in the county by the State College farm, Roy Tarwater and others. Since 1920 lespedeza has been an important hay crop.

Life on the Rutherford County farm though still capable of enrichment is much more pleasant today than formerly. Better schools, improved highways, and a variety of farm organizations have added materially to the happiness of the rural population. The Tennessee Valley Authority and the Rural Electrification Administration have been especially busy in the county. The Middle Tennessee Electric Membership Corporation reports that nearly half of the farms in the county are being served with electricity and the number is rapidly increasing. Many of the homes now have bath rooms, electric refrigerators and other conveniences. The use of farm machinery while increasing does not equal that of many other counties. This is because so many Rutherford farms are too small for expensive machinery. This is in part taken care of by a number of farmers who do custom work with combines, pick-up bailers and other machines.

There is, however, still a dark side to the picture. Rutherford County has always ranked high in farm tenancy. The percentage in 1925 was 51.4. This meant that a majority of the farmers were tenants. Rutherford County was outranked in this respect by the cotton counties of west Tennessee. It is safe to say that the readjustment years following the depression brought no great change in the precentage of farm tenancy. This despite the fact that many farmers were encouraged to purchase some of the lands which they farmed. Many of the best farms of the county have been passed on in the same family from generation to generation. In prosperous times men whose primary interests lie in other business fields sometimes venture fabulous prices in order to obtain a farm as a secondary pursuit. Seldom does the tenant or share-cropper rise beyond the station in which these circumstances fix him.

TRADE AND INDUSTRY

Many years before Rutherford County was established, there was a trading post near the Black Fox Spring where traders from the Cumberland settlement came to exchange goods with Chief Black Fox and other Indians. Hunters in search of food also explored the area soon to become Rutherford County. These early excursions into the beautiful Stone's River Valley encouraged the Tennessee pioneers to turn their attention toward the fertile fields of this new area. Soldiers, farmers, tradesmen and homemakers, who came from the "already crowded" banks of the Cumberland, and from North Carolina and Virginia, had begun to establish homes and business enterprises some time before the county was organized.

One of the earliest business establishments was a grist mill which opened for business in 1799. This was some four years before Rutherford County was organized. The business was owned by Thomas Rucker and was known as Cave Mill. Best accounts indicate that the first "trade store" was opened in the year 1803 by William Nash. The store was located near Jefferson and according to Goodspeed the stock in trade consisted of "a little drygoods, some groceries, a little powder and lead and the inevitable barrel of whiskey." Since money was a very scarce item, a barter system was used by Nash in exchanging store goods for products of field and farm. Large ox hides were valued at four dollars. Wolf scalps could be used to pay taxes. Produce, collected by Nash, was sent to New Orleans by flatboat. This journey usually required more than a month. Whenever the first settlers did use money for exchange, they frequently had to cut dollars into quarters or halves and use these parts of the dollar for change. It is said that the terms "two bits", "four bits", and "six bits" originated with this custom.

A second grist mill was built in the county in 1804. This was owned by Louis Anthony and was built on Stone's River near Jefferson. From this date on, the construction of grist mills and saw mills became a regular feature of the industrial life of Rutherford County. By 1820, more than twenty-five mills of one sort or another had been authorized by the county court. Most of these were operated by waterpower, although there were a few tread mills. Stills also sprang up along with mills.

In the year 1806, John Nash Read opened a tavern near Jefferson. Descendants of this man built the famous Read house in Chattanooga. After Read's Tavern opened, many others sprang up to accommodate the travelers who made slow journeys into the new county. By 1820, inns and taverns were being operated by William Mitchell, William Nash, Harvey Page, Charles O'Flynn, Hugh Good, James Hill, William Hamborough, W. R. Hearn, Thomas Mayfield, Peter Williams, William Rather, Thomas Goodrich and others. In early stage-coach days, the second stop on the Nashville to Murfreesboro run was Gregory Inn, near Smyrna. One writer said of Gregory Inn that "commodious rooms, nightly dances, fiddling and heavily laden banquets were widespread elements of the place."

The first cotton gins in Rutherford County were built by William Lytle and James Rucker about 1808. It was not long, however, before others were constructed and most of these continued in successful operation for many years. Thomas Woods opened a blacksmith shop on Overall's Creek in 1807 and enjoyed good business from the beginning.

The "hawker" or "peddler" was a familiar sight on the paths of Rutherford County in early days. The state legislature acts of 1833 contained the following provision: "Be it enacted, that Hartwell Miles, of Williamson County be authorized to hawk and peddle within bounds of the congressional district composed of the counties of Williamson and Rutherford, without obtaining license therefor." This was only one of many such acts and these acts indicate something of the customs of the day in salesmanship.

After the industrial revolution struck America, the South including Tennessee and Rutherford County, tried to follow New England in the establishment of manufacturing plants. Most of these attempts, however, ended in failure. In 1831, the Washington Cotton Factory was opened by a Mr. Lowry. The motive power for this industry was known as a head-wheel and was driven by one horse. In order to keep the industry going Mr. Lowry was forced to bring several partners into the business. Despite the combined efforts of these men and the purchase of a twenty-five thousand dollar engine, the organization proved to be a complete financial failure and in a few years the entire business was sold for less than fifteen hundred dollars. It was used as a cotton gin by John Primm and later as a saw mill by Ransom and Kirkpatrick. In later years the Perkins Lumber Company occupied the site of this business and today it is occupied by Young and Ogilvie Lumber Company.

According to Goodspeed's history, "In 1833, a report was made to the city council on the feasability of establishing a system of waterworks. A favorable report was made and the estimated cost was $1,000. It was proposed to raise the water from the Sand Spring in large tubs to be conveyed to the top of Capital Hill upon a wooden railway; the same to be elevated by horse-power. The water was to be led from Capital Hill by cedar tubs into an air-tight tank in the court-yard square; thence by hydrants to the places of business." It seems that this work was completed and the Rose Water Works went into operation about 1834. The venture, however, proved to be impractical and operation was discontinued after a short while.

In describing the shift of industry from Jefferson to Murfreesboro, Goodspeed said that Capt. William Lytle built a mill, blacksmith shop and afterward a cotton gin near Murfreesboro in 1808. The first house was built within the corporate limits of the town in 1811.

A. Carmichael built the first tavern in Murfreesboro near the Pump Spring. Col. Joel Dyer moved his tavern from Jefferson to Murfreesboro in 1812; this building stood untill burned in 1854. Col. Robert Jetton built a tavern on South Main Street of cedar logs, that stood till burned in 1853. J. Renshaw also built a tavern on South Main Street of cedar logs, that stood till burned in 1853. The town was now growing rapidly. A public warehouse was built near the creek on Main Street in 1813. In 1818, the market house was built, which, with some improvement stood till destroyed by the soldiers. Hugh Cabel was made sealer of weights and measures for town and county. In 1818 the town well was ordered begun, but was not finished untill 1824.

The year 1837 was apparently a prosperous one for Murfreesboro. By this time, Jefferson had begun to lose some of its early prestige and the center of activities had shifted to Murfreesboro. As late as 1830, Jefferson was a thriving community and the focal point for many enterprises, but later on in this decade began to lose its importance as a trade center. In 1837 the first "genuine" grocery store was opened in Murfreesboro by John Decker. In this same year, H. H. Tredway opened a drug store and not many months later another was opened by Avent and Carney. The latter was eventually sold to J. H. Nelson. The first carriage manufacturing plant was also opened in 1837. Murfreesboro had begun to reap the profits of the "internal improvements" movement that was sweeping the western communities. The town boomed and business establishments sprang up in rapid order. Other parts of the county also began to enjoy prosperity. Milton and Salem were particularly fortunate in this respect as business establishments of importance were established in these communities. A short while later the Christiana, Fosterville, Lavergne, Smyrna, and Eagleville communities began to enjoy a prosperous business development.

In 1840 census indicated that there were some twenty dry goods establishments in the county along with an equal number of grocery stores. In the same year thirty-one men were employed in cotton manufacturing (Washington Cotton Manufacturing Company), there were twelve tanneries employing forty men, some dozen men were employed in the manufacture of hats and caps and there were twenty distilleries producing 18,000 gallons of whiskey and employing forty men. It is significant to note, too, that in this same year four men were employed in the manufacture of small fire arms valued at two thousand dollars. There were two printing offices and twelve men were employed in making carriages and wagons. There were also in the county thirty grist mills and twenty-five saw mills and ten men were employed in the manufacture of furniture. The total value of all homemade goods in 1840 was approximately $210,000.

It is interesting to note, however, that this figure never again reached this high total, because homemade goods were replaced with those imported from other communities or those made in the new factory establishments. Improved transportation helped to decrease the quantity of home made goods. By 1860, there were thirty-five or more manufacturing establishments in Rutherford County with approximately $142,300 capital invested and spending $133,020 annually for raw products. These establishments employed one hundred thirty-six men and the annual cost of labor amounted to approximately $38,000. No women were employed in Rutherford County industries at this time.

Other important businesses established in Murfreesboro between 1830 and 1860 included a hardware store owned by John C. Spence, a jewelry store owned by F. Garland, James Reed, and R. D. Reed, a book store by Craig and Fletcher, a livery stable by Todd and Carnahan, and a carriage shop by R. and S. Smith. In 1855, W. S. Huggins and Company constructed a building to house the Rio Mills. This business was constructed at a total cost of $25,000. The building was a large four-story brick and it is claimed that the mill had a capacity of about 200 barrels of flour per day. The Rio Mills were later sold to William Spence and a distillery was added in 1860. Goodspeed's history states that this place fed many "hogs". The first gas works were started in Murfreesboro in 1857. Apparently efforts were made to make gas from resin oil and cotton seed. The mains for transmissions were laid, but the war interfered with the experiment and it was not attempted in this manner again.

The Cedar Bucket Factory was opened in 1854 by John C. Spence. Although this business was forced to operate on a limited scale during the war and was eventually taken over by the Stone's River Utility Works, it was the forerunner of an industry that was to prove highly important for the county.

A student of the military history in middle Tennessee would probably come to a quick conclusion that Murfreesboro and Rutherford County were practically devastated during the war between the states. Such a conclusion might not be far from right. One historian says that "Murfreesboro was poverty stricken after the war." Others point out that Rutherford County was the scene of some of the bloodiest fighting of the entire war and claim that the inhabitants were "sorely beset" in early days after the conflict. Coupled with the destruction caused by the armies was that of a raging fire that swept the square of Murfreesboro on April 15, 1869. This fire destroyed a number of business houses and for many years was referred to as the "great fire."

The year 1868 saw the establishment of an enterprise that was called the "greatest in Rutherford County" up to that date. It was known as the Tennessee Central Agricultural and Mechanical Association. This organization was apparently designed to encourage greater farm production and the use of mechanical equipment. A kind of county fair was conducted each year by this organization. One historian said that "Although not recovered from the effects of the war, the people entered into this combined institution of profit and pleasure with enthusiastic spirit." Despite this enthusiasm, however, the business was not a success and in 1884 all grounds and buildings were sold to the Rutherford Fair Association.

Other important business organizations to open in Rutherford County immediately after the war included the livery, feed, and sale stable of James H. Allen, the carriage and buggy business of Osborn, Bock and Co., the tin shop of Alfred M. Cawthon, the merchandise business of Thomas G. Ivie, the merchandise business of McFadden and Son, the dry goods store of Morris G. Rosenfeld, the hardware business of Street, Byrn and Co., and the jewelry firm of William R. Bell.

By 1870 there were sixty-four small manufacturing establishments in Rutherford County. These establishments had $187,250 of capital investment. They paid out $71,945 in wages and the total sales of all products amounted to $796,370. Only a few of these sixty-four small manufacturing establishments were incorporated but it is interesting to note that by this time some women workers were being employed in these industrial plants.

John M. Childress, James M. Haynes, Jefferson M. Leatherman, S. H. Sanders, M. Parsons and associates were incorporated in 1867 under the firm name of Murfreesboro Manufacturing Company. This organization was to have the same powers and privileges as previously granted to the Nashville Cotton Mills. It is not known just how long this organization continued in operation.

By 1870 the Nashville, Chattanooga and St. Louis railroad was back in full operation and doing a better than fair business. The annual report of the company for the year 1869 revealed that approximately two hundred and fifty citizens of Rutherford County owned stock in this company.

In discussing the business organization of W. B. Earthman and Company, established in the late seventies, Goodspeed said, "For the past eight years Murfreesboro has grown to be a cedar market of greater importance and reputation than any other city in the country, considerably overshadowing many other cities of a much larger population. This result has been attained on account of the superior advantages Murfreesboro has in locality, being surrounded by immense cedar groves, and because the above named firm has had the necessary capital, capability and push. The business of this firm reaches out over a large extent of territory; their chief markets are St. Louis, Cincinnati, Louisville and Indianapolis."

By the turn of the century cedar slats by the millions were being turned out by the mills of the county. These slats were made for the most part from cedar rails some of them almost one hundred years old. Prior to the first world war many of these slats were sent to Germany and found their way back to America as pencils.

The "gay nineties" brought increased business activities to Murfreesboro and Rutherford County. New store houses were built and new enterprises were undertaken in this decade. P. P. Mason, B. L. Ridley, and Dr. J. E. Tompson started the new Murfreesboro Waterworks in 1891. In the same year Mason built Mason Court, a building which still stands, just off the square on East Main Street.

P. P. Mason must have been one of the big business men of Murfreesboro back in the nineties. He entered into at least one business venture however, which proved to be a financial failure. In 1895 Mason started a soap factory in Murfreesboro. It seems that the large out-of-town soap manufacturing companies then flooded Murfreesboro stores with all kinds of soap at ridiculously low prices. Mason's venture into the soap business lasted for only a few months.

The National census of 1900 indicated that Rutherford County had within its borders a total of ninety-four small manufacturing establishments. Many of these firms were owned, managed and operated by one person. Most of them were not incorporated. The ninety-four firms employed a total of two hundred and forty-five laborers. The value of all products manufactured by these firms was approximately $750,000. By this date the population of Murfreesboro had increased to near the forty-five hundred mark and the population of the Murfreesboro district was considerably more than five thousand.

A great flood swept Murfreesboro and other parts of Rutherford County in the closing days of March in 1902. Several hundred thousand dollars worth of damage was done to business houses and dwellings in the county. A tornado in 1913 caused considerable destruction especially on the north side of the square. By 1920, the county had approximately a dozen manufacturing establishments that were valued at more than $35,000 each.

Before the advent of electricity into this area Murfreesboro streets, business houses, and some homes were lighted by gas produced at a plant on South Maple Street.

An important event took place in the city in 1890 when Jim Perry established an electric plant. For various reasons this new business did not enjoy success in the beginning. Apparently the people were afraid to use new power despite its improvement over the crude gas lighting. Perry eventually sold his business to J. H. Reed and in 1901, Reed sold to Dr. J. H. Nelson. Dr. Nelson made many improvements and Murfreesboro began to be a well lighted city. Davis and Elam purchased the business from Dr. Nelson and these men in turn sold to J. C. Beesley, George Beesley and R. B. Roberts. This transaction took place in 1919 and these men continued to improve and enlarge the plant and services until they sold to the Tennessee Electric Power Company for a sum reputed to be over a half million dollars. The Tennessee Electric Power Company continued to render services to Murfreesboro and surrounding communities until the advent of the Tennessee Valley Authority. Now Murfreesboro owns its own electric power distributing system and in a few short years of operation has accumulated more than a two hundred thousand dollar surplus. This surplus has been brought about in spite of lower rates for both domestic and industrial consumption. The Middle Tennessee Electric Corporation also sells electric power to farm areas in Rutherford and adjoining counties. Rural areas in middle Tennessee are being furnished with electric power at low rates. There is little reason for farm areas of Rutherford and other counties not making use of this valuable product.

Before Rutherford County went "dry" in 1903 there were fourteen saloons on the public square in Murfreesboro. Among the owners of these establishments were Dick Hill, J. Bloomenthal, Guggenheim, Mose Nelson, Sam Cranor, Jim Miller, J. B. Kirk, and E. B. Hunt.

A handbook published in 1922 by the Mutual Realty and Loan Company listed several of the most important business establishments of the county. At that time the Sunshine Hosiery Mill was manufacturing 12000 pairs of hosiery each day. Other firms listed in the handbook included the Putnam Overall Manufacturing Company, called the "largest clothing factory from St. Louis to the coast," the Tennessee Rubber Company, manufacturers of the "Ezy-on" lace boot for tires, the Elrod, Hargis Manufacturing Company, maker of women's dresses and the Tennessee Red Cedar Woodware Company, manufacturers of pencil slats and oil of cedar, red cedar buckets and churns.

During the 1920's Murfreesboro attempted to branch out in manufactures. Much stock was sold to local citizens in a silk mill. The venture was a failure and heavy losses were suffered. The property was later taken over by the Wellwood Company which has been quite successful.   The blanket mill organized some years earlier was successful for a time but poor management caused it to close its doors with further loss to investors.

The turbulent early thirties brought disaster to other business establishments in Rutherford County.   By 1940, however, many others had been organized to take the place of those that were forced to close their doors during depression years and the unemployment problem was largely a thing of the past.   With the outbreak of the second world war, several industries were able to gear production to the needs of the United States Government.   The Wellwood Silk Mills manufacturers of ribbons and rayons, made parachutes for Uncle Sam.   The Air Utilities Corporation made products that were used in the manufacture of the atomic bomb and the Sunshine Hosiery Mill sent thousands of pairs of hosiery to the armies and navies of our allies.   These organizations and others made valuable contributions to the war effort.

The latest statistics available on manufacture and trade for the county are to be found in the federal census of 1939.   During that year Rutherford County had twenty-five manufacturing establishments which produced goods valued at $4,219,887.   The county ranked nineteenth in the state in this respect.   In addition to those establishments already mentioned for processing milk there are others that depend upon agricultural products.   Murfreesboro has two flour mills and is rapidly becoming a center for manufacturing meal and stock feeds.   In other parts of the county are numerous smaller mills, some operated by water, which manufacture flour, meal and feeds.   The Middle Tennessee Bakeries, one of the largest in the state, supplies many middle Tennessee counties with a variety of products.

Among the more recent establishments to locate in the county were the Novelty Furniture Company, the American Textile Machine Corporation and various plants for making cement blocks.

Although Murfreesboro has overshadowed other towns in the county in industry several communities deserve mention.   Eagleville, since Chesley Williams established a general merchandising store before the Civil War, has had many prosperous businesses.   The Owen Tobacco Company for years furnished many southerners with twist chewing tobacco and other tobacco products while Crosslin Brothers today carry on a large mercantile business.   The Puckett store between Eagleville and Rockvale has long been regarded as one of the most successful country stores in middle Tennessee.   Smyrna has also been the site of many successful business firms.   One of the most important in recent years was the Smyrna Lumber Company, operated by Bryan Jordan and Will Coleman. It had a buisness that was carried into several foreign countries.

Notwithstanding the successful manufacturing plants in the county it will be noted by comparison with other counties in the state that Rutherford County has a definite lag in this respect. Although many think that too many manufacturing plants, especially those that employ a low type of laborer, might be a definite disadvantage to a community, a few more well chosen plants would maintain a better balance with agriculture and make a broader market for farm products.

In 1939 the county had twenty wholesale firms which did a business of $3,337,000. The county was sixteenth in the state in this respect. It is in the wholesale grocery business that Murfreesboro has been outstanding. Henry King and the Raglands were pioneers in this field. Henry King later moved to Chattanooga where he was one of the leaders in his field while Hardin and Allen Ragland moved to Nashville and operate one of the largest wholesale businesses in the state. Outstanding wholesale grocery firms in Murfreesboro have been King, Ragland and Company; Henry King and Company; Ragland, Potter and Company; and J. W. Fletcher and Son. The last two are still in business.

A few years ago a live stock market was opened in Murfreesboro. It has sales every Friday and boasts a business of nearly a million dollars a year. Wilson and Company have for a number of years operated a large produce house in the city.

Murfreesboro has always been a retail center of considerable importance not only for the county but for several adjoining counties. In 1939 the county's 339 retail establishments sold over six million dollars worth of merchandise to make the county tenth in the state in that respect.

In mentioning outstanding business men that Rutherford County has contributed to other sections of the country one should not overlook H. C. Alexander, one of the partners of the famous New York firm of J. P. Morgan and Company, and J. F. Jarman, founder of the General Shoe Corporation.

TRANSPORTATION

"It is ordered by the Court that Thomas Bedford oversee the clearing out and keeping of lawful repair the part of the road leading 'thro' the forks of Stone's river to Nashville from the place where said road now crosses the west fork of said river downward to the county line, and that the hands in the following bounds work with him: All on the lower side of the road leading from Hurricane Creek to Captain Howell's mill, all on the lower side of the road cut by John Cummins from said mill, to the west fork of said river, all on the west side of said west fork to its junction, thence including Alexander McCulloch, the settlement about John Miller and William Nash, thence down to Kimbros at the mouth of Hurricane Creek."

The quotation above was taken from the Court Minutes of the Rutherford County Court, which met on January 4, 1804, in the home of Thomas Rucker, one of Rutherford's pioneers. It affords insight into the methods and processes used to construct and maintain the roads of the day.

As soon as the county was established numerous dirt roads were laid out by the county court. Some of these led to the seat of government located at Jefferson and others to the important grain mills located on the streams.

When Murfreesboro became the permanent seat of government, another wave of building followed, with roads radiating from this newly established town to other parts of the county. These roads were not hard-surfaced, and transportation in bad weather was almost impossible. They were worked by able-bodied men, on the orders of the county court, and the only expense to the county was an occasional crowbar and sledge hammer.

In many respects the road building campaigns in Rutherford County were but a part of the internal improvement's schemes that gripped the state early in its history. As early as 1799 the state legislature appropriated "a sum not to exceed $1,000 for the construction of the Walton Road over the Cumberland Plateau." This was only a crude dirt road. During the same year, a corporation was chartered to build a turnpike connecting middle and east Tennessee. The venture was only partly successful. In 1804, the state legislature passed a law stating that "Every County Court within this State is hereby authorized and empowered to call on any person or persons in their respective counties to account for any monies such person or persons may have in his or their hands by virtue of any 'difrefs' heretofore made for default of working on any road in such county and all monies to receive and apply toward keeping in repair the roads and bridges on which such default was made".

While the state legislature was in session in Murfreesboro in 1824, a charter was granted to a company for the construction of a hard surfaced toll road from Nashville to Murfreesboro and ultimately to Shelbyville. Several attempts were made to construct this road, but no real work was done until 1831, and the road was not completed until 1842. Rates of travel were fixed by the state legislature, and tolls were paid at toll gates established at five-mile distances along the route. The following were some of the toll charges:

20 head of sheep_____20 cents
20 head of hogs_____20 cents
20 horned or beef cattle_____50 cents
4 wheel pleasure carriage_____25 cents
Loaded wagon_____25 cents
Empty wagon_____$12\frac{1}{2}$ cents
Man and horse_____ $6\frac{1}{4}$ cents
Cart_____$12\frac{1}{2}$ cents
Hogshead of tobacco_____$12\frac{1}{2}$ cents

The next road out of Murfreesboro to be undertaken was to Manchester and ultimately to Winchester. This road was chartered in 1837. Soon toll roads were radiating from Murfreesboro in all directions.

In a *History of Tennessee* published by the Goodspeed Publishing Company in 1886, the statement is made in reference to Rutherford County, "It is doubtful if any county in the State can boast of as many and good pikes or more efficient and accommodating officials." An old Murfreesboro paper in the Library of Congress contains the following interesting information: "In the stage and mail coach days of the 1820's and 1830's, the route used from Sparta was through McMinnville, Danville (later named Woodbury); thence eight miles to Readyville, twelve miles to Murfreesboro, ten miles to Jefferson, then to Nashville. The distance from Knoxville 203 miles." Another route from Huntsville, Alabama, to Nashville was "through Fayetteville, Shelbyville, and Murfreesboro, on to Nashville by way of Jefferson."

It must not be supposed that all the interest in transportation in early Rutherford county history was centered in the building of roads. The coming of the steamboat had a tremendous effect upon commerce in Tennessee. In 1818, a steamboat came up the Cumberland River, but was forced to unload part of its cargo at Harpeth Shoals and wait for a rise in the river before it could go on to Nashville. This event, along with the trouble east Tennessee was experiencing in floating goods down the Tennessee, aroused a demand for making the rivers in the state navigable. All kinds of schemes were suggested. A canal connecting the Hiawassee and the head waters of the Coosa, as well as connections between the lower Tennessee and other Alabama rivers were discussed. Many acts were passed by the legislature declaring rivers as navigable and prohibiting obstructions, meaning, of course, dams, from being erected. This caused a protest from those desiring to build grain and saw mills.

Between 1801 and 1815 many navigation companies were chartered by the legislature, while in 1817 a Board of Managers to superintend the Holston and Tennessee Rivers was appointed. About $12,000 was appropriated for this Board. In 1819, however, a bill to appropriate one half million dollars for improving river navigation was defeated. It was supported almost unanimously by east Tennessee, but opposed by middle Tennessee which was rapidly becoming the most populous and the wealthiest section of the state. A similar act was defeated in 1827. In 1830, however, a modest appropriation was voted for improving river transportation, chiefly on the Tennessee. By this time, steamboats were operating on the Tennessee, but it was impossible to make a continuous run from its mouth to Knoxville. The usual practice was to tie up below Muscle Shoals and transport the cargo around the Shoals by land, and reload it for shipment. Except in times of high water, it was necessary to unload farther up stream and reship in smaller boats in order to reach Knoxville. In 1838 the legislature authorized the issuing of $300,000 in state bonds for improving rivers, but the bonds could not be sold and little was done till 1842 when $100,000 of Federal money distributed to the states was set aside for rivers. None of this money was spent in middle Tennessee.

For a time, many thought that Stone's River would become an important artery of commerce. As early as 1807, it is reported that a flat bottom boat carried a 40 ton cargo from Cummings' Mill down the river to the Cumberland and then to Nashville at a very low cost. Although authoritative information is lacking, various reports indicate that Jefferson was a port of considerable importance for flat bottom boats. Even after Murfreesboro became the county seat, Jefferson continued to prosper as a port. The legislature, in 1817, as well as orders of the County Court, about the same time, authorized the establishment of warehouses at Jefferson for inspecting corn meal, cotton, hemp, tobacco, and other products. Stone's River was declared by the legislature to be a navigable stream, much to the disgust of those who wished to build dams for operating mills. In 1827, Stone's River was included in those for which lotteries might be held to secure money for improvements.

In 1824, a steamboat of 100 tons was built at Jefferson by Constant Hardeman and was floated down the river to Nashville where machinery was installed. It was soon discovered, however, that the river was too shallow for steamboat navigation, and the county became interested in other means of transportation.

After 1830, the railroad fever enveloped the country. Immediately it became apparent that a railroad would be more practical than a canal for connecting Tennessee with the Atlantic Seaboard.

South Carolina, under the leadership of Robert Y. Hayne, interested east Tennessee in such a project, though Memphis also became interested in connecting with the Atlantic Seaboard about the same time. It seems that middle Tennessee was interested at first in a road through the center of the state from Mississippi to east Tennessee. A meeting in the interest of this project was called at Columbia in 1834. David Graham of Rutherford County presided at this meeting.

In 1836, after prolonged and heated discussion, a law was passed by the state legislature whereby the state agreed to subscribe to one-third of the stock of railways and turnpike companies, provided the companies complied with certain specific regulations of the act. Later this act was changed to allow the state to subscribe to as much as one-half of the stock of these "internal improvements" companies.

In 1841, the people of Murfreesboro were given the privilege of investing in a new method of transportation. In discussing the Nashville, Chattanooga and St. Louis Railway, Goodspeed says: "The railway was completed from Nashville to Murfreesboro in 1851. A large subsidy in the form of stock was voted by the State, and large sums were given by private citizens. Among those most influential in building the road, outside the county, were Gov. James C. Jones, Col. V. K. Stevenson and the distinguished Robert Y. Hayne of South Carolina. So eager were the people for the road that they seemed to vie with each other as to who should donate most liberally toward the road. The first passenger coach over the road from Nashville arrived on the 4th of July, 1851. Flowers and festoons decorated the little city, and a dinner and speeches commemorated the great event. A new world of business was opened up; a communication between the manufacturing cities of the north and the rich fields and sea board cities of the south. The road extends through the County a distance of nearly thirty miles, entering near the northwest corner of the county at LaVergne and passing out near the southeast part of the county at Fosterville. The road is one of the best and most profitable thoroughfares of the country." Goodspeed might have added that Col. James H. Grant of Maine, the engineer who built the railroad, was a distant relative of President U. S. Grant. In 1857, Col. Grant moved to Christiana and lived there for several years. It is interesting to note that two of the most successful presidents of the Nashville, Chattanooga and St. Louis Railway are identified with Murfreesboro. John W. Thomas, Sr. and John W. Thomas, Jr. both served as presidents of the road, and both enjoyed outstanding success in this position. The father was educated at and taught mathematics in Union University, and the son was born in Murfreesboro. A statue still standing in Centennial Park in Nashville, is a tribute to the honor of John W.

Thomas, Sr. and a recognition of his services in promoting and carrying to success the celebration of Tennessee's Centennial.

It seems that the railroad was a success from the very beginning. There was one period, however, when it did not enjoy the prosperity that has marked most of the years of its operation. In reconstruction days business was at a standstill in most of the towns along the line. The same situation prevailed during the cholera epidemic which gripped Murfreesboro and many other southern communities. For a number of years after the War Between the States, there was a sharp decline in the volume of business done by the Nashville, Chattanooga and St. Louis Railway. The companies' reports show, however, that by 1875, business was again on the upgrade. Nearly five thousand bales of cotton were being shipped from Murfreesboro each year, and other large shipments were being made from Lavergne, Smyrna, Florence, Christiana, and Fosterville. In addition to the one and a quarter million pounds of freight being shipped from Murfreesboro at this time, passenger traffic was also increasing. Goodspeed, writing of the railroad in an 1886 publication, said, "From official information it is learned that the railroad business alone at Murfreesboro amounts to $30,000 in passenger traffic and $50,000 annually in freight, with about $5,000 additional at Lavergne, Florence, Christiana, and Fosterville. Of 10,000 or 12,000 bales of cotton raised in the county 6,000 or 7,000 are shipped by rail, and in addition there are shipped 1,000 car loads of cedar lumber, 200 car loads of other grains and 500 car loads of miscellaneous freight."

No story of the history of transportation in Rutherford County would be complete without some reference to the famous velocipede of the seventies and eighties. This was a tricycle affair and was very popular in Murfreesboro. It was followed by the "high bicycle" with its high front wheel and low rear wheel. The mounting and peddling of one of these vehicles was an accomplishment within itself, but the young swain of the late eighties enjoyed riding up to the home of his "Lady Fair" on a shining new "High Bicycle". One of the favorite jaunts of the young folk of 1885 was a "High Bicycle" ride from Murfreesboro to Lebanon to Nashville and back to Murfreesboro. The young man who fell out along the route was never allowed to forget it.

It would also be impossible to pass over the history of transportation in Rutherford County without some reference being made to Murfreesboro's "famous" street railway. In 1892 P. P. Mason, B. L. Ridley and T. B. Fowler incorporated a business known as the Murfreesboro Street Railway. The company owned eight cars, twenty-four mules, two miles of tracks, a number of barns and other equipment necessary for operating this enterprise. The corporation continued in existence for about a year, but it is said by those who should know that it lost money every day.

It was some years after the coming of the automobile into Rutherford County before the highway picture was changed to any extent. Natives point out that some of the old turnpikes were still being used in 1920. Jim Reed and George Darrow claimed the distinction of owning the first automobile brought to the county. Crowds gathered around the square to witness the performance of this early canvas top car, and we can well imagine that the two young owners of the car were advised many times to buy a horse. Col. B. B. Kerr likes to tell of the famous Stoddard-Dayton automobile that was purchased by a citizen of Murfreesboro around 1910. Young couples of the town enjoyed borrowing this car to drive to near by towns to have the marriage ceremony performed. Col. Kerr made such a trip to Wartrace in 1911.

Automobiles began to come to the county in large numbers sometime before the first world war. There was considerable activity in repairing roads and building new ones at this time. The war of course, interrupted this progress. Immediately after the war, however, the highway program got into full swing and the early twenties witnessed a vast expansion in the net work of roads all over the county. Federal and state construction projects brought great relief to many sections and the automobile business boomed. As a result of this highway building program paved roads radiate out of Murfreesboro in all directions at the present time. The Dixie Highway leads tourists to all parts of the Southland and the Broadway of America opens up the whole country for pleasure travel and industrial commerce.

The farm-to-market road program of the New Deal Administrations brought some improved roads to the country. Unfortunately some of these were not well-constructed and many are in bad repair at present time. Most of them could not stand up under the heavy pounding received during the army maneuvers in middle Tennessee.

Trucking companies, some of them with headquarters in Murfreesboro, have enjoyed success in operating fleets of trucks for industrial transportation. The most successful of the Rutherford County transports are those of the Hoover Line owned and operated by Eph Hoover, and the fleet owned by the Wilson Brothers. The Cason-Miller Bus lines operating between Murfreesboro and Nashville and between Murfreesboro and other nearby points enjoyed unusual success in the twenties before the business became a part of the Southeastern Greyhound system. Murfreesboro now has over one hundred busses arriving or departing daily with direct connections with Nashville, Chattanooga, Knoxville, Lebanon, Smithville, Hartsville, Fayetteville, Columbia, and Centerville.

One could not conclude a discussion of transportation in Rutherford County without referring to the interest of the people in aviation. The first airplanes to be examined by the citizens of the county came to the county fairs. Soon a few of the more daring did more than examine and finally decided to "go up". After that it was not unusual to find aviators landing on some field and conducting two or three days business of taking spectators on sight-seeing trips over Murfreesboro.

A large airport called Sky Harbor was constructed on the Nashville Highway about six miles from Murfreesboro, in 1929. On the day of the official opening highways were blocked for miles as people came from far and near to witness the parachute jumps and loop-the-loop performances of Jimmy Doolittle and other outstanding aviators. Sky Harbor continued in operation until the opening of Berry Field, near Nashville. During the years of its use many celebrities visited Murfreesboro. For the past few years, the buildings have been used to house machinery used in the production of war goods.

The discontinuance of Sky Harbor as an airport has not dampened the ardor of the local citizenry for aviation. Some have enrolled in classes at Middle Tennessee State College and take daily flights from the college airport, which is located on the college campus. A few own their own planes. Steps are now being taken for the construction of a municipal airport on the Lebanon road.

The large field established near Smyrna by the army during the late war for the training of aviators to man four motored bombers will no doubt become a commercial airport if the army decides to discontinue its use as a training center.

The latest means of communication to come to Murfreeboro has been radio station W G N S owned and operated by Cecil Elrod.

BANKING

The history of banks in the state of Tennessee and in Rutherford County somewhat parallels that of internal improvements. The Nashville Bank, which was the first to be authorized by an act of the state legislature, received its charter in 1807. This bank opened its doors for business in March, 1810. Although the state was authorized to subscribe to three hundred shares of stock in this banking business, it apparently did not take advantage of the opportunity.

In 1811 the Bank of the State of Tennessee was authorized by the legislature. The state subscribed to four hundred shares of its stock. By 1815 banks had been authorized for Clarksville, Columbia, Jonesboro, Fayetteville and Franklin. In 1817 a branch of the Bank of Tennessee was established in Nashville.

The first bank in Rutherford County was opened in 1817. The first session of the 12th general assembly meeting at Knoxville passed an act stating, "There shall be a bank established in the town of Murfreesborough, in the county of Rutherford by the name and style of the Murfreesborough, Tennessee Bank." The act provided that the bank at Murfreesboro might have the privilege of becoming a branch of the state bank or the Nashville bank. It further provided that twenty thousand dollars in capital stock be subscribed before the bank opened and required that business transactions be published regularly in either a Murfreesboro or Nashville newspaper. The directors for Rutherford County's first bank were Edward Jones, John Smith, William Barfield, Nicholas Tilford, Joel Childress, Benjamin McCulloch, Elisha B. Clark, John Clapper, Samuel P. Black and John Fisher. Benjamin McCulloch was president and Samuel P. Black, cashier.

An editorial in the Nashville *Banner and Whig*, August 16, 1826 stated that all branches of the Nashville Bank except that at Rogersville had been closed by 1826. Later in the article, it was stated that the bank at Murfreesboro was about to be closed. Other articles state that the bank closed as early as 1824. What finally happened is not clear, but best accounts seem to indicate that the bank closed sometime late in 1826.

The panic of 1819 taxed the banks to their utmost and many suspended specie payments. In 1820 an institution called the Bank of the State of Tennessee with its main office at Nashville and agencies in each county was established by the legislature. Some writers referred to this institution as a state loan office, but it was commonly known as the "New State Bank". This manner of doing a banking business did not prove popular. The agents were accused of enriching themselves at the expense of the public whom they were supposed to serve as well as using the business for encouraging particular political movements that fitted well into the scheme of things. By 1826 the "New State Bank" had served its purpose and steps were soon taken for its liquidation. Phelan in his History of Tennessee said, "The State Bank of 1820 was one of those expedients to tide over an era of depression in business transactions, of which there are numerous examples in the history of our country."

In 1836 a bank to be known as the Planters Bank was authorized for Murfreesboro. It is not known just how long this bank continued in operation.

It was not unusual to find the residents of Rutherford in the forties and fifties doing business with banks outside the county. The Merchants Insurance and Trust Company organized in Nashville in 1840 apparently attracted much business from Murfreesboro and Rutherford County.

In 1850 the Murfreesboro Savings Institute was organized. Several outstanding business men incorporated this business. These included L. H. Carney, William Spencer, John Leiper, Robert E. Currin, Charles Ready, E. A. Keeble, H. M. Burton, William D. Hicks, William A. Reid and John Jones.

The Exchange Bank was established in the summer of 1852. It was started by William and Joseph Spence under what was called the free banking system. The bank was started with a capital stock of $50,000, but this was later increased to around $125,000. For a time it seemed that this bank would be a most prosperous one. For five years after its opening, it did a most profitable business. Goodspeed claims that the managers became embarrassed as a result of some improper management in 1857 and closed the doors of the bank for about a year. It reopened in 1858 but apparently the public had lost confidence in the enterprise and there were few depositors. After a few weeks, the bank was permanently closed. It is claimed that several citizens lost large sums of money and much dissatisfaction with banking was expressed by the people of the community.

In 1859 another Planters Bank with John W. Childress as President and William Ledbetter as cashier started operation in Murfreesboro. At the outbreak of the war the business of this firm was transferred to a Nashville bank. It did not reopen after the war.

The State of Tennessee attempted to get its financial institutions in better condition in 1860 just prior to the outbreak of the war. Phelan said of the General Banking Act of 1860, "It was important that it showed that the state had finally arrived at the correct idea of the relations which should exist between itself and its banks."

In 1866 E. L. Jordan, J. B. Kimbro and associates of theirs were authorized to establish the Murfreesboro Savings Bank. It is not known just how far this group went in organizing for business or how successful they were. These men immediately became interested in organizing the First National Bank under an act of Congress passed during the war.

The First National Bank was established in March of 1869. The capital stock of the organization was $100,000. The first board of directors had in its membership several who had been interested in other banking enterprises. Board members were J. B. Kimbro, W. N. Doughty, J. W. Richardson, J. R. Collier, J. R. Dillon, J. E. Dromgoole, J. B. Palmer, W. A. Ransom, M. L. Fletcher, W. B. Lillard and A. M. Alexander. John Bell Kimbro, first president of the bank died in 1872 and was succeeded by E. L. Jordan. Except for depression years of the later seventies and early eighties, this bank enjoyed an ever growing business. It continued in operation until the early years of the "great depression."

The Stone's River National Bank opened for business in Murfreesboro on May 1, 1872. Members of the Board of Directors for this institution were W. N. Doughty, J. P. Rice, W. R. Butler, W. C. Eagleton, T. C. Goodrich, Theodore Smith, J. I. C. Haynes, D. D. Wendel, and C. B. Huggins. William Mitchell was the first president, D. D. Wendel the first cashier and C. B. Huggins the first teller. In 1917 under the stress of war-time conditions, the Stone's River National Bank was merged with the First National Bank to form one of the strongest institutions of its kind in middle Tennessee. John M. Butler became president of the First National Bank. J. C. Beesley was vice-president. C. B. Bell, cashier and W. B. Carnahan, assistant cashier.

The Murfreesboro Bank and Trust Company was organized in 1905 with B. F. Moore as its first president, Leland Jordan as cashier and D. L. Ledbetter as teller. This bank started with total resources of around $125,000. By 1923 this had increased to near two million dollars. The officers at this time were A. L. Todd; president, C. D. Ivie and N. C. Maney; vice-presidents, R. T. Bell, Jr, cashier, H. C. Beasley and Miss Bess Reeves; assistant cashiers. This bank has enjoyed continued success from the very beginning. Today the bank has the highest deposits and greatest resources of its history. R. T. Bell, Jr. former cashier has been president of the bank for a number of years.

For the most part in recent years the banks of the smaller communities of Rutherford County have been branches of Murfreesboro Banks. The citizens of Smyrna, however, organized their own bank in 1904. This institution was chartered under the name Bank of Smyrna. It enjoyed a good business for a number of years. The First National Bank of Smyrna replaced it. The Bank of Readyville, another independent was absorbed by the Commerce Union Bank in 1928. B. H. Carter of the Readyville bank was brought to Murfreesboro to manage the Commerce Union Bank. This bank is doing a good business today. Prior to the establishment of the Commerce Union Bank, its quarters were occupied by a bank called the Rutherford County State Bank. This enterprise had replaced the Citizens Bank, another institution that did business for only a short while. The business of the Rutherford County State Bank was taken over by the Commerce Union in 1925. The Lascassas bank is now a part of the Murfreesboro Bank and Trust Company as is that at Eagleville.

The banks of Murfreesboro and Rutherford County with the exception of one, weathered the hectic days of the "great depression" in fine style. The First National Bank closed its doors. It became apparent in later years, however, that this bank might have come through the siege had not its managers and directors fallen victim to the hysteria that was beginning to grip the country. Depositors were paid such a high per cent of their deposits that many people have pointed to this fact as an indication that the bank need not have discontinued business at all. Other people say that Murfreesboro would hardly have noticed the depression at all had it not been for the closing of the First National Bank. Others say that the failure of the bank "sho wiped out class distinction in Murfreesboro."

The bank holiday, as in other places, was followed by a period of "script dealing". It was not long, however, before the banks of Rutherford County were doing business at the same old stand in the same old way. "New Deal" banking legislation brought a new confidence in banking all over the United States. This confidence is reflected in the record deposits in the three Murfreesboro banks, the Commerce Union, the Murfreesboro Bank and Trust Company and the Federal Savings and Loan Bank in the years following the depression. The banks in the other communities also began to show increased business. By the time of the start of the second world war, the people of Rutherford County had deposited record breaking sums of money in its banking institutions. The deposits now are approaching fifteen million dollars.

Bibliography

Allred, C. E. et al., *Tennessee, Economic and Social*. (University of Tennessee, 1929).

Drake, E. L., *Annals of the Army of Tennessee*. (A. D. Haynes, 1878).

Biographical Sketch of Tennessee Governors. (J. S. Jones, 1903).

Biographical Directory of the American Congress. U. S. Printing Office, 1920).

Bond, John, *History of the Concord Baptist Association*. (Graves, Marks and Co., 1860).

Clayton, W. W., *History of Davidson County*. (J. W. Lewis, 1880).

Dictionary of American Biography. (Scribner's Sons, 1935).

Dictionary of National Biography. (Oxford University Press, 1922).

Fitch, John. *Annals of the Army of the Cumberland*. (Lippincott, 1864).

Folmsbee, S. J., *Sectionalism and Internal Improvements in Tennessee*. (Knoxville, 1939).

Foster, A. P., *Counties of Tennessee*. (Department of Education, Nashville, 1923).

Galloway, J. J., *Geology and Natural Resources of Rutherford County*. (Tennessee Geological Survey, 1910).

Goodspeed Publishing Company, *History of Tennessee*. (1886).

Hale, W. T. and Merritt, Dixon, *History of Tennessee*. (Lewis, 1913)

Hamer, P. M., *Tennessee: A History*. (American Historical Society, 1933).

Haywood, John, *The Civil and Political History of Tennessee*. (Heiskell, Brown, 1823).

Henderson, C. C., *The Story of Murfreesboro*. (News-Banner, 1929).

Historical Survey Records, *Tennessee*. Number 74, Rutherford County. (Nashville, 1938).

Hughes, Mary B., *Hearthstones*. (Mid-South Publishing Company, 1942).

Long, Minnie Rutherford, *General Griffith Rutherford and Allied Families*. (Cuneo Press, 1942).

McFerrin, J. B., *History of Methodism in Tennessee*. (Southern Methodist Publishing House, 1869–1879).

Methodist Church South, *Journal*, 1845–1927.

Moore, J. T. and Foster, A. P., *Tennessee, the Volunteer State*. (S. J. Clark, 1923).

National Baptist Register.

Parks, Edd W., *Charles Egbert Craddock*. (University of North Carolina Press, 1941).

Pittard, Homer, *Legends and Stories of the Civil War in Rutherford County*. (Master's Thesis, Peabody College, 1940).

Putnam, A. W., *History of Middle Tennessee*. (Nashville, 1859).

Ramsay, J. M. Q., *Annals of Tennessee*. (Walker, 1853).

State Teachers College, Murfreesboro, *History of Rutherford County*. (Mimeograph, 1938).

Stephenson, A. P., *The Battle of Stone's River*. (J. R. Osgood, 1884).

Tennessee Planning Commission, *County by County Compilation of Resources*. (Nashville, 1943).

University of Tennessee, *Soils of Rutherford County*. (Stubley, 1924).

U. S. Bureau of Census, 1810–1946.

Walker, F. R., *Ten Years of Rural Health Work, Rutherford County, Tennessee*. (The Commonwealth Fund, 1935).

White, R. H., *Tennessee's Four Capitals*. (Mimeograph).

Williams, S. C., *Dawn of Tennessee Valley and Tennessee History*. (Watauga Press, 1937).

Williams, S. C., *Early Travels in the Tennessee Country*. (Watauga Press, 1928).

Williams, S. C., *Tennessee in the Revolutionary War*. (Tennessee Historical Commission, 1944).

Index

www.ingramcontent.com/pod-product-compliance
Lightning Source LLC
Chambersburg PA
CBHW021858020426
42334CB00013B/386

* 9 780893 087005 *